TELEVISION AND THE
PUBLIC INTEREST

BROADCASTING STANDARDS COUNCIL

5–8 The Sanctuary
London SW1P 3JS

Tel: 071–233 0544
Fax: 071–233 0397

TELEVISION AND THE PUBLIC INTEREST

Vulnerable Values in West European Broadcasting

edited by
Jay G. Blumler

ⓈSAGE Publications
London · Newbury Park · New Delhi
in association with the Broadcasting Standards Council

First published 1992

SAGE Publications Ltd
6 Bonhill Street
London EC2A 4PU

SAGE Publications Inc
2455 Teller Road
Newbury Park, California 91320

SAGE Publications India Pvt Ltd
32, M-Block Market
Greater Kailash – I
New Delhi 110 048

British Library Cataloguing in Publication data

Television and the public interest: Vulnerable
values in West European broadcasting.
   I. Blumler, Jay G.
   302.23094

   ISBN 0-8039-8649-1
   ISBN 0-8039-8650-5 pbk

Library of Congress catalog card number 91-050990

Typeset by Photoprint, Torquay
Printed in Great Britain by Biddles Ltd, Guildford, Surrey

Contents

Foreword

Lord Rees-Mogg, Chairman of the Broadcasting Standards Council

The Broadcasting Standards Council has a responsibility under the Broadcasting Act 1990 for monitoring the portrayal in programmes of violence, sexual conduct and matters of taste and decency. The responsibility extends to those programmes which reach this country from overseas, of which the rising number of European satellite services provide a good illustration. In addition, the Council may be asked by the Government to represent it at international meetings where the setting of television standards is under discussion.

On both counts, therefore, the Council has a continuing connection with the development of broadcasting in Europe and elsewhere. Standards are not, in practice, divisible by programme category. Their observance generally is a reflection of the broadcasters' aspirations to good professional practice in all fields.

From this springs the Council's involvement in the present publication. What are the values against which standards in broadcasting are set? How do nations set about preserving those values when they have the will to do so? And how effective can those attempts to preserve and protect be in the fast-changing conditions, economic and technical, in which broadcasters must operate today?

These are some of the questions outlined in the pages which follow. Answers are provided from the perspectives of scholars from eight European countries. In matters such as these, it is the Council's wish to stimulate an important debate rather than itself to offer solutions. Where solutions exist, they may be national in character, but they may instead be European, an expression of that coming-together of the nations which, in Europe, has given the final decades of the twentieth century one of their special characteristics.

Lord Rees-Mogg

Acknowledgements

The Broadcasting Standards Council wishes to acknowledge the help of the John and Mary R. Markle Foundation which provided funds for a conference at Liège in December, 1990, and so brought into existence the collection of papers from which the present selection has been made. The conference was organized by Professor Yves Winkin of the University of Liège, with further financial assistance from the Belgian National Fund for Scientific Research and the French Centre National de la Recherche Scientifique, and the Council's thanks are also due to them. Finally, the Council expresses its gratitude to all those whose reflections at the conference influenced the final shape of the work.

1

Introduction: Current Confrontations in West European Television

Jay G. Blumler

For more than half a century assurance and pride were hallmarks of West European broadcasting. The appropriateness of public service principles, as legitimizing creed and policy guide, was unquestioned. Criticisms of performance were more often particular than general. Controversy and proposals for change focused more on institutional arrangements than on ideological beliefs. New developments were introduced incrementally, avoiding radical breaks with the past.

By the late 1980s, however, this serene climate had been displaced by a more stormy season. Caught in a veritable blizzard of technological, economic, structural and legal change, all the societies of Western Europe are today grappling with profound and (for them) unfamiliar issues of electronic media policy. They are having to come to terms with a host of essentially novel conditions: termination of the monopoly sway of public service broadcasting bodies; an invasion of transnational forces at corporate, production and distribution levels; a shift from spectrum scarcity to multi-channel abundance; the unleashing of unprecedented competition for revenue and viewing shares; uncertainties about how the programming patterns on offer will be affected; associated uncertainties about likely shifts of audience preferences and tastes in response. Moreover, the past approaches of these societies to broadcasting administration offer little guidance for coping with the resulting problems (McQuail et al., 1990):

1   how to regulate private television to ensure its conformity to the public interest (however defined);
2   what roles to envisage for public television in the new competitive conditions;
3   how to adjust the expectations, obligations and resources of public and private broadcasters to each other;

4   how to hold the proliferating broadcasting authorities and services effectively accountable for their policies and performance.

Three features of the situation deserve preliminary notice.

First, it has been marked, not only by a break-up of the old public service monopolies, but also and more profoundly by a loss of consensus over the purposes that broadcasting should serve and how it should be organized to achieve them (see especially Wolton's comments on this in Chapter 10 below). In most European countries two broad frameworks of outlook and organization face each other in contention, even contradiction. One of these approaches broadcasting from a standpoint of social ethics, associating it with a cluster of values to be pursued purposively, whilst trusting (or hoping) that the audience will be content with the programming outcome. The other regards capture of the audience-as-market as the prime normative and pragmatic goal of the broadcasting business, with an implication for other values *either* that they will naturally tend to be realized in a system of extended provision and choice; *or* that they must simply take their chances in the rough and tumble of commercial life; *or* that they may even have to go to the wall as now out of date.

The several countries of Western Europe are presently reacting to this division in a variety of ways. In essence, it appears that *Germany* is striving to reconcile the two broadcasting modes under a constitutionally mandated framework of overarching principles. *Britain*, having unleashed powerful market forces, is nevertheless endeavouring so to control them that serious damage to social values can be prevented. For a long period *Italy* was much less bothered, regarding the disparity of broadcasting types as natural, tolerating the ensuing anarchy and letting the two modes develop in line with their respective proclivities in a 'horses for courses' spirit (only tidying things up belatedly in a 1990 Broadcasting Act). *Sweden*, *Switzerland* and *the Netherlands* are striving to shore up the public service components of their broadcasting systems as best possible, while accepting that significant advances of market-based television are inevitable. Recent governments of *France* appear to have been moved by a mixture of enthusiasm for market principles and nostalgia for public service values, supporting the latter, however, with legal forms that some critics regard as little more than fig leaves. French-speaking *Belgium* has seemingly singled out one threatened value – maintenance of a strong indigenous production industry – for priority support. And in some countries – *Austria*, *Portugal* and *Spain* come to mind as examples – few policy makers have yet grasped the nettle presented by the opposed perspectives.

Of course these are simplified characterizations of far more complex states of affairs, fuller accounts of which are presented in Part II of this book. They are also snapshots of fluid and unstable situations that could eventually look quite different as the systems continue to evolve.

Second, certain peculiarities of broadcasting organization complicate the policy task for Europeans today. Although national television service no longer emanates from a monopoly provider of the public utility kind, neither can it be easily brought into line with a conventional model of market performance. Though a highly consumer-oriented good, television programming is very different from most other such goods (like cars, toasters, washing machines, electricity or telephones). Whereas the latter provide the means, the former trades in the meanings of life. Consumer responses to programmes have no immediate impact on supply as they tend to do in most other industries. Audience feedback is delayed, much mediated (particularly by advertisers in commercial systems) and subject to crude, summary, at times even arbitrary, interpretation by schedulers and programmers. Mechanisms for perfecting broadcasting markets through direct individual payment for programmes (so-called 'pay-per-view') are probably suited only to extraordinary offerings (for example, major sporting events and first-run films), not more run-of-the-mill output. Moreover, television cannot be regarded as only a source of relaxation and a thriving entertainment business. It is also a vehicle of political power; an omnifarious source of cultural experience; and 'a chief means through which . . . society observes and evaluates itself' (Seymour-Ure, 1991: 13).

This last characteristic leads to a third important yet relatively neglected feature of the European broadcasting scene at present. As formerly dominant public service broadcasting systems have undergone structural change, much academic and journalistic attention has focused on impulses of technological advance, multichannel expansion, commercialization and sharpened competition. In many of the societies concerned, however, such trends have formed only one side of the policy story. In addition, markers have been put down by legislators, policy makers, broadcasters, civic groups and media observers for values thought to be at risk in the new conditions, and safeguards of a regulatory or institutional kind have been sought for them.

It is to that effort that this book, an outcome of international collaboration, is devoted. In November 1990 a conference of 17 scholars of mass media organization was convened by Professor Yves Winkin at the Université de Liège in Belgium on the theme of 'Vulnerable Values in Multichannel Television Systems: What European Policy Makers Seek to Protect'. This was made possible by support from the Belgian National Fund for Scientific Research, the French National Centre for Scientific Research, the John and Mary R. Markle Foundation in New York City and the Broadcasting Standards Council in Britain. The topic was approached in two stages. First, the situations in eleven different countries were outlined in substantial papers, eight of which, revised after discussion, form Part II of this book. (For space reasons, it was not possible to include the excellent analyses of Simon-Pierre de Coster and Robert Stephane for French-speaking Belgium, Hans Heinz Fabris for Austria and Manuel José Lopes da Silva for Portugal.) Second, the broader implications were reviewed more analytically, identifying widely shared value concerns, ways of upholding them and problems experienced in trying to do so. Parts I and III reflect much of this discussion.

Readers will find that four aims have shaped our work:

1 to identify the principal values and related programming forms that European policy makers are striving to protect from marketplace pressures;
2 to examine the array of regulatory measures that are being adopted for this purpose;
3 to assess the likely effectiveness of such measures in the light of certain enforcement problems that may be anticipated; and
4 to consider ways of countering such problems and of preserving vulnerable values more effectively in a mixed television economy.

We are particularly preoccupied with the likely fate in the new scheme of things of the reduced but still sizeable public service broadcasting organizations, which appear to face a Scylla-and-Charybdis-like dilemma. On the one hand, they may be tempted to try to offer a fully comprehensive service, even when diminished resources could limit their chances of doing that well. On the other hand, they will not wish to slip into the marginal role of merely filling whatever gaps are left untended by the commercial broadcasters. New ideas about public service commitments that could avoid these extremes are urgently needed.

Fresh thought is also needed, however, on overall television system governance. In the public service era, dominated by only a few state-fashioned organizations, broadcasting was a relatively stable sector of policy formation, influence channels and feedback.

Processes of public accountability came into being, which, though open to criticism as narrowly based, were nevertheless quite effective in obliging those in charge to explain and defend their records. Since these are now being disrupted and bypassed by the electronic media revolution, a difficult question arises: what new forms of accountability are required, and along what lines might they be modelled?

Other analysts have examined broadcasting system performance, policy and change from a variety of perspectives: that of *market economics* (Owen, Beebe and Manning, 1974); *technology* as a prime determining factor (Forester, 1985); *ideology* as a critical influence (Negrine, 1988); neo-Marxist emphases on *private owner-ship influences* (Murdock, 1990); the sociology of *media industry organization* (Tunstall, 1991); and the politics of *neo-pluralism* (Dyson and Humphreys, 1990). The authors of this collection have adopted yet another analytical stance – that of *the social values at stake* in how broadcasting is organized. Identification and clarifica-tion of such values – what they might mean and how they could fare in multichannel competition – are essential for facing the three central challenges of modern European broadcasting policy. One is the problem of regulating the burgeoning private television sectors: to what ends can regulation be used and how effective can it be? A second is the problem of course-steering for the public service bodies: whether to offer a comprehensive or more slimmed-down service and how to go about it. The third is the problem of devising new forms of accountability appropriate to the changed times in which television authorities and providers must now operate.

References

Dyson, Kenneth and Humphreys, Peter (eds) (1990) *The Political Economy of Communications: International and European Dimensions*. London and New York: Routledge.

Forester, T. (ed.) (1985) *The Information Technology Revolution*. Oxford: Basil Blackwell.

McQuail, Denis and the Euromedia Research Group (1990) 'Caging the Beast: Constructing a Framework for the Analysis of Media Change in Western Europe', *European Journal of Communication*, 5 (2/3): 313–31.

Murdock, Graham (1990) 'Redrawing the Map of the Communication Industries: Concentration and Ownership in the Era of Privatization', in Marjorie Ferguson (ed.), *Public Communication: The New Imperatives*. London, Newbury Park and New Delhi: Sage. pp. 1–15.

Negrine, Ralph (ed.) (1988) *Satellite Broadcasting*. London: Routledge and Kegan Paul.

Owen, B.M., Beebe, J. and Manning, W. (1974) *Television Economics*. Lexington, MA: Lexington Books.

Seymour-Ure, Colin (1991) *The British Press and Broadcasting since 1945*. Oxford: Basil Blackwell.

Tunstall, Jeremy (1991) 'A Media Industry Perspective', in James A. Anderson (ed.), *Communication Yearbook 14*. Newbury Park, London and New Delhi: Sage. pp. 163–86.

PART I

WEST EUROPEAN TELEVISION IN TRANSITION

2

Public Service Broadcasting before the Commercial Deluge

Jay G. Blumler

Concerns about the impact of change on vulnerable values emerge from an interplay of social forces and broadcasting traditions. Since the 1920s European broadcasting has conformed to a public service model. Despite many constitutional, linguistic, cultural and political differences among the several host countries (plus differences of size and sheer resources, of course), until the early 1980s most of the broadcasting services shared six features that sharply distinguished them from the more market-oriented model prevalent in the United States.

The Public Service Legacy

A comprehensive remit
First, West European television was shaped by an ethic of comprehensiveness. This was in direct contrast to American public television, which always saw itself as an island of welfare in an ocean of commercialism (Blumler, 1986). Whereas in the United States the commercial networks have provided *Dallas* and public television has provided Pavarotti, in Europe public broadcasters have provided both (Rowland, 1991). Their omnibus services embraced such multiple goals as education, information *and* entertainment; range, quality *and* popularity (Nossiter, 1986).

At root this ethic of comprehensiveness emanated from the broadcasters' financial reliance (wholly or predominantly) on licence fees levied on each household with a radio (later a television set). As O'Brien explained for Britain: 'The BBC as a public service form of broadcasting, acquiring its funds through equal payments by considerable numbers of the public, has a clear obligation to discover and satisfy, so far as it is possible to do so, the common denominator of broadcasting demand' (1937: 96).

It is true that a modest degree of specialization set in as more public channels went on air from the 1960s onwards (the current West European norm is between two and three, though Britain boasts four and Norway still has only one). There was a tendency for majority tastes to be served on one channel, while more minority interest and regional/local audience programming was presented on the others. Even so, most majority channels incorporated some demanding materials in their schedules, while the minority channels aimed to include at least some large audience attractions in theirs.

Generalized mandates
Second, in their juridical founding documents (whether in the form of a charter, a licence, a concession, a basic law or a contractual agreement with the state) the public broadcasting corporations were all given quite broadly worded mandates, affording much flexibility of interpretation and little need for legalistic application. In Britain, for example, a triad of information, education and entertainment applied. In Sweden, Sveriges Radio was required to 'promote the basic principles of democratic government, the principles of the equality of man and the liberty and dignity of the individual'. The Dutch broadcasting companies were expected to provide culture, information, education and entertainment. Austrian television was asked to provide a service of comprehensive general information; popular, youth and adult education; arts and sciences; unobjectional entertainment; and to stimulate an interest in active sports (Fabris, 1990).

In most systems (though the Netherlands is an exception), enforcement and supervision of broadcasters' activities were entrusted to politically appointed Boards, which were built into the structure of the very organizations they oversaw. In Britain, for example, the Board of Governors of the BBC was expected 'to intervene, chide or even discipline the broadcasters in the public interest' (Annan Committee, 1977). Nevertheless, the Board had much latitude to determine, within a framework of certain broad norms – objectivity, impartiality, decency, good taste and respect for law and order – what the 'public interest' required in policy terms at any given time. In some countries additional bodies were created to deal with complaints or allegations of remit violations of defined kinds (the most formed example is Sweden's Radio Council; others may be found in Britain, Switzerland, Austria and Portugal), giving rise to something resembling case law for their specific areas of concern. But even such bodies were exceptions to the more usual discretionary rule; they operated only after the broadcast fact in response only to submitted complaints; they could wield only relatively weak sanctions (typically publicity given to negative verdicts by the offenders); and more often than not they found in favour of the broadcasters.

More to the point, a considerable amount of freedom and authority was consequently bestowed on high-minded and liberally oriented television executives and professionals, who were allowed to plot their own courses, so long as they did not steer too closely toward dangerous political reefs and sensitivities. With exceptions in times of crisis and political trouble of course, this meant that the broadcasters could by and large regard themselves more as communicators of meaningful experience than as marketeers of products or propagandists for creeds. Interviews with a large number of British broadcasters in the mid-1980s illustrate the kind of scope they believed a public service framework afforded (Nossiter, 1986). There was, for example, the current affairs producer who described British broadcasting as 'the principal forum which enables the whole nation to talk to itself'. There was a concern to communicate something intelligibly about culture, arts and science to an audience reaching well beyond the cognoscenti and the already involved, illustrated by the arts programmer who proclaimed: 'Never before has there been the opportunity to speak to all the people or to make available to them the whole of British culture.' There were producers in the regional ITV companies who saw their work partly in terms of nourishing networks of geographical identities and ties – 'sustaining community in parts of Britain that are sparsely populated and remote from London', as one put it. There was the soap opera producer who said: 'We are trying through our serial to make people think about relationships and the problems around us – whether it's race or teenagers and their parents or caring for the elderly' (Nossiter, 1986: 18–19; 37).

Diversity, pluralism and range
Third, all the West European public television systems were pluralistic in a thorough-going and multifaceted sense. In Germany, for example, the Federal Constitutional Court has repeatedly emphasized the need for a diversity of communication offerings, reflecting the concerns of all relevant social forces and groups, the opinions that may be expressed on contested issues, and a broad range of programme forms. According to the Broadcasting Research Unit, a core tenet of British public service broadcasting was 'to provide programmes of wide range and diversity over a

reasonable span of time for practically all kinds of taste for large groups and small' (1985: 3). The pillarized Dutch system was constructed to enable each ideologically oriented sector of society to provide programming in line with its own beliefs. The Swiss Broadcasting Corporation provides a full service for each of the country's three main linguistic elements – in German, French and Italian. In Belgium, there are separate public television services for the French (RTBS) and Flemish-speaking (BRT) areas of the country, respectively. The governing boards of many European broadcasting corporations are composed of representatives of a wide range of social, political and cultural groups.

Thus, European public service television has been conceived in pluralist terms at several levels: in the multiplicity of audience types served and audience images catered for; in respect of programme making, striving to match it to the heterogeneity of the viewing public and ensuring that each programme form has sufficient resources to be good of its kind; and in respect of responsiveness to society, implying that all significant sectors of the community, divided by interests, values and identities, are entitled to have their main concerns reflected in a tolerably authentic way in programme output. Crucial for the realization of such pluralism has been a readiness to structure budgets in line with different programmes' needs, instead of obliging them to make do with what they could earn in the marketplace. As Sir Brian Young, a former Director-General of Britain's Independent Broadcasting Authority, once put it: 'The output must consist not only of programmes that pay their way. The same source that puts out cheap and popular programmes must also put out programmes that are expensive and ambitious.' (1983). Actual cross-subsidizing applies in Switzerland, where much French- and Italian-language television is paid for in effect by its German-speaking population.

This pluralist broadcasting model contrasts with the more majoritarian model of television provision that is fostered by advertising-financed systems. In the latter, pride of place tends to be given to satisfaction of the personal and immediate gratifications of as many individual audience members as possible, with resources flowing toward programmes in close proportion to their audience drawing power.

Cultural roles

Fourth, most European public television systems were imbued with a cultural vocation. As Rowland and Tracey have explained: '[In Europe] broadcasting was originally seen principally as a cultural enterprise . . . . Broadcasting organisations were taken to be part of the sector of society which is responsible for generating and disseminating its linguistic, spiritual, aesthetic and ethnic wealth' (1988: 6–7). Partly this was envisaged as a responsibility for sustaining and renewing the society's characteristic cultural capital and cement. Partly it reflected an assumption that television should be available to artists, musicians, dramatists, writers and intellectuals generally – the best and brightest of a nation's cultural talent – as a vehicle for disseminating their creative work more widely. Partly the aim was to enable viewers to enjoy the fruits of such talent.

Conceptualization of this cultural mission took many forms. There was the idea that broadcasters in charge of a public, society-wide medium 'should recognize their special relationship to national identity, . . . community [and in some cases language]' (Broadcasting Research Unit, 1985: 7). The BBC was styled for many years (even after a rival Independent Television service was set up) 'the national instrument of broadcasting'. French Presidents sometimes termed their television service 'the voice of France'.

There was the idea of television as a centripetal, societally integrative force. In Katz's (1985) words, it offered 'the opportunity of shared experience . . . contributing to authenticity by connecting the society to its cultural center and acquainting the segments of society with each other'.

There was the notion of the broadcaster as the viewer's guide to whatever was culturally worthwhile. A classic statement was Lord Reith's assertion of a BBC responsibility 'to carry into the greatest possible number of homes everything that is best in every department of human endeavour and achievement'. A less overtly paternalist version was Alasdair Milne's expressed view (when BBC Director-General in the 1980s) that 'public service broadcasting must make the popular worthwhile and the worthwhile popular'. In line with this role were tendencies for Britons to refer to the BBC as 'Auntie' and Italians to RAI as 'Mamma'.

All this was tied to a concept of worthwhile viewing experience. Television, it was believed, could and should be able to do more for the average audience member than merely divert him or keep her abreast of the headline news. Although such needs for relaxation and digestible information should not be short-changed, it was assumed that in a well-run public service system television should at least occasionally present audience members with material that would stretch their minds and horizons; awaken them to less familiar ideas and tastes in culture, the arts and the sciences; and perhaps even challenge some of their uncritically accepted assumptions about life, morality and society. Television should enhance the viewer's quality of life instead of merely receding 'into the back-ground of life . . . a placebo, a resort against boredom, a reference point for information' (as was supposedly more common in the United States: Forman, 1987).

Many of these ideas were fused in public service-based notions of programme quality, conceived as enabling an enriched viewing experience. Lady Warnock, a philosopher and past Member of the Independent Broadcasting Authority, for example, has defined 'a quality programme' in terms of its 'depth-giving and fascinating' aspect with the 'effect of making [the viewer] feel that horizons are being opened and that there is more to be discovered because his imagination and that of the programme-maker are working *together*' (1990: 16). Such aspirations were also linked to notions of pro-gramme range, however, according to which prime time (for example) should not be regarded as almost exclusively 'fun time' (as in the United States) but rather as an opportunity to sample across a more kaleidoscopic span of offerings catering for a more varied set of viewing gratifications.

Place in politics
Fifth, as creatures ultimately of the state, public service broadcast-ing corporations were highly politicized organizations – even in those societies where safeguards of their editorial independence had been carefully crafted. This has been a complex source of strength, preoccupation and weakness for all of them.

On balance, the civic sphere has benefited greatly from this feature, being taken far more seriously by European public service broadcasters than by journalists working for the popular and tabloid press of their own countries or by journalists in more commercially driven television systems elsewhere (for example, the United States). European television has typically assumed some responsibi-lity for the health of the political process and for the quality of public discourse generated within it. News, current affairs and political programming has often been treated like a protected species (Blumler, 1990a), putting on a range of interviews, panel discussions, phone-ins, debates, issue analyses and (more occasion-ally) exercises of investigative journalism in what has become a national political forum. Debates, Leader exchanges and policy announcements in national Parliaments have been covered promi-nently in television news. Considered principles of political access have evolved, giving the main parties free quotas of air time during elections and at other times. News coverage of election campaigns has been extensive and substantive, presenting much issue and policy information and not reducing them to mere horse races or elaborate strategic games as in the United States (Semetko et al., 1991).

Nevertheless, the politicization of European television has plagued its practitioners with many problems. For one thing, just because public broadcasters were supposed to be impartial, avoid undue offence, not interject their own opinions into the debate, and in other ways serve the public interest, they were correspondingly and readily open to accusations of impropriety, bias, and neglect of duty, some sincerely voiced, others cloaking the more naked pursuit of partisan advantage. For another, broadcasters were often constrained to prudence due to their dependence on governments of the day for decisions vital to their continuing survival and welfare (Blumler, 1980). They have trimmed some of their programming (though not invariably) to interests of the state (as in coverage of the IRA in Northern Ireland and presentation of the 'Royal Question' in the early post-war years in Belgium: cf. Burgelman, 1989). For yet another, public service broadcasting organizations are singularly lacking in self-sufficiency. They badly need outside support, much of it political, to keep afloat in turbulent societal seas. It was for such reasons that the late Sir Charles Curran, former Director-General of the BBC, proclaimed a need for senior broadcasters continually to engage in what he called 'the politics of broadcasting'. As he put it: 'The broadcaster's life has to be one of continuous political ingenuity' (Curran, 1979: 319). Most seriously, in some systems broadcasting was structurally under many political thumbs, subjected either to ministerial interference in programming matters (as most blatantly in Greece but also in France), to detailed parliamentary supervision (as in Italy) or (most commonly) to a distribution of senior positions, directorships of channels and news editorships among the leading political parties (as in Italy, Germany, Denmark and Belgium: cf. Burgelman, 1989, for Belgium).

This is not to imply that the dichotomies of political control/accountability vs broadcaster independence have been organized on identical lines throughout Europe. On the contrary, Kelly finds three different forms of television linkage to politics:

1) formally autonomous systems, in which mechanisms for distancing political organs from broadcaster decision-taking have been adopted – as in Britain though also in Ireland and Sweden;
2) politics-in-broadcasting systems, in which the governing bodies of the broadcasting organizations include representatives of the country's main political parties as well as of social groups loosely affiliated with them – as in Germany, Denmark and Belgium;
3) politics-over-broadcasting systems, in which state organs are authorized to intervene in broadcaster decisions – as in Greece and Italy and France in the past. (1983: 73)

Non-commercialism
Sixth, European broadcasting was structured in an awareness of tensions between culture and commerce with a corresponding attempt to keep market forces at bay and to ensure that they did not unduly dominate or distort programme making. As Sepstrup has put it, whereas television advertising was treated 'in the USA as a guest of honour', in Europe it was 'a tolerated visitor with a more humble place at the table' (1986: 383). Even though in some systems licence revenues were significantly supplemented by the sale of commercial time (yielding up to a half of their income for some public broadcasters), until the advent of private television there had been no *competition* for advertising support. Furthermore, the amount and placement of the commercials were subject to strict controls. In some cases, stringent minutage limits applied – down to as little as 20 minutes per day. In others, spots within programmes were disallowed, and commercials would appear only in blocks at a few specified times. This is not to imply a blissful indifference among public broadcasters to the economics of their trade: the allocation of resources, control of costs and their relationship to a calculus of ratings. However, such material and monetary factors were not normally treated as decisive but took their place within a broader framework of principled decision-taking.

Of principle and power
In its prime, then, European public television had become a fascinating meeting ground of idealism and realism; of Platonic high-mindedness and toughly pragmatic power politics; of disinterest and organized interest; of self-policing and political policing. It cannot be understood by ignoring one or the other side of this coin, the relative importance of which varied by system, across periods of time and over different programming sectors and episodes of conflict. On the one side, public service broadcasters were obliged at times to adjust their offerings to political forces that could significantly steer or stay their hands. On the other side, many public broadcasters subscribed to certain values of communication welfare which they had absorbed and were keen to apply in their work.

Points of Vulnerability and Weakness

Monopolistic television systems dominated by Brobdingnagian corporations, however public spirited, could not evade fundamental change in the 1980s. The impact of new communication technologies (notably cable and satellite), offering both a vastly expanded channel capacity and a simultaneous transmission of programmes and advertising from external sources into the homes of more than one national audience, was inherently destabilizing. As an influential member of a British policy review committee put it: 'The status quo is not an option' (Hetherington, 1987). Even the most stalwart supporters of the public service model – for example, former purists in Sweden (see Hadenius, Chapter 8 below) and the initially staunchly resistant German Social Democrats – eventually had to concede at least some need to introduce market forces into their countries' broadcasting arrangements. In these circumstances, the ability of public broadcasters to defend their corners was enfeebled by certain inherent sources of vulnerability.

Politicization
Three chinks in the armour of public service television were exposed by its place in national political orders.

First, it was tied to a declining vision and fabric of more organic state–society–citizenry relationships that, ironically, the spread of television had itself very probably helped to dissolve. A Dutch reliance on pluralistic 'confessional television', for example, was being unsettled by a social process of 'depillarization' (McQuail, 1991, and Chapter 7 below). A process of 'laicization' was 'de-ideologizing' Italian politics (Mazzoleni, Chapter 6 below, and 1987: 82). In Britain a 'secularization' of electoral politics was under way, in which the role of the voter was becoming more like that of a consumer or juror than that of a religious adherent (Crewe, 1983). Throughout Western Europe faith in political institutions was declining, party identifications were weakening and electoral volatility was on the increase (see Hadenius, Chapter 8 below). At the same time that 'formerly more solid and enduring . . . élite-mass relationships' were weakening (Blumler, 1990b: 102), single-issue pressure groups were proliferating, basing their influence and claims more on broad-ranging media publicity than on linkages to a single party, while (as Saxer notes in Chapter 9 below) an overall ethos of consumerist hedonism was suffusing the expectations of mass publics. In such a climate the traditional forms of service offered by public television could appear old-fashioned and their traditional clients appear a declining constituency.

Second, precisely because they were politicized, public service broadcasting organizations were open to attack by critics with alternative and less conventional views of the political roles they should be performing. Syvertsen (1991) has classified these as including a public acountability critique of public television (for a paucity of popular involvement in the governance of broadcasting); a cultural liberalist critique (for allowing only a limited range of cultural forms to be presented on the screen); a critical intellectual perspective (for broadcasters' complicity, through their close links to state power centres, in legitimizing capitalism); a public enlightenment critique (for disseminating too little information useful for popular understanding and participation in politics and culture); and a regionalist/localist critique (for undue commitment to metropolitan cultural perspectives at the expense of periphery interests). For beleaguered public broadcasters this was unfortunate, since many of the groups concerned shared only a common distaste for the 'privatization of public communication'. Consequently, (as Syvertsen soberly concludes) 'the best hope [for] public broadcasters' is a 'negative alliance' in their support (1991: 111–12).

Third, politicization ensured that public broadcasters were often snared in a 'damned if they do and damned if they don't' trap, open alike to accusations of undue passivity and of obtrusive intervention in politics (Blumler et al., 1986). When apparently free to take independent initiatives, images of arrogance, complacency and an 'over-mighty subject' were triggered. But when they endeavoured to be responsible and discreet, equally damaging images of timidity, subservience and abdication of journalistic norms came to the fore.

All this strengthened the appeal of a liberal-utopian vision of an infinite number of communication channels, in which all would-be programme providers would be free to pursue their own creative and political stars without fear of state control.

Economic factors

Parallel trends were simultaneously undermining the financial footings of old-style public television in Europe. Licence fee income increases, resulting over much of the postwar period from the diffusion of first black-and-white and then colour sets throughout the population, had reached a ceiling in the 1970s. With the onset of inflation, coupled with proportionately steeper increases in programme production costs, licence fee revenue then began to decline in real terms – for example, by 30 per cent from 1972–3 to 1983–4 in Sweden (Nowak, 1991). This not only pinched the prospects for a vigorous public service fightback; because they could not afford it, any real involvement of public broadcasters in the new media revolution was also ruled out – except here and there, as exemplified by the German satellite services of ARD and ZDF, or, as with teletext, on only a modest scale. This left most of the pioneering interventions in the hands, then, of national and international private entrepreneurs. An instructive 1990 example was the inability of BSB, the British satellite operation licensed as a public service by the Independent Broadcasting Authority, to survive in competition with Skytelevision (a Rupert Murdoch venture) as the financial stakes became increasingly prohibitive. In addition, the revenue/cost crunch has increasingly impelled public broadcasters to seek co-production projects and international marketing deals, with corresponding risks of diluting their programming distinctiveness.

Meanwhile, economic and financial criteria have been playing an ever more central part in the standards of evaluation by which public television performance is measured. Thus, by far the most influential part of the Peacock Committee report (1986) on British policy appeared in Chapter 4, entitled 'The "Comfortable Duopoly"', in which it was argued that neither the BBC nor ITV was under a sufficient financial discipline to keep its costs down. From this diagnosis stemmed recommendations (all subsequently accepted by the Government) to: oblige both BBC and ITV to commission by 1992 at least 25 per cent of their programming from independent producers not in their employ; to break the ITV companies' monopoly grip on television advertising by allowing Channel 4 to sell its own commercial time and by introducing a fifth, advertising-finance terrestrial channel; and to award licences for Channels 3 and 5 to the highest bidder in a sealed-envelope auction (among applicants who first passed a quality threshold). This inversion of priorities contradicted the prerequisites of quality programming as public broadcasters had previously understood them. Hence, Forman's (1987) *cri de coeur* about a 'change in the mood towards television – not [among viewers] . . . but [in] the mood of our masters, who have come to see television as an industry, and an industry in need of reform' and his call for a political will that would 'show as much interest in good television as in cheap television'. As a result, public service broadcasters have been thrown onto the defensive, having to justify themselves on issues where they were relatively weak and virtually having to keep silent about their traditional strengths.

Relations with the audience

In its heyday, the relationship of European public television to its mass audience of individual viewers compounded two somewhat opposed elements. On the one hand, the broadcasters felt a close bond with an audience for which they were striving to do so much – one that they could also imagine was broadly reciprocated. On the other hand, there was a strain in its programming profiles against the grain of mass taste. Everywhere there was some gap between the shares of scheduling time devoted to different kinds of programming and the shares of audience time devoted to watching them. In some systems this may have been less pronounced than in others. Blumler, Brynin and Nossiter argued that British television stood up quite well by this criterion:

> Despite a lingering Reithian legacy, a great strength of public service broadcasting, as practised in Britain, has been how it has carried the mass audience along with it: often catering for popular tastes with high-quality production standards and offering diversity to stretch interests and horizons without creating an impression that uplift was being imposed. (1986: 354)

In the absence of such a blend, however, the new entrepreneurs were able to present themselves as the people's champions against entrenched and stuffy élites. Mazzoleni considers that the arrival of competition in Italy, for example, jolted RAI out of its monopolistic 'inertia' and made it aware that 'the public demanded modifications of programmes in terms of quantity, novelty, and service', precipitating a 'conversion from a heavy cultural perspective to a more commercial one' (1991: 229–30).

With an increase in channels and national and foreign competition, three problems ensued for public broadcasters. First, the pursuit of their cultural mission became less straightforward and more subtle. As McQuail points out in Chapter 7 on the Netherlands below, there could no longer be any question of paternalistically imposing such a mission on a captive audience. Viewers would have to be carried along at every stage and instance of its provision. On this matter (as well as on many others in the new media environment), the coping problems for broadcasters in smaller states – with fewer resources to lavish on domestic talent and appealing production values – are particularly acute (Trappel, 1991).

Second, the blast of commercial-populist competition was so strong in some countries that the very survival of the public broadcasting organizations seemed at risk. Policies of trying to beat, or at least match, the competition on its own terms have been adopted, cramping if not abandoning the public service remit in prime time at least. Early examples included RAI's responses to Berlusconi's three networks of uncontrolled private television in Italy as well as the emergence of what was called 'Trossification' in Holland (see Mazzoleni, Chapter 6, and McQuail, Chapter 7 below). Creeping signs of 'self-commercialization', with some convergence of the programming offered by public and private broadcasters, have also been reported in France, Spain, Switzerland and (relatively slightly) in Germany. In Flemish-speaking Belgium, a drastically plummeting fall in public television viewing following the launch of a private terrestrial channel has compelled BRT to concentrate on fighting like with like (de Bens, 1991).

Third, a demographic weakness underlies these other difficulties. Audience statistics repeatedly show that when new and privatized services are introduced, they are patronized particularly heavily by younger elements of the population – which are precisely the segment that advertisers wish to reach and are prepared to pay premiums for. The long-term threat to public broadcasters' bonds with their audiences could be serious.

Back to their masters
Finally, it would be understandable if many European broadcasters felt somewhat let down by the politicians who were ultimately responsible for policies to effect the transition from public service-dominated regimes to the mixed public/private economies of 1990s television. The situation was complex and variable, but politicians often seemed to give a higher priority to the international telecommunications competition, to new media development as industries, to pressures to economize, and to their own partisan advantage, than to the maintenance of programme quality and range. In Britain, for example, although the Government designated the BBC the 'cornerstone' of public service broadcasting for the 1990s (Home Office, 1988), it has been exerting pressure on its licence fee support (awarding a rise in winter 1991 3 per cent below the increase in the retail price index). A glaring example of such political indifference was the willingness of the Italian political parties to allow private broadcasting to lapse into 'a state of lawlessness' for more than a decade (Mazzoleni, 1991: 214). If Germany is distinctive for the relative care and consideration shown the interests of its public broadcasters, this may have something to do with the fact that the key decisions were taken, not by party politicians, but by judges of its Federal Constitutional Court.

References

Annan Committee (1977) *Report of the Committee on the Future of Broadcasting.* Cmnd 6753. London: HMSO.

Blumler, Jay G. (1980) 'Mass Communication Research in Europe: Some Origins and Prospects', *Media, Culture & Society*, 2 (4): 367–76.

Blumler, Jay G. (1986) 'Television in the United States: Funding Sources and Programming Consequences', in *Research on the Range and Quality of Broadcasting Services*. London: HMSO. pp. 73–152.

Blumler, Jay G. (1990a) 'Television and Politics: The British Public Service Model', paper presented at the Aspen Institute Conference on Television Coverage and Campaigns: Models and Options for the US–USSR Commission on Television, Wye Woods, Maryland.

Blumler, Jay G. (1990b) 'Elections, the Media and the Modern Publicity Process', in Marjorie Ferguson (ed.), *Public Communication: The New Imperatives*. London, Newbury Park and New Delhi: Sage. pp. 101–13.

Blumler, Jay G., Brynin, Malcolm and Nossiter, T.J. (1986) 'Broadcasting Finance and Programme Quality: An International Review', *European Journal of Communication*, 1 (3): 343–64.

Blumler, Jay G., Gurevitch, Michael and Nossiter, T.J. (1986) 'Setting the Television News Agenda: Campaign Observation at the BBC', in Ivor Crewe and Martin Harrop (eds), *Political Communications: The General Election Campaign of 1983*. Cambridge: Cambridge University Press. pp. 104–24.

Broadcasting Research Unit (1985). *The Public Service Idea in British Broadcasting: Main Principles*. London.

Burgelman, Jean-Claude (1989) 'Political Parties and their Impact on Public Service Broadcasting in Belgium: Elements from a Political-Sociological Approach', *Media, Culture & Society*, 11 (2): 167–93.

Crewe, Ivor (1983) 'The Electorate: Partisan Dealignment Ten Years On', *West European Politics*, 6 (4): 183–215.

Curran, Charles (1979) *Broadcasting: A Seamless Robe*. London: Collins.

de Bens, Elsa (1991) 'Flanders in the Spell of Commercial Television', *European Journal of Communication*, 6 (2): 235–44.

Fabris, Hans Heinz (1990) 'Liberal Protectionism: The Case in Austria', paper presented at a conference on Vulnerable Values in Multichannel Television Systems: What European Policy Makers Seek to Protect', Liège, Belgium.

Forman, Denis (1987) 'Will TV Survive the Politicians and the Media Mercenaries?', *The Listener*, 16 July.

Hetherington, Alastair (1987) Lecture to Conference on the Future of Broadcasting after Peacock, York.

Home Office (1988) *Broadcasting in the '90s: Competition, Choice and Quality*. Cmnd 517. London: HMSO.

Katz, Elihu (1985) 'The New Media and Social Segmentation', paper presented at a conference on The Individual and New Communication Technologies, Heidelberg.

Kelly, Mary (1983) 'Influences on Broadcasting Policies for Election Coverage', in Jay G. Blumler (ed.), *Communicating to Voters: Television in the First European Parliamentary Elections*. London, Beverly Hills and New Delhi: Sage. pp. 65–82.

McQuail, Denis (1991) 'Broadcasting Structure and Finance: The Netherlands', in Jay G. Blumler and T.J. Nossiter (eds), *Broadcasting Finance in Transition: A Comparative Handbook*. New York and Oxford: Oxford University Press. pp. 144–57.

Mazzoleni, Gianpietro (1987) 'Media Logic and Party Logic in Campaign Coverage: The Italian General Election of 1983', *European Journal of Communication*, 2 (1): 81–103.

Mazzoleni, Gianpietro (1991) 'Broadcasting in Italy', in Jay G. Blumler and T.J. Nossiter (eds), *Broadcasting Finance in Transition: A Comparative Handbook*. New York and Oxford: Oxford University Press. pp. 214–34.

Nossiter, T.J. (1986) 'British Television: A Mixed Economy', in *Research on the Range and Quality of Broadcasting Services*. London: HMSO. pp. 1–71.

Nowak, Kjell (1991) 'Television in Sweden 1986: Position and Prospects', in Jay G. Blumler and T.J. Nossiter (eds), *Broadcasting Finance in Transition: A Comparative Handbook*. New York and Oxford: Oxford University Press. pp. 235–59.

O'Brien, Terence H. (1937) *British Experiments in Public Ownership and Control*. London: George Allen and Unwin.

Peacock Committee (1986) *Report of the Committee on Financing the BBC*. Cmnd 9824. London: HMSO.

Rowland, Willard D. Jr (1991) 'Public Service Broadcasting: Challenges and Responses', in Jay G. Blumler and T.J. Nossiter (eds), *Broadcasting Finance in Transition: A Comparative Handbook*. New York and Oxford: Oxford University Press. pp. 315–34.

Rowland, Willard D. Jr and Tracey, Michael (1988) 'The Apple's Worm: Current Challenges to Public Service-Broadcasting Worldwide', paper presented at the International Institute of Communications Annual Conference, Washington, DC.

Semetko, Holli A., Blumler, Jay G., Gurevitch, Michael and Weaver, David H. (1991) *The Formation of Campaign Agendas: A Comparative Analysis of Party and Media Roles in Recent American and British Elections*. Hillsdale, NJ: Lawrence Erlbaum Associates.

Sepstrup, Preben (1986) 'The Electronic Dilemma of Television Advertising', *European Journal of Communication*, 1 (4): 383–405.

Syvertsen, Trine (1991) 'Public Television in Crisis: Critiques Compared in Norway and Britain', *European Journal of Communication*, 6 (1): 95–114.

Trappel, Josef (1991) 'Born Losers or Flexible Adjustment: The Media Policy Dilemma of Small States', *European Journal of Communication*, 6 (3): 355–71.

Warnock, Baroness (1990) 'Quality and Standards in Broadcasting', in Nod Miller, Cresta Norris and Janice Hughes (eds), *Broadcasting Standards: Quality or Control?* Manchester: University of Manchester School of Education. pp. 5–24.

Young, Sir Brian (1983) *The Paternal Tradition in British Broadcasting 1922–?*. Edinburgh: Heriot-Watt University.

3

Vulnerable Values at Stake

Jay G. Blumler

The blizzard of change has *partially* transformed the European broadcasting landscape. Free market models have been introduced for the first time on something like their own terms; yet they also cohabit with many other forces and logics. Although commercial principles and private services have advanced everywhere, such gains were often preceded by intense, heated and prolonged policy debate over issues that continue to stir controversy and concern (see for examples the Part II chapters on Britain, Germany, Italy and Sweden). Nowhere has the market philosophy of television provision scored a clean sweep.[1]

The Appeals of a Market Approach

The march of the market has taken many forms. New private channels of terrestrial television have been (or are about to be) licensed in all the countries covered by this study (except Switzerland). The cabling of households – first diffused extensively in Belgium and the Netherlands; spreading rapidly at the time of writing in Germany, Sweden and Switzerland; but still making little progress in Britain and Italy – has increased viewers' exposure to external as well as domestic sources of commercial television. Satellite services, designed for transnational marketing and available to viewers over cable or directly to homes that have bought suitable reception dishes, have 'invaded' most domestic broadcasting systems, reaching an increasing number of households and in some cases posing sharp challenges to past broadcasting polices (see especially McQuail on the Netherlands and Hadenius on Sweden, Chapters 7 and 8 below, respectively). Otherwise, a major public channel has been privatized in France (TF1). In French-speaking Belgium, the public broadcaster (RTBS) was allowed to sell advertising for the first time in 1989 (de Coster and Stephane, 1990). In Ireland, a ceiling has been imposed on the amount of income that the public broadcaster (RTE) can earn from commercials, in order to help a newly licensed private channel to sell advertising. In

Britain, competition for advertising has been introduced for the first time by allowing the innovative Channel 4 to sell its own commercial time; and licences for the established Channel 3 franchises will normally be awarded in a sealed-envelope auction to the highest qualified bidder. Some details of the main commercial inroads may be consulted in Tables 3.1 (on the introduction of private channels), 3.2 (for cable penetration) and 3.3 (on the creation of satellite services).[2]

A mixture of principled considerations and well-mobilized interests has paved the way for these commercializing trends (see Hoffmann-Riem, 1990, for a systematic review of the influences at work).

Some part was played by the technological argument that the overcoming of frequency scarcity undermines the regulatory rationale or at least makes regulation less essential when there is no longer a single monopoly broadcaster. In any case, policy makers could not stand in the way of channel abundance once it was technically feasible; and the opportunity to exploit it mainly fell into private hands, since Government decisions ensured that few of the financially squeezed public broadcasters could afford to invest in its provision.

Increased competition was also justified by appeals to principles of economic and political liberalism. Whereas the previous shortage of frequencies had 'frozen' the freedom of entrepreneurial broadcasting, its elimination enabled such freedom to be more fully activated. Political liberty would also be advanced, it was hoped, by pushing state-supported television over to one side. Pluralism and diversity might be achieved more freely in an 'external' form across the promised multitude of channels instead of through managerial feats of balanced scheduling, channel by channel, in its historic 'internal' form. For its part, the British Peacock Committee on Financing the BBC viewed the introduction of an open and competitive programming market as a step toward the realization of consumer sovereignty in broadcasting, arguing that:

> It is a good general principle that any service to the public should be designed to promote its satisfaction. If this principle is to govern the provision of a service, it can be shown that, provided certain conditions are fulfilled, the public are best served if able to buy the amount of the service required from suppliers who compete for custom through price and quality. In addition, the stimulus of competition provides further benefits to the public through the incentive given to offer new and improved services . . . . The fundamental aim of broadcasting policy should [therefore] be to increase both the freedom of choice of the consumer and the opportunities available to programme-makers to offer alternative wares to the public. (1986: 28)

Table 3.1   *Mix of public and private terrestrial channels:*
Selected European countries, 1990

Country	No. of channels			Remarks
	Public	Private	Total	
Austria	2	–	2	Government policy to introduce private television.
Belgium				
Flanders	2	1	3	No country-wide channels.
Wallonia	2	1	3	No country-wide channels.
France	2	4	6	
Germany (West)	3	4	7	One public channel regionally structured. Not all private channels country-wide.
Italy	3	6	9	Three private Berlusconi channels. Also some local stations.
The Netherlands	3	–	3	
Portugal	2	–	2	Government policy to introduce at least two private channels.
Spain	2	2	4	Eight regional governments have also authorized public channels.
Sweden	2	–	2	Government policy to introduce one advertising-financed channel.
Switzerland	3	–	3	Linguistically distinct (German; French; Italian). Draft law for eventual private television.
United Kingdom	2	2	4	Private channels regarded as part of public service system in past. 1990 Act relaxes controls and authorizes another private channel.

Sources: Gliebel et al. (1990); *Medeien Jahrbuch* (1990) vol. 1, Ulm

Industrial policy considerations, fed by images of television as a rapidly globalizing medium (Ferguson, 1990), were a third force for commercialization. Regulatory supervision should be relaxed, it was argued, to boost the export potential for communication hardware and for domestic broadcasters, programme producers and ancillary media companies to gain readier access to the international market and to be more competitive in it.

Table 3.2 *Penetration of cable television: Selected European countries, 1990*

Country	TV households (millions)	Cable households (millions)	Per cent cabled
Austria	2,749	0,613	22.3
Belgium	3,266	3,262	99.8
France	20,000	0,278	1.4
Germany (West)	32,532	7,250	22.3
Italy	20,000	–	–
Netherlands	5,800	4,580	79.0
Portugal	3,185	–	–
Spain	10,540	0,030	0.3
Sweden	3,314	1,152	34.8
Switzerland	2,400	1,800	75.0
United Kingdom	21,700	0,312	1.4
All Western Europe	133,820	22,019	16.4

Source: *Media Spectrum* (1991), no. 4, p. 46

The international dissemination of commercial broadcasting was facilitated by a fourth factor: the emergence of a 'television without frontiers' policy for an unimpeded circulation of advertising and programmes among member countries of the European Community. Culminating in the adoption of a European Community Directive in 1989 (after five years of cross-national discussion, bargaining and compromise), this obliged all member states to admit channels and services originating in other Community countries, provided that they conformed to certain minimum standards. Commercials, for example, should take up no more than 15 per cent of broadcasting time per day on average (no more than 20 per cent in any clock hour). Closer restrictions on advertising in certain types of programming (feature films, news, current affairs, documentaries, children's and religious programmes) were specified as allowable. The Directive's provisions on programme content mainly centred on protection of the physical, moral and mental development of minors from exposure to pornography and gratuitous violence. Countries were also strongly urged to ensure that a majority of their programmes would be of European origin, though this was to be achieved 'progressively', 'where practicable' and 'on the basis of suitable criteria'.[3] Possibilities of broadcasting system control were weakened in two ways. For one thing, a fair wind was given to satellite-carried commercial programming, so long as it emanated from other European countries and did not violate the above-mentioned standards. In some countries, the hold of public service broadcasters on their national audiences was seriously threatened as a

Table 3.3   Satellite television services operating in Western
Europe, 1990

Service	Owner	Program-ming	Language	Remarks
BBCTV Europe	BBC	General	English	
SVT1/SVT2	Sveriges TV	General	Swedish	
TVE Int'l	RTVE	General	Spanish	
RAI1/RAI2	RAI	General	Italian	
A2	Antenne 2	General	French	
3-Sat	ZDF/ORF/SRG	General	German	3-nation; German language
TV5 Europe	TF1/A2/SRC/TVA/ FR3/RTBF/SSR	General	French	Multinational; French language
La Sept	French Government	Culture	French	
Sky One	News Int'l	Entertain-ment/news	English	
Superchannel	BetaTV/Virgin	Entertain-ment/news	English	
RTL Plus	CLT/Bertelsmann	Entertain-ment/news	German	
Sat 1	Kirch/Springer	Entertain-ment/news	German	
Pro 7	Kirch/Ackermann	Entertain-ment/news	German	
Tele 5	Telemünchen/CLT	Entertain-ment/news	German	
TF 1	Bouygues/Maxwell	Entertain-ment/news	French	
Canal Plus	Havas	Movies/sport	French	Pay-TV
La Cinq	Hersant/Fininvest	Entertain-ment/news	French	
M6	CLT/Lyonnaise	Entertain-ment	French	
TV3	Scansat	Entertain-ment	Swedish, Danish, Norwegian	Scandinavian
KTL 4 Veronique	CLT	Entertain-ment	Dutch	
Galavision	Euro Visa Ltd.	Entertain-ment	Spanish	
Nordic Channel	Karissima AB	Entertain-ment	Swedish	
FilmNet	Esselte	Movies	English	Pay-TV
Sky Movies	News Int'l	Movies	English	Pay-TV
Teleclub	Kirch/Ringier	Movies	German	Pay-TV
SF Succe	Svensk Film Time–Warner	Movies	Swedish	Pay-TV

Table 3.3 continued

Service	Owner	Programming	Language	Remarks
TV 1000	Kinnevik	Movies	Swedish, Danish, Norwegian	Pay-TV
Children's Channel	British Telecom	Children	English	
Kindernet	W.H. Smith	Children	Dutch	Pay-TV
Canal J	Hachette	Children	French	Pay-TV
Eurosport	News Int'l	Sports	English, German	
Screen Sport	Smith, ESPN	Sports	English	
Sport Kanal	Smith, MHV, CCR	Sports	German	
TV Sport	Smith, GDE	Sports	French	
EBC	AWF	Business inform'n	English, German	
MTV Europe	Viacom, Mirror	Pop videos	English	
CNN Int'l	Turner	News	English	
Worldnet	USIA	News	English	
Lifestyle	W.H. Smith	Women's	English	
Discovery Channel	UAE, Discovery Channel	Nature documentaries	English	Pay-TV

Source: *SZV/ASE Bulletin* (1990), no. 3, p. 13

result (see the chapters on the Netherlands, Sweden and Switzerland in Part II). In addition, doubt was cast on the legality of certain protective measures that national policy makers might wish to adopt – for example, the French-Belgian community's attempt to exact special levies from foreign broadcasters' earnings within its borders, to be channelled to a fund for indigenous audio-visual production (de Coster and Stephane, 1990).

Finally, powerful interests, formerly excluded from much involvement or profit in national broadcasting systems, lobbied hard on behalf of liberalization, commercialization and deregulation. In some countries (for example, Germany), it was initially newspaper publishers who forced their way into the broadcasting field, seeking a new sector of operations in which to invest their often substantial profits, expecting to have good start-up chances due to their media expertise. In others, (for example, Britain), it was advertising interests, who argued that an expansion of commercial time on television would lower the extortionate rates they claimed they were being charged and would invigorate the economy generally. At the same time, increasing influence was being asserted throughout Western Europe by large multi-media conglomerates, winning places for themselves in certain national systems (for example, France) on the strength of their supposed ability to advantage the country concerned in the international television marketplace.

Doubts about Fully Competitive Television

Nevertheless, many reservations caused European policy makers to stop well short of injecting a full-blown commercialism into 1990s televison.

One was a set of prudential considerations. Whatever its limitations and however open to criticism, European public service broadcasting had many widely appreciated achievements to its credit. Few viewers would thank any politician who proposed to cut off such benefits at an abrupt stroke of policy. Nor would it be advisable to jeopardize them for the sake of free market doctrine before the extent of its fruits could be witnessed on household screens. The resulting pitch for change-with-preservation was exemplified by the White Paper in which the British Government presented its ideas for restructuring broadcasting: 'The Government understands and values the rich heritage of British broadcasting: although its proposals are radical they preserve strong elements of continuity. Our broadcasting system has had notable successes. One of the Government's main objectives is to maintain and strengthen its quality, diversity and popularity' (Home Office, 1988: 4). There was also something rather grand – worth taking pride in and keeping alive somewhere – about that 'high moral ground' which public service broadcasters had tried to occupy in the past (see Hearst, Chapter 5 below).

Second, most European societies lack the kind of capitalist culture which, in the United States, leads almost automatically to the equation of greater business competition with more diversity, freedom, consumer welfare and democracy. McChesney (in press) notes how 'Capitalism has been off-limits as a topic of political discussion' in the United States 'since at least the First World War and arguably as far back as the 1890s'. This has made it extremely difficult for critics of American television to question its predominantly private ownership and the pervasive role of advertising in it. Regulation has been so closely equated with government interference and control that, from the 1930s onwards, spokespersons of commercial broadcasting could claim virtually without challenge: 'that a free radio and a free democracy are inseparable; that we cannot be a controlled radio and remain a democracy; that when a free radio goes, so also goes free speech, free press, freedom of worship, and freedom of education' (Sarnoff, 1937). In contrast, most European countries have hosted strong (and sometimes ruling) socialist and social-democratic parties, and more goods have been reserved for public support for fear of neglect or damage by unbridled market forces. Consequently, the principle that a democratic society should have some say in the direction of its broadcast media, taking account of their enormous potential for sociopolitical influence, has been more readily accepted.

Third, although the internationalization of television has unleashed deregulatory impulses, it has also made many Europeans feel culturally beleaguered. The large public broadcasting organizations might offer stronger defences against an imported flood of Hollywood series and movies than upstart private operators, eager to buy cheap but popular programmes off US shelves. As the research department of NRK, the Norwegian public service broadcaster, urged: 'The answer to the challenge from abroad is to have more and better national television' (cited in Rowland and Tracey, 1988: 25).

Fourth, caution was counselled by awareness of the cultural and representational power of mass media generally and television specifically in modern society (Blumler, 1987: 65). Mass communication is now widely regarded as an influential 'part of the larger social process of creating meaning' and a 'key vehicle through which the various . . . individuals and organisations that make up society try to define themselves and others' (Turow, 1991: 224–5). This has prompted determined efforts by many interest and cause groups to influence the symbolic contents of the mass media, sensitized to them as possible 'purveyors of stereotypical images of their identities, be they related to gender, ethnicity, class, age or sexual preference, which it is then in their interest to challenge and displace' (Blumler, 1990a: 105). In such a competitive climate of image maintenance, public television has decided advantages over commercial television for groups concerned about their communication destinies. With more time available for public affairs, there should be more ample chances to put their own views across. With less responsiveness to ratings pressures, there should also be less submission to those simplifying and sensationalizing tendencies that establish and entrench stereotypes of all kinds.

Fifth, national public broadcasting organizations drew strength from the roots sunk into their social structures in the period when they alone provided radio and television service. An outstanding example is the Netherlands, where each recognized broadcasting association was supposed 'to represent some clearly stated societal, cultural, religious or philosophical stream' (in McQuail's words, Chapter 7 below). In other systems, a host of groups were represented in public broadcasting governing bodies or advisory councils. Several chapters in Part II (for example, those on Switzerland, Britain and the Netherlands) draw attention to the loose coalitions that were mobilized to defend public service principles in the face of advancing commercialism, ranging from cultural conservatives to more left-wing elements, churches, parents' groups, writers' and artists' associations, plus articulate public broadcasters themselves.

Finally, perceptions of a sizeable gap between the promise and the performance of commercially fuelled multichannel television in the United States may have contributed to European hesitancy over market influences. Viewed from afar, the over-commercialization of American television looked to be at least partly responsible for its political communication system's 'crisis of cynicism, ignorance and apathy' (McChesney, in press). And so far as diversity was concerned, the market model appeared to pivot on a built-in tension. Supposedly suited to the promotion of external pluralism, it also breeds pressures that limit it. In light of recent research in the United States, the new television marketplace has been termed a 'skewed system', showing a decided 'hedonistic bias' that privileges 'entertainment programming and related production values, with a corresponding tendency to limit expenditure on other program types and qualities or to oblige them to conform to entertainment criteria' (Blumler, 1991a). Many social, creative and personal values could indeed be vulnerable in such a system.

Vulnerable Values Identified

Market pressures could jeopardize many features of television programming that West Europeans had previously taken for granted. Participants in the Liège conference of November 1990 concluded that West European policy discussion had concentrated most often on seven sets of values as sufficiently likely to be at risk in competitive multichannel conditions to deserve institutionalized protection in their emergent mixed broadcasting systems.

Programme quality
Notions of programme quality have become 'increasingly central to discussions of broadcasting purpose and policy in many countries', including those of Western Europe (Blumler, 1991b: 191; see also Ang, 1991: 136). However, the concept of quality in television has 'multiple meanings' (Ishikawa and Muramatsu, 1991: 209). This

follows from the fact that quality is best understood as 'a relation between sets of [programme] characteristics and sets of [assessment] values', which cannot be reduced to some single criterion (Rosengren et al., 1991: 50). What matters for good broadcasting arrangements, then, is not that some particular criterion of quality should prevail over all others (elevating subjective preference to the status of a dominant principle) but (a) that the system as a whole should regard the pursuit and evaluation of programme quality as a priority goal and (b) that a wide-ranging spectrum of the several types of excellence to which programme makers could aspire should be encouraged.

The chapters in Part II illustrate this diversity in the thinking of European policy makers about impending challenges to quality television, as they understand it. There has been an all-embracing conceptualization, exemplified by the proposition that: 'Good programme-makers will seek to make in all categories programmes that are "good of their kinds"' (Broadcasting Research Unit, 1989: 6). Quality has been given an upmarket meaning, associated with the traditional cultural vocation of public service broadcasting, in which contributions were expected 'to the development of culture, including the handing down of tradition, the creation of new cultural forms, and the promotion of education, cultural activities and sports' (Ishikawa and Muramatsu, 1991: 211). It has also been expressed as antipathetic to a preponderance in the schedules of 'fast-food-like', standardized programming – to a 'Dallasification' of European television (as Flemish-Belgian de Bens, 1991, puts it), in which 'all the new channels' might 'be filled with simple home-made game and entertainment shows and with American soap operas' (in Hadenius' words from Sweden).

In Western Europe it is widely feared that commercial incursions will undermine support for quality aspirations.[4] Such concerns are particularly marked in the larger countries, where more resources were always available to support a tradition of high production standards (in Britain, for example, where Hearst, Chapter 5, notes that respect for quality is 'firmly embedded' in the national culture, and in Germany) and in countries proud of their reputations as cultural powers (for example, Austria, according to Fabris, 1990). One reason for anxiety is that there could be less readiness to invest generously in quality television when something less expensive and less creatively satisfying might yield the same (or even a higher) ratings reward.[5] Another is that risk-taking for innovation will become less common when every rating point counts. Then, as multichannel competition heats up, the production environment could change, subjecting programme makers' creative impulses to:

rationalistic/calculative approaches to program planning and production; the frantic search for audience-maximising formulae; . . . the difficulty of 'knowing' one's audience, except through stereotypical images, when programs are destined for acceptance in multiple markets; factory systems of production . . .; and executive interference with program decisions in the uncertain pursuit of higher ratings. (Blumler, 1989: 25)

Decision-taking power could also shift from executives with programming experience to executives from business, sales and accounting backgrounds. In such conditions, what Hearst (Chapter 5) calls 'the best minds and talents in the country' might no longer be so attracted to work in television.

Diversity

Pluralism of many kinds – regional, linguistic, political, cultural, and in taste levels – was a hallmark of public service broadcasting organization and programming throughout Western Europe. If society is diverse in composition, it follows that each of its sectors should be able to find materials in the schedules reflective of its interests and with which it can identify. Individual audience members, differing in tastes and concerns, should also have a wide range of selection and choice, while the chance of coming into contact with the interests and ways of life of others should encourage the understanding and tolerance on which democracy depends (Blumler, 1991b; Ishikawa and Muramatsu, 1991).

The chapters in Part II are laced with many illustrations of commitment to this value. The Spanish broadcasting law of 1980, for example, enjoined 'respect for political, religious, social, cultural and linguistic pluralism'. According to McQuail (Chapter 7), 'pluriformity of structure and diversity of content' was 'the most distinctive and most fundamental value upheld' by the Dutch broadcasting system. Hoffmann-Riem (Chapter 4) describes how seriously the German Federal Constitutional Court has taken this value, ruling that private broadcasting is constitutional only within the framework of a dual and interdependent broadcasting order, in which a particularly full-blown notion of diversity is assured, comprising at least five dimensions: plurality of opinions aired, group standpoints presented, issues covered, territorial interests reflected and 'format diversity' (a balanced range of programme types) scheduled.

In essence, the West European fear is that the advent of commercial television will shift the emphasis from a *principled* to a *pragmatic* pluralism, yielding only that amount and those forms of diversity that are likely to pay. At risk could be poorly placed segments of the population: the underclass; the less informed;

children; the elderly; minority cultural interests; and holders of less orthodox opinions. Less popular programmes could be disadvantaged over resources (having to make do with less than before), scheduling (pushed out of prime time slots) and maintenance of stylistic integrity (under pressure 'to offer entertainment in other guises', as Blumler, 1991a, puts it).

Cultural identity
Collective identities are in turmoil throughout the world. Multiple identities vie with each other inside geographic and psychic spaces alike. Political forces throw their weight behind or cultivate support from allegiances to congenial identities. Extending communication networks are stirring this pot ever more vigorously, heightening awareness of change and challenge. There is associated ethical confusion over the relative claims of more cosmopolitan and more communally parochial standards. Conceptualization of the complex issues that have resulted is often unclear or inexplicit (Schlesinger, 1991).

   Western Europe is no exception. It has been rich in national and regional identities, interwoven with distinctive cultural traditions, historic memories, customs, social values, and styles of linguistic and artistic expression (for a sustained discussion, see especially Wolton's perspective from France in Chapter 10). Its national and regional services were regarded as prime sources of such expressions of identity, not only in news, current affairs and documentary output, but also in entertainment programming. As Buonanno explains:

> *television tells stories*, drawing on and expanding . . . ancient traditions which have their roots in myth. There is a great hunger for stories, and the tales told on television satisfy a deep need, the pleasure of listening, of letting oneself be carried away (in a 'suspension of disbelief') by the flow of the story; but at the same time, these stories are about *us*, or rather about the society and culture they spring from . . . . [Such] fiction [is] very useful for understanding and deciphering values, expectations, attitudes, dreams and fears, ways of seeing the world, which at any one time go to make up the cultural entity of a society. (1991)

In domestically produced television fiction, then, national audiences shared not only diversion and amusement, but also depictions of their societies' characteristic role patterns, issue frames, social conflicts and moral dilemmas. Today, despite watching many foreign programmes with pleasure, without wishing to cut themselves off from the outside world, and even whilst embarking on paths of more closely knit European integration, many Europeans are still primarily wedded to their historic national and regional identities, seen as particularly under threat. This explains Wolton's insistence on the need to strengthen the role of television 'as a social link *inside* a national community' and Europe-wide acceptance of the proposition that 'a country ought to produce from its own resources as high a proportion of the materials shown on its television services as possible' (Pragnell, 1985: 14).

The coming of commercial television seems to pose a double threat to this value. National communication systems are 'at risk of being subverted by a bland and homogeneous international media culture' (as McQuail puts it), when private satellite and terrestrial channels are stocked with foreign (chiefly American) series, films and game shows. It is also more difficult to sustain a strong indigenous production industry when resources flow toward the international media giants (see de Coster and Stephane, 1990, and Trappel, 1991, for discussion of the impact of this problem on smaller states, like Belgium and Austria).

Steps taken to defend this value have included licensing obligations on channels to strengthen and promote the national language; creation of services for national regions with distinctive cultures and tongues (in, for example, Spain, Switzerland, Belgium and for Wales in the United Kingdom); and quotas requiring both public and private channels to screen set proportions (often rising over time) of domestically produced programming.[6] In French-speaking Belgium a particularly ambitious programme to strengthen national production capacity has been mounted. An audiovisual development fund has been created, financed by levies on the revenues of the various players in its television system, private and public. Private stations must comply with certain quotas for production or co-production with French-Belgian companies. Sums that must be invested in different categories of such production have been fixed. Foreign services distributed in Belgium must pay levies to the audiovisual fund, proportionate to their audience ratings averaged over the year. Percentages of their advertising revenues are also being exacted for contributions to French-Belgian production. RTBS (the public broadcaster) is also expected to devote a significant proportion of its own advertising income to projects that will improve the quantity and quality of specified types of home-produced programmes (de Coster and Stephane, 1990).

Independence of programme sources from commercial
influences
The continuing force of anti-commercial sentiment in West European cultures is mentioned in many chapters in Part II. According to Hadenius (Chapter 8), for example: 'For many people in

Sweden, freedom from advertising has been the most important and the most vulnerable value in the broadcasting media.' Mazzoleni (Chapter 6) puts protection of the integrity of creative works (such as feature films) from interruption by advertising at the top of his list of values that Italians are keen to preserve in the new broadcasting order. According to McQuail (Chapter 7), 'non-commercialism' has been evinced in the Netherlands in a 'strong fear' that certain cultural and religious values could be threatened by 'submission to . . . commercial goals'. Among important historic influences on the evolution of the United Kingdom broadcasting system, Hearst (Chapter 5) mentions 'distrust of what the British opinion-forming classes called "commercialism"'. Saxer's specification of the values that underlie Swiss controls on television advertising (Chapter 9) applies to most European countries.

In some cases Europeans' mistrust of excessive commercialism has been quite comprehensive. In Sweden, for example, the proposed introduction of an advertising-financed terrestrial channel has been resisted for its potentially deleterious impact on *all* the values that television should serve: quality, diversity, objectivity in news reporting, cultural identity, etc. Elsewhere, a more focused approach to anti-commercial damage limitation has been taken. Certain programme forms (educational, cultural, news and public affairs, religious, childrens, feature films, etc.) have been singled out for protection from interruption by overly frequent commercial breaks. Elaborate codes on sponsorship have been drafted to defend both the integrity of programme content (for example, prohibiting sponsors' support for programmes that could have the effect of promoting their products or interests) and transparency (by requiring credits clearly indicating who the sponsors are). Under some codes, certain kinds of programmes may never be sponsored. In some countries, there are restrictions on advertising that masquerades as programming (teleshopping and what Americans call 'infomercials'). Finally, the viewer's interest, as a consumer of *programmes*, in not being the target of a veritable bombardment of distracting commercials has been safeguarded by a host of rules, setting maximum limits on advertising minutage per hour or day, and regulating the placement of commercials (whether in blocks or spots and if the latter how frequently).

The integrity of civic communication
So far few notes of alarm have been sounded in European policy circles specifically about this undoubtedly vulnerable value. In many countries, legislators appear to have been content to carry over the established requirements of impartiality, objectivity and non-

editorializing from the old broadcasting regime to its newer services (relaxed a little in some cases, but actually tightened a little in others).

Nevertheless, concerns to sustain the level of support that European television has hitherto accorded the civic sphere have surfaced in some countries under broader normative umbrellas: the British conception of quality, for example; the Swedish view of a broadcasting system little tainted by commercialism; and the German notion of diversity. This value happens to have a particularly firm constitutional basis in the German system, where (as Hoffmann-Riem explains in Chapter 4) freedom of broadcasting is not just conceived in terms of rights of expression, as in the US First Amendment, but also of 'the freedom of recipients to inform themselves comprehensively'. This requires 'the conveyance' in turn 'of information and opinions of all kinds', as well as safeguards against concentrations of informational power in the broadcasting sector. The British public service broadcasting model has recently been characterized in terms of such features as: 'a sense of some responsibility for the health of the political process and for the quality of public discussion generated within it'; a 'privileged status' for 'news and current affairs departments in the broadcasting system'; a ban on political advertising in television and radio; and 'a meticulous approach to impartiality, fairness and party balance' (Blumler, 1990b). According to Escobar-Lopez, the Spanish public broadcaster (RTVE) is expected to encourage viewers to identify with the values of freedom, justice, equality and political pluralism, promoting these not merely passively but actively for the health of democracy itself. The Swedish broadcasting law requires television and radio to 'uphold the basic concepts of democratic government'. According to Saxer (Chapter 9), Swiss broadcasting norms reflect the 'civic ideal of the politically interested and active citizen'.

The commercialization of European television could threaten the integrity of civic communication in several ways. The priorities of providers and viewers alike could shift from information toward entertainment. News bulletins could concentrate on presentation of the most dramatic and arresting events, short-changing analysis and discussion. Current affairs programmes could lose their cachet, and their producers could cater more for viewers' spectator interests than their citizen roles. Political competition could increasingly be presented through horse-race models and chess-like scenarios. Slogans, images and racy soundbites might take precedence over substance, information and dialogue.

Certain attempts to avoid these perils are noted by the authors of the chapters in Part II. In most European countries the sale of time for political advertising on radio and television is still prohibited (though Finland has recently legislated to allow such commercials in the future). Italy's long pending law to regularize and regulate its private television sector obliges the commercial networks to put on daily news programmes. The British Broadcasting Act of 1990 requires holders of commercial television licences to ensure:

> that a sufficient amount of time is given in the programmes included in the service to news programmes and current affairs programmes which (in each case) are of high quality and deal with both national and international matters, and that such news programmes are broadcast at intervals throughout the period for which the service is provided and, in particular, at peak viewing times.

Welfare of children and juveniles

The disparity between public and commercial provision is probably nowhere so dramatic and stark as in children's programming. Public broadcasters throughout the world have aimed to provide a goodly amount of educative fare, intended to inform, stimulate and broaden the horizons of children. Private broadcasters have concentrated instead on cartoon programmes, featuring robots, animated and stuffed animals, dolls and a range of animated adventure characters, including space fantasy heroes. Crass commercialism has been extraordinarily blatant in this area, shown in the United States by the screening of massive amounts of advertising in and around children's programmes, commercials delivered by programme presenters, and close ties between leading programme characters and toys on sale in the shops (Kunkel, 1988).

European recognition of children as potentially vulnerable viewers presumes the validity of three related values: respect for their developing educative needs; fairness in the sense of not exposing them to sophisticated advertising messages before they have developed a protective awareness of persuasion; and avoidance of exposure to overly adult fare. For the first of these concerns, Europeans are likely to depend mainly on a continuing commitment of their public broadcasters to educative programming for children, though in Britain, the 1990 Act requires commercial licence holders to give 'a sufficient amount of time' to 'programmes intended for children'. As to the second, several countries have banned advertising before, during and following children's programmes (for example, in Italy) and promulgated rules intended to restrict programming produced primarily to promote toys (though much vigilance and monitoring by parents' and consumers' bodies may be needed to keep regulators on their toes in this difficult area to police). On the third concern, so-called 'watershed' scheduling times now apply in most European societies – that is, certain specified hours before which broadcasters should presume that children will be in the audience and should not therefore be inadvertently exposed to more adult portrayals.[7]

Maintenance of standards
Though varying in approach and degrees of stringency, most European public television corporations had aimed to avoid deep offence to popular sentiment in the fields of violence, sex and use of bad language. It is presumed, however, that in more competitive conditions downward pressures might be exerted on such standards. Certain channels offering pornographic films to pre-paying subscribers have already appeared. More generally, as the need sharpens to attract and hold viewers' attention against rival attractions in the many other channels, producers of all kinds may rely increasingly on the shock troops of sex and violence. In the United States such a tendency has given centre stage 'to an ability to shock, scandal, prurience, titillation and combative confrontation' in certain genres of so-called 'reality programming' and 'tabloid television' (Blumler, 1989: 26).

European responses to such tendencies have been complicated, however, by changing and more permissive social attitudes toward moral conduct in the postwar period (as most of the authors in Part II, writing independently of each other on this point, note). In characterizing the Italian scene, for example, Mazzoleni (Chapter 6) declares that: 'Nowadays, however, conventions have changed, channels have multiplied, authors have become more daring, and live transmissions have increased in number, all making vigilance more difficult.' According to Fabris (1990), 'the social climate towards pornography' in Austria 'has in general become considerably more liberal in the 1960s and 1970s'. According to McQuail (Chapter 7), the Netherlands underwent a 'very marked social-cultural upheaval' in the same period, which transformed a 'traditional and rather culturally conservative society . . . into a standard bearer of change'. According to de Coster and Stephane (1990), a 'radical evolution of public morality' took place in Belgium in the 1970s. Saxer (Chapter 9) describes a gradual diffusion of hedonistic values in Swiss society over the postwar period.

European cultures also differ over what arouses greatest concern. According to Hadenius (Chapter 8), for example, the Swedish public has a 'high level of tolerance for erotic films', 'but the limits are far stricter when it comes to violence'. British viewers are reportedly more bothered by bad language on television than by violent or erotic episodes (Independent Television Commission, 1991). A diffuse nonchalance may be more prevalent in Italy, where, according to Mazzoleni (Chapter 6), there has been 'much indulgence toward certain forms of social and individual deviance from accepted moral standards'.

Nevertheless, the impending commercialization of television has been responsible for some tightening of supervision over standards in most West European countries. In Germany, for example, articles protecting juveniles and barring incitement to racial hatred, the glorification of violence and dissemination of pornography have been incorporated into the Interstate Treaty on public and private broadcasting. The Austrian draft law for the regulation of private television includes a clause forbidding pornographic or gratuitously violent content (Fabris, 1990). The Italian Broadcasting Act prohibits scenes of gratuitous violence and pornography and stipulates closure of a station as a penalty for transmitting films classified as not to be shown to young people under the age of 18. In advance of the pending introduction of two private channels in Portugal, much concern is being voiced about the need for television to uphold 'the fundamental values of the family', including a right 'to be protected from abuses [concerning] violence, pornography and eroticism' (Lopes da Silva, 1990). What is probably the most active intervention in this area has been initiated in Britain, however, where the Government has created a new body, the Broadcasting Standards Council, to oversee it. This was required to produce a Code of Practice on the presentation of violence, sexual conduct and bad language, to consider complaints from members of the public about alleged infringements (with requirements on offending broadcasters to publish unfavourable findings) and to undertake research into related issues of public taste and media effects.

From the General to National Particulars

The foregoing discussion has elaborated the theme of vulnerable values in the developing multichannel television systems of Western Europe in relatively abstract terms. In each case it has sought (a) to define the value concerned, (b) to illustrate how it has been expressed by those who care about it, (c) to explain why competitive commercialism is regarded as potentially threatening to it, and (d) to mention some of the measures that have been taken to realize or defend it. What such an analysis cannot show is how these concerns have arisen – and are treated as objects of debate, politicking and law making – in complex and fluid social and organizational settings. That is what the authors of the national case studies in Part II richly provide, fleshing out the historical origins, the varying priorities, the dynamics of sociopolitical and media change and the enforcement problems in which those values are concretely embedded. The chapters have not been pressed into a standard mould but reflect instead the individualities of different national cultures and circumstances and of their author-observers. However, they each tell a fascinating story – one that is still unfinished – blending genuine commitments with real predicaments.

Notes

1. A possible exception to this generalization is the special case of Luxembourg, where broadcasting was always in the hands of a private company (Compagnie Luxembourgeoise de Télédiffusion or CLT) – that is, before as well as after the onset of the new media revolution.

2. The data in these tables were compiled by Friedrich Krotz of the Hans-Bredow-Institut für Rundfunk und Fernsehen, Hamburg.

3. Similar provisions for most other West European nations were incorporated into a Convention of the Council of Europe. For further discussion of the European dimension of television regulation, see Papthanssopoulos (1990) and Wedell and Lange (1991).

4. Even the Dutch Broadcasting system, initially depicted by McQuail as little oriented in the direction of intrinsic cultural quality, is described by him as nevertheless putting 'a high value on artistic culture in general and also on science and information of all kinds, not only because of its own traditions but also because it has to make a living in the world by the application and handling of many forms of information'.

5. As a Canadian regulatory body argued in a recent report, 'While a program's costs are not always proportionate to its quality, there is generally a relationship between the two' (CRTC, 1989).

6. Due to EEC rules, such quotas are always expressed as percentages of programming from domestic *or* European Community sources.

7. These appear to range from 9:00 p.m. to 11:00 p.m.

References

Ang, Ien (1991) *Desperately Seeking the Audience*. London: Routledge.
Blumler, Jay G. (1987) 'Paradigm Lost', in Michael Gurevitch and Mark R. Levy (eds), *Mass Communication Review Yearbook*, vol. 6. Newbury Park, London and New Delhi: Sage. pp. 65–6.
Blumler, Jay G. (1989) *The Role of Public Policy in the New Television Marketplace*. Washington, DC: Benton Foundation.

Blumler, Jay G. (1990a) 'Elections, the Media and the Modern Publicity Process', in Marjorie Ferguson (ed.), *Public Communication: The New Imperatives*. London, Newbury Park and New Delhi: Sage. pp. 101–13.

Blumler, Jay G. (1990b) 'Television and Politics: The British Public Service Model', paper presented at the Aspen Institute Conference on Television Coverage and Campaigns: Models and Options for the US–USSR Commission on Television Policy, Wye Woods, Maryland.

Blumler, Jay G. (1991a) *Public Television in an Expanded Media Landscape*, monograph prepared for The Association of America's Public Television Stations, Washington, DC.

Blumler, Jay G. (1991b) 'In Pursuit of Programme Range and Quality', *Studies of Broadcasting*, 27: 191–206.

Broadcasting Research Unit (1989) *Quality in Television: Programmes, Programme-makers, Systems*. London and Paris: John Libbey.

Buonanno, Milly (1991) *Il Reale e Immaginario*. Turin: Nuova ERI.

CRTC (Canadian Radio-Television and Telecommunications Commission) (1989) *Local Television for the 1990s*, Public Notice 1989–27. Ottawa: CRTC.

de Bens, Elsa (1991) 'Flanders in the Spell of Commercial Television', *European Journal of Communication*, 6 (2): 235–44.

de Coster, Simon-Pierre and Stephane, Robert (1990) 'Measures Taken to Maintain the Quantity and Quality of Audiovisual Production in the French-Speaking Community of Belgium', paper presented at a conference on Vulnerable Values in Multichannel Television Systems: What European Policy Makers Seek to Protect, Liège, Belgium.

Fabris, Hans Heinz (1990) 'Liberal Protectionism: The Case in Austria', paper presented at a conference on Vulnerable Values in Multichannel Television Systems: What European Policy Makers Seek to Protect, Liège, Belgium.

Ferguson, Marjorie (1990) 'The Mythology of Globalization', paper presented at 18th Telecommunications Policy Research Conference, Airlie, Virginia.

Gliebel, T., Hubert E., Krotz, F. and Schuler-Harms, M. (1990) *Mediensysteme in Europe und Nordamerika: Eine Ubersicht*. Arbeitsberichte-Dokumentation No. 4 des Hans-Bredow-Instituts für Rundfunk und Fernsehen. Hamburg.

Hoffmann-Riem, Wolfgang (1990) *Erosionen des Rundfunkrechts: Tendenzen der Rundfunkrechtsentwicklung in West Europa*. Munich: C.H. Beck.

Home Office (1988) *Broadcasting in the '90s: Competition, Choice and Quality*. Cmnd 517. London: HMSO.

Independent Television Commission (1991) *Attitudes to Television in 1990*. London.

Ishikawa, Sakae and Muramatsu, Yasuko (1991) 'Quality Assessment of Broadcast Programming: Research Subjects for Future', *Studies in Broadcasting*, 27: 207–19.

Kunkel, Dale (1988) 'Children and Host-selling Television Commercials', *Communication Research* 15 (1): 71–92.

Lopes da Silva, Manuel José (1990) 'Vulnerable Values in Multichannel Television Systems: The Case of Portugal', paper presented at a conference on Vulnerable Values in Multichannel Television Systems: What European Policy Makers Seek to Protect, Liège, Belgium.

McChesney, Robert W. (in press) 'Off-limits: An Inquiry into the Lack of Debate Concerning the Ownership, Structure and Control of the Mass Media in U.S. Political Life', *Communication*.

Papthanassopoulos, Stylianos (1990) 'Broadcasting and the European Community: The Commission's Audiovisual Policy', in Kenneth Dyson and Peter Humphreys (eds), *The Political Economy of Communications: International and European Dimensions*. London and New York: Routledge. pp. 107–24.

Peacock Committee (1986) *Report of the Committee on Financing the BBC*. Cmnd 9824. London: HMSO.

Pragnell, Anthony (1985) *Television in Europe: Quality and Values in a Time of Change*. Manchester: European Institute for the Media.

Rosengren, Karl Erik, Carlsson, Mats and Tägerud, Yael (1991) 'Quality in Programming: Views from the North', *Studies in Broadcasting*, 27: 21–80.

Rowland, Willard D. Jr and Tracey, Michael (1988) 'The Apple's Worm: Current Challenges to Public Service-Broadcasting Worldwide', paper presented at the International Institute of Communications Annual Conference, Washington, DC.

Sarnoff, David (1937) 'Broadcasting in the American Democracy', in C.S. Marsh (ed.), *Educational Broadcasting 1936*. Chicago: Chicago University Press. pp. 146–55.

Schlesinger, Philip (1991) *Media, State and Nation: Political Violence and Collective Identities*. London: Sage.

Trappel, Josef (1991) 'Born Losers or Flexible Adjustment: The Media Policy Dilemmas of Small States', *European Journal of Communication*, 6 (3): 355–71.

Turow, Joseph (1991) 'The Challenge of Inference in Interinstitutional Research on Mass Communication', *Communication Research*, 18 (2): 222–39.

Wedell, George and Lange, André (1991) 'Regulatory and Financial Issues in Transfrontier Television in Europe', in Jay G. Blumler and T.J. Nossiter (eds), *Broadcasting Finance in Transition: A Comparative Handbook*. New York and Oxford: Oxford University Press. pp. 382–404.

PART II

NATIONAL EXPERIENCE

4

Protecting Vulnerable Values in the German Broadcasting Order

Wolfgang Hoffmann-Riem

The possibility of affording protection in the broadcasting order to values of importance to the individual or society as a whole is influenced by the overall structure of the broadcasting system. This chapter opens therefore with a brief description of the most important features of the German broadcasting order.

Dual Broadcasting System

Development of the German broadcasting order
During the establishment of a democratic state following World War II, considerable value was placed in the Western zones of occupation on an independent broadcasting system representing the diversity inherent in society (Bausch, 1980; Humphreys, 1990: 128ff.). Serving as a model was the BBC in Britain, where broadcasting was conceived of as a public service. In the Soviet zone of occupation, on the other hand, a state broadcasting institution was set up, which was employed as a means for realizing the socialist order and thus for exercising political control over citizens (Gerber, 1990).

In the West, broadcasting was financed by user fees (whereas the East relied on state subsidies), which were supplemented in the mid-1950s with advertising revenues. After decades of debate (Humphreys, 1990: 195ff.; Montag, 1978), private radio and television companies began to be licensed in the West in 1984. In the East, the monopoly over state broadcasting remained intact until 1990; nevertheless, programmes originating in the West, including broadcasts on private channels, were in recent years able to be received without interference. The decentralization of broadcasting in the GDR commenced in 1990, paving the way for the licensing of private broadcasters. The subsequent accession of the GDR to the Federal Republic of Germany has resulted in an adaptation to the Western broadcasting system (Hege, 1990).

At present, Germany is characterized by a co-existence of non-profit-oriented public broadcasting with private broadcasting, which is virtually exclusively dependent on advertising revenue. Pay-TV is in its inception and has thus far only been offered by private broadcasters. Public and private broadcasting alike are regulated by the special broadcasting laws of Germany's formerly 11, now 16 states (*Bundesländer*); these are accompanied by treaties between the states, such as the Interstate Treaty on Broadcasting of 3 April 1987 (Ring, 1990), revised 31 August 1991. The Federal Government itself has no jurisdiction over the broadcasting sector – apart from the field of foreign broadcasting. Because the broadcasting laws enacted by the states often deviate in substance from one another, the state of the law is far from uniform (Hesse, 1990; Ricker, 1985). Since it is not possible to describe these differences in detail here, the following will be limited to basic outlines.

The Federal Constitutional Court as substitute legislature
The development of West German broadcasting has been markedly influenced by the case law of the Federal Constitutional Court. In the course of resolving a number of fundamental disputes over broadcasting structure, it has established certain essential guidelines for the broadcasting order in a manner comparable to a legislature. The Court has based its decisions on a mandate, inherent in the basic right of freedom of communication (Article 5 of the Basic Law), that the legislature should specify the structure of the broadcasting order by law. Such laws must ensure the free formation of individual and public opinion in a broad sense, that is, not limited to mere news coverage or the conveyance of political opinions but rather encompassing the conveyance of information and opinions of all kinds (Bundesverfassungsgericht, 1961: 260; 1971: 326; 1973: 222–3; 1981: 319). From the standpoint of constitutional law, entertainment programmes are also of significance. The underlying assumption is that broadcasting is able to have an effect in all of its programmes on the individual and collective orientations of citizens and that it can be of importance in all areas of life. In addition to the freedom to express opinions and allegations of fact, the freedom of recipients to inform themselves comprehensively is also important. In short, freedom of broadcasting serves the freedom to form opinions. Realization of this

freedom, however, may be endangered by certain interests and is in need of special protection. On the one hand, freedom from state dominance and influence must be ensured; but also to be averted are other forms of abuse stemming from the one-sided exercise of influence over public opinion, especially by private interests. Powerful organizations in possession of transmission frequencies and the requisite financial means must be prevented from dominating the process of public opinion formation (Bundesverfassungsgericht, 1981: 323). In addition to such 'negative' defences, 'positive' institutional guarantees are also necessary to ensure that the diversity of existing opinions is conveyed as widely and completely as possible and that comprehensive information is provided. Broadcasting must not be left to the free play of forces, since, in the view of the Court, this free play – particularly in the economic marketplace – is incapable of preventing the concentration and abuse of power in the broadcasting sector.

The concept of freedom of broadcasting as serving other freedoms, as well as the necessity for statutory commitments ensuring diversity and independence in forming public opinion, are justified in much the same way as in most other Western broadcasting systems: with reference to the scarcity of frequencies and the great financial expenditure still required for effective broadcasting (Bundesverfassungsgericht, 1961: 261; 1971: 326; 1981: 322; 1986: 154). But even if these conditions were no longer applicable in the future, statutory precautions would still be necessary to ensure the independence and diversity of opinion: the possibilities for a concentration of power over opinion and the risks of misuse by one-sided interests are far too great (Bundesverfassungsgericht, 1981: 322–3). The Federal Constitutional Court thus considers broadcasting to be an agent of power and regards limitations on such power as indispensable. Since it does not believe that the economic market alone can achieve this, it has called upon the legislature to guarantee a variety of communication structures that are also able to satisfy minority interests.

The Court has made a sceptical prognosis over the range and quality of the programming likely to be offered by private broadcasters. In the private television sector, the Court does not expect a spectrum of programming that is broad in substance:

> since suppliers are virtually exclusively dependent on revenues from commercial advertising for the financing of their operations. These will flow in all the more lucratively when private programming achieves sufficiently high ratings. Suppliers thus are faced with the economic necessity of offering programmes with the highest possible mass appeal – which is accomplished by successfully maximizing viewer and listener

shares – at the lowest possible costs. Programmes that are only of interest to a limited audience and require great expense – as is often the case for particularly high-quality cultural programmes – will normally become a rarity, if not altogether absent. (Bundesverfassungsgericht 1986: 155–6).

It requires no detailed explanation that such diagnoses and prognoses by the Court and the conclusions drawn from them in political discussions are highly controversial (Engels et al., 1989; Mestmäcker, 1988). The heated policy debate over the licensing of private broadcasting, which was conducted in the Federal Republic in the 1980s (Humphreys, 1990), has left a number of deep scars. Even after the political course was settled, the battles continued on a different level, such as over interpretation of what the laws required concerning the supervision of broadcasting. In fact, the media sector is still riddled with controversy. The lack of a basic consensus impedes the practical application of statutory norms and thereby the protection of vulnerable values as well.

Constitutional guarantee of the dual broadcasting order
Despite the above-described reservations, the Federal Constitutional Court has held private broadcasting to be constitutional, but only within the framework of the dual broadcasting order. It proceeded from the assumption that diversity of opinion and independence can still be best ensured through fees-financed public broadcasting, since this is not subject to the dictates of viewer ratings or dependent on the advertising industry. So long as it provides comprehensive, diverse information, the statutory requirements on private broadcasting may be relaxed – but not abandoned (Bundesverfassungsgericht, 1986: 157–8; 1987: 325–6; 1991: 297–7). Only when the existence of public broadcasting is assured, may private broadcasting be exempted from some of those requirements. Thus, it must be guaranteed that public broadcasting retains its present transmission possibilities and mandate; that an adequate financial basis is provided for it; and in addition that it can enjoy full access to future technological developments (for example, HDTV, or high-definition television), including not only the technical but also the financial means to utilize them (Bundesverfassungsgericht 1987: 326).

Public broadcasting as such – though not necessarily any individual broadcaster – together with its largely market-independent financing is thus accorded a constitutional guarantee, that is, one not amendable by simple legislation. The Federal Constitutional Court apparently does not believe that private, market-oriented broadcasting can in the long run serve as a trustee for all societal interests and protect vulnerable values sufficiently, and it has therefore taken great pains to ensure such a lasting trusteeship role for public broadcasting to provide sufficiently broad, high-quality programming for all sections of the population. The dual broadcasting system is thus constitutional only if its public pillar is solid and secure.

A corresponding guarantee has not been accorded private broadcasting. But if it is permitted, then its ability to function must be ensured. The operation of private broadcasting should be subject to special licensing and to ongoing supervision by a state media authority. The legal requirements for the licence and the broadcaster's conduct need not differ according to mode of transmission technology. Cable broadcasting, for example, is subject to the same requirements as terrestrial broadcasting. In addition, there are no fundamental differences between radio and television.

Freedom of information and the free flow of communication

The Federal Constitutional Court has recognized that the international broadcasting market has effects on the national broadcasting order, which also influence the possibility of protecting vulnerable values. Since the Basic Law also protects the freedom to receive information, the Court respects transborder broadcasting. For practical reasons, it imposes less demanding requirements on the mere retransmission of programmes by cable than on terrestrial broadcasting (Bundesverfassungsgericht, 1986: 197–9; Hesse, 1990: 209–16). This refers both to programmes originating abroad and to programmes from broadcasters licensed in other German states. The level of protection in cable transmissions is consequently reduced. But here too the Court has called for safeguards to ensure that a 'minimum of substantive balance, neutrality and mutual respect' is guaranteed.

European Community norms take precedence over national broadcasting law. The Federal Constitutional Court will not measure such norms against German basic rights when comparable guarantees for the rights concerned are established in EC law. Although it has not yet had the opportunity to rule on whether Article 10 of the European Convention on Human Rights in conjunction with the basic rights recognized in the constitutional orders of the member states constitutes such a guarantee, it would undoubtedly assume this to be the case. Correspondingly, the Television Directive of the European Community must be observed in Germany.

Protection of Vulnerable Values in Broadcasting Laws

Vulnerable values

The state parliaments, which are responsible for promulgating broadcasting laws, have introduced the dual broadcasting system and in so doing followed the requirements set down by the Federal Constitutional Court. All broadcasting laws, whether for public or private broadcasting, contain norms for the protection of vulnerable values. These usually make no distinction between radio and television. The norms can be divided into two groups: from a negative standpoint, whether they ward off dangers for vulnerable values; or from a positive standpoint, whether they seek to ensure the provision of certain programme offerings that would not otherwise be produced at all or in the desired quality.

A number of broad social values which may be infringed by television programming are protected by the legal system in general. These include such values as rights of privacy and copyright, respect for religious feelings, public morals and – within narrow boundaries – national security, but not standards of taste and decency. Such values are protected by so-called 'general laws'. Freedom of communication is limited by these 'general' laws (Article 5 (2) of the Basic Law). Such limitations are permissible so long as their application complies with principles of proportionality, necessity and reasonableness (Hoffmann-Riem, 1989a: 432–7). Although these limitations occasionally appear in broadcasting laws as well, they are more often located in other norms, such as those of the Criminal Code.

The sound development of juveniles, for example, enjoys special protection (Hege, 1989; Jung and Müller-Dietz, 1981; Stefen, 1986). This is provided for not only in general juvenile protection laws but is mentioned in Article 13 of the Interstate Treaty on Broadcasting as well. Article 13 also contains a broad prohibition of incitement to racial hatred, glorification of violence and dissemination of pornography. The norm reads:

> Programmes shall not be permitted when they: (1) incite to racial hatred or portray cruel or otherwise inhuman acts of violence against persons in a manner glorifying or belittling such acts of violence or depicting the cruelty or inhumanity of the act in a form violating human dignity; (2) glorify war; (3) are pornographic; or (4) are clearly capable of posing a serious moral threat to children or juveniles. Programmes that are capable of interfering with the physical, mental or emotional well-being of juveniles may not be transmitted, unless the broadcaster takes precautions with regard to the time of broadcast or in some other manner ensures that children or juveniles of pertinent age are normally not able

to view the programmes; the broadcaster may assume this to be the case for programmes broadcast between 11 p.m. and 6 a.m.

These rules apply to the depiction of violence not only in fiction but also in news bulletins, in current affairs and documentary programming (Brockhorst-Reetz, 1989; Hartstein et al., 1990: 572–606). However, the relevant passages of the Act are so formulated that news coverage of real-life violence may not be forbidden (Brockhorst-Reetz, 1989: 44–5; Scharf, 1989). The boundary between permitted and prohibited violence consequently turns on whether it is 'glorified or belittled'. In uncertain cases, the decision must be made in favour of freedom of news coverage.

In addition to generally protected values, one also finds special values that are only protected in broadcasting laws, because they relate to the ability of the broadcasting order to function appropriately. These primarily have to do with the independence and diversity of communication offerings. The Federal Constitutional Court has repeatedly stressed that diversity is not a purely quantitative category. In interpreting its position, I have distinguished between at least five dimensions of diversity: (1) substantive, opinion-oriented diversity in programming, that is, especially the coverage of opinions on socially relevant issues and the exclusion of one-sided power over opinion; (2) individual- and group-oriented diversity, that is, providing important societal forces and groups with opportunities to express themselves; (3) issue-oriented diversity, that is, covering a sufficiently broad spectrum of issues in programmes; (4) territorial diversity, that is, coverage of views and news from the various local, regional, national and supra-national areas; and (5) format diversity, that is, a balanced provision across the various programming categories, particularly information, entertainment, education and advice (Hoffmann-Riem, 1989a: 492–3). The legislature is provided with discretion in regulating diversity and need not protect all of the above dimensions to the same degree. It must, however, provide stronger guarantees for public broadcasting than for private broadcasting, although a minimum amount of opinion and issue-oriented diversity is also required from the latter.

Consequently, broadcasting laws include norms about the general programming mandate that refer to these dimensions of diversity. They are accompanied by norms regulating how programming is to be structured, such as duties regarding thorough, conscientious researching, the separation of commentary from factual presentation in news and current affairs programmes, and journalistic fairness. In public broadcasting, diversity of opinion is particularly ensured by the requirement that in each channel the responsible broadcaster should provide all socially relevant forces and groups with an opportunity to articulate their positions, that is, to offer an internally pluralistic programming menu. In the case of private broadcasting, however, a certain degree of one-sidedness is permitted, so long as the offerings as a whole are sufficiently diverse (achieving external pluralism). Such diversity is usually assumed to be ensured when several – generally at least three – broadcasters are competing with one another, unless the supervisory authority determines that this is still insufficient to guarantee a plurality of opinion expression. If diversity of opinion is not ensured, then each broadcaster must provide for adequate diversity in its own programming.

Other norms serve to protect the recipient against excessive or manipulative television advertising. These primarily deal with such requirements as the separation of advertising from programming, the grouping of commercials into 'blocks' and the designation of commercials as advertising, as well as the prohibition of excessively frequent commercial interruptions. These norms were recently brought into line with the EC Television Directive.

Measures of protection
The broadcasting order recognizes a number of ways to protect vulnerable values. In essence, two types of regulation must be distinguished (Hoffmann-Riem, 1990: 16–23). One model works with command and control regulation, in which direct attempts are made to steer the conduct of broadcasters, including the content of their programming, through particular requirements, orders and prohibitions, with violations being negatively sanctioned. The other regulatory model sets up a structural framework – such as the basic economic structure (for example, a market-based economic order; designation of a certain source of finance) or rules specifying a pluralistic organizational structure – which is expected to influence conduct indirectly.

Command and control regulation is particularly employed to protect those values that are enforced by the legal system generally. Examples include prohibitions concerning threats to privacy rights, copyright and the healthy development of juveniles. In the broadcasting sphere specifically, however, this model covers such matters as the prohibition of broadcasting without a licence, the imposition of advertising restrictions and the enforcement of certain duties to provide diverse and balanced programming.

Nevertheless, some values cannot be protected by direct requirements and prohibitions alone. It has been recognized in many areas of society that reliance on requirements and prohibitions has had only a limited success in controlling conduct. As a result, more emphasis is being put on structural constraints. The Federal Constitutional Court recognized this at an early stage and stressed that organizational and procedural guarantees are needed to ensure independence and diversity in communication (Bundesverfassungsgericht, 1981: 320). The effectiveness of such structural provisions is greater to the degree that they activate the potential of organizations or groups of persons to develop self-regulatory mechanisms.

For example, public broadcasting is provided in Germany by broadcasting authorities, which are supposed to be organized pluralistically. Within this structure, there are collegial organs – the Broadcasting Council (*Rundfunkrat*) and the Council of Administration (*Verwaltungsrat*) – composed of representatives from a range of social forces and groups, the internal variety of which is intended to prevent any single element from exercising a one-sided influence (Herrmann, 1975; Hoffmann-Riem, 1979; Lerche, 1979). The statutory stipulation on public broadcasting finance is designed to ensure that programming is not unduly influenced by economic considerations, such as a drive to increase advertising revenue, or at least that – since advertising is permitted to a certain degree – the orientation to the advertising market does not predominate. This is to make it possible, for example, to continue to produce high-quality cultural programmes and to serve minority interests.

The private broadcasters, however, are at liberty to make their own decisions about sources of finance and forms of organization. In their field, the rationale for encouraging market-based competition is that the resulting free competition over programmes and audiences should help to realize diversity. Precautions are nevertheless necessary against imperfections in the market due to excessive concentration. This is principally achieved through application of the general norms of competition law, especially monopoly law, that is, the Act against Restraints of Competition. Monopoly law primarily serves to limit mergers and prohibits the abuse of market-dominant positions (Spieler, 1988). However, this is of only limited applicability to broadcasters. Therefore, to combat undue concentration in television and radio, special supplementary measures are needed in broadcasting laws (Bundesverfassungsgericht, 1986: 172ff.). These particularly include restrictions on multiple ownership and cross-ownership (though only to a limited degree in the latter case). However, even these provisions are relatively weak. Since, in the view of the Federal Constitutional Court, the market is insufficient as a regulator, additional precautions are needed against threats to diversity of opinion. The laws do not stipulate these in close detail but instead provide broadcasters with a margin of discretion. Licences are usually granted only to so-called *Anbieter-gemeinschaften*, undertakings in which a variety of different persons or enterprises must hold shares. This is based on the hope that the diversified composition of the broadcaster will ensure that its programming gives coverage to diverse interests. In addition, the media laws of some states entitle representatives of cultural interests to present their programming proposals to the broadcasters concerned and to secure considered reactions to them. Also mentioned is the possibility of establishing pluralistic councils, similar to the Broadcasting Councils of the public broadcasting authorities, that could play a counselling or even a decision-making role in programming matters. In some states, the law also encourages organizational guarantees of journalistic autonomy by stating that they may count in the broadcaster's favour when the franchise is to be renewed; this is based on the expectation that when journalists are enabled to act autonomously, the influence of their professional values will support plurality and the civic needs of the general public.

Supervision
Norms alone do not suffice for obtaining the desired results. It is also necessary to provide for their enforcement, for which there are a number of possibilities.

Some norms are enforced through the usual legal channels. For instance, the violation of criminal norms can be sanctioned by the prosecutor and the criminal courts; that of norms concerning privacy can be sanctioned by the injured party initiating a suit in the civil courts. When anti-monopoly laws are violated, the monopoly authorities can intervene. For protection of juveniles, Germany has, on the one hand, a state institution, a Federal Review Office, to review both written works (books, the press) and video recordings (*Bundesprüfstelle für judgendgefährdende Schriften*), and, on the other hand, a Voluntary Agency for the Self-Regulation of the Film Industry (*Freiwillige Selbstkontrolle der Filmwirtschaft*) for classification of theatrical films (Stefen, 1986). Both these bodies, however, have only a limited authority over television (Bundes-verwaltungsgericht, 1990: 933; Hartstein et al., 1990: 580 ff.). In particular, enforcement of the special juvenile protection norms is not their province but that of the broadcasting authorities (Hege, 1989).[1]

In public broadcasting, responsibility for the observance of norms in general (that is, not merely those of juvenile protection) is mainly entrusted to the Broadcasting Councils, though occasionally to the Councils of Administration as well (Herrmann, 1975). The Broadcasting Councils are expected particularly to monitor whether programming duties are being followed. In the event that these Councils do not fulfil their tasks, a state supervision authority may step in, which, however, has only limited sanctions (Berendes, 1973). Moreover, the Broadcasting Councils can challenge such rulings in the administrative courts.

For private broadcasting, special licensing and supervisory institutions (that is, so-called state media authorities) have been created in all states as part of the German broadcasting order. These bodies are independent of the Government. They are administered by a director and (usually) a pluralistically composed executive board. They decide on licence applications and monitor day-to-day conduct. They have been provided with relatively large staffs in order to be able to supervise programming in well-defined areas. Although German citizens lack formalized rights of participation in programming supervision, they may submit complaints to the state media authorities, which are free to decide how to react, both procedurally and substantively, to the charges made. When exercising their licensing responsibilities, the state media authorities review whether the applicant can be expected to observe the norms of the broadcasting and other relevant laws, and they can attach conditions to the licence, for example, to improve the chances for plurality. If they decide that norms have been violated, they can issue directives to eliminate the violations and, if necessary, revoke the licence, which is granted for a limited period of time. They can also enforce their directives by imposing fines. However, their decisions concerning the revocation of licences, the setting of conditions, the issuance of directives or the imposition of penalties can all be challenged before the administrative courts.

Effectiveness of Measures for the Protection of Vulnerable Values

Germany has a differentiated system for the legal regulation of broadcasting. By way of its – world-wide, undoubtedly unique – interpretation of the basic right of freedom of communication, the Federal Constititutional Court has formulated a position according to which the rules of the broadcasting order are not regarded as interfering with the broadcasters' freedom of communication; rather, they serve to structure that freedom in such a way that it is also ensured for recipients. As a result, the legislature's margin of discretion when setting up this structure is correspondingly broad. However, when freedom of communication is restricted in order to protect values that are already protected in the legal system generally, then this is said to constitute an 'interference' with freedom of broadcasting. Nevertheless, if such interference follows from the above-mentioned 'general laws', it may still be deemed lawful.

In line with the German tradition of rule of law, the norms that set out the statutory commitments on broadcasters are quite detailed; they establish sanctions and provide injured parties with remedies. At first glance, this does not appear to be a system of 'light-handed' regulation. A second glance, however, calls for a more reserved appraisal in view of the relatively limited effectiveness of much of this regulatory framework.

Public broadcasting
It has often been observed that for public broadcasting, the objectives desired by the laws have not always been obtained. For example, despite the guarantee of independence, political parties have been able to gain a decisive influence in the pluralistically composed Broadcasting Councils; this influence has then been exploited politically – often in cooperation with the respective state government – as in decisions on the hiring of top personnel or over programming matters (Kabbert, 1987; Menningen, 1981; Starck, 1970). In parliamentary democracies, it seems that many interest groups (as are principally represented in the Broadcasting Councils) tend to form coalitions along party lines. Political parties create platforms on which diverse interests can find some common ground. It has also been noted that the Broadcasting Councils often experience difficulty in monitoring programming effectively. Sometimes they are too reticent (leading to control deficits); sometimes they intervene too intensively and intimidate journalists. The often dysfunctional consequences include self-censorship and, in particular, a preponderance of orientations converging on the 'mainstream'.

Nevertheless, the system of countervailing checks and balances among the various forces has had some positive effects, in particular having given rise to relatively balanced programming. Minorities continue to be served by public broadcasting, and high-quality cultural and political programmes are quite often transmitted in prime time, even when they only obtain relatively low ratings. On the whole, German programming has achieved a world-wide reputation for high standards of quality. The instances when vulnerable values have been violated are relatively few. Nevertheless, competition with private broadcasting has prompted public broadcasters to make greater efforts to achieve high viewer ratings, in order, on the one hand, to avoid losing political legitimacy and, on the other, to generate the highest possible advertising revenues in the (limited) commercial period of the broadcasting day. As a result, one can witness a certain (limited) convergence in the programming offered by public and private broadcasters (Schatz et al. 1989), although there are still fundamental differences (Krüger, 1989; Stock, 1990).

Private broadcasting
The presence of public broadcasting and its competition with private broadcasters also have effects on the latter. In many areas, such as informational programming, they cannot avoid being measured against the model of public broadcasting and are encouraged to emulate it. Nevertheless, one notices that the programming of these broadcasters is resembling that in countries that have long had externally pluralistic private broadcasting. Predominant are mass-appeal entertainment programmes; informational programmes are not so highly represented; and minority programmes are a rarity (Krüger, 1988; 1989: see also Faul, 1989; Gellner, 1990: 265 ff.). Programmes with much violent content are more numerous than in public broadcasting. Late-evening schedules sometimes include erotic programmes (without being legally classifiable as pornography).

The institutions charged with licensing and supervision – the state media authorities – have experienced great difficulties in discharging their supervisory roles effectively. In view of the large number of broadcasters and amount of programming to be monitored, the practical administration of supervision is problematic. Since whatever supervisory action might be taken usually runs counter to the broadcasters' interests, considerable opposition from them can normally be expected. Although the supervisory authorities operate in a constitutionally and politically sensitive field, they also lack workable, easily enforceable norms. In spite of the fact that they contain quite detailed requirements, the laws often employ general clauses and vague legal terms, which necessitate much diagnostic and prognostic appraisal and entail quite broad decision-making discretion (Ziethen, 1989). Supervision of broadcasting involves uncertain decisions; nevertheless, it is subject to judicial review. Because of a lack of clear standards, there is a considerable risk that the supervisory decision will be rescinded in a court battle. It must also be borne in mind that the pluralistic supervisory organs are themselves composed of interest representatives, some of which may be sympathetic to the broadcasters being monitored. These broadcasters are often able to organize political support against supervisory interference with their operations. Furthermore, since many of the supervisory standards vary from state to state, the broadcasters are occasionally able to play the different supervisory bodies against each other. To counter this, however, the state media authorities make an effort to coordinate their supervisory activities.

Through such experience, the state media authorities soon realized that successful supervision often depends on close co-operation with the broadcasters being supervised. Only thus can they gain access to the information required for effective super-vision. Cooperative supervision is also less troublesome than con-frontational control. But even in a context of cooperative relations, it can be difficult to achieve effective supervision. For example, it is impossible to take action against concentration without precise information about ownership patterns. But there are so many ways to circumvent and to cloak the true participation data, via figure-heads, complex interlocking of companies and direct-control con-tracts, that the monitoring institutions are unable to obtain an adequate overview (Hoffmann-Riem, 1989c: 252–5; Thaenert, 1990). When advertising restrictions are violated, the broadcasters have a number of possibilities for side-stepping supervisory action, or even when they refrain from the specifically prohibited conduct, they can still devise other ways of pursuing their ends that undercut the objectives of the norms (Hoffmann-Riem, 1989c: 255–7). The norms for juvenile protection contain unclear standards, and every intervention is at once a problematic interference with broadcaster autonomy and programming freedom. Consequently, only flagrant violations are sanctioned. The excessive violence found in some cinematic films and US series normally remains unremonstrated, despite the fact that experts on juvenile protection predict substan-tial dangers. On many occasions, violent programmes have been granted exemptions from the scheduling time conditions laid down in the Interstate Treaty on Broadcasting (Hege, 1989: 32). All the same, the monitoring of juvenile protection does not appear to have been without result (Hege, 1989: 33–4).

Although the diversity-based programming duties are binding, they are difficult to translate into tangible demands and mainly have the force of mere exhortation. In some respects, the laws rely on fictions – such as the fiction of diversity when at least three broadcasters are competing with one another. In view of the difficulties involved in the operationalization of norms and the risks of abuses of supervisory power, the control bodies often practise restraint when enforcing norms, justifying this by the presumed desirability of not limiting the openness and robustness of public debate. It is evident, however, that those broadcasters who do not belong to the economic and cultural-political establishment are more likely to be reprimanded for neglect of their programming duties.

As is similarly the case in other broadcasting systems (Hoffmann-Riem, 1989b), one can observe that the German supervisory authorities are most reluctant to resort to formal supervisory action and endeavour where possible to take informal steps. They take great pains to establish a relationship of mutual trust with the broadcasters being monitored, mainly employing an informal policy of 'raised eyebrows'. In this manner, they can resolve some infractions discreetly, most likely those which the broadcaster can forego without having to abandon its own interests. Since the supervisory authorities assume co-responsibility for the broadcaster's conduct when granting the licence, they are often interested in ensuring the 'success' of the licensee. Subsequently, they may at times be willing to pay greater respect to the broadcaster's interests than is called for by the broadcasting norms. In any case, the supervisory authorities tend to accord a sort of 'protected status' to holders of licences once they have been granted. This leads to close interrelationships, sometimes even a 'camaraderie', that approaches a condition of 'capture'. On occasion, one can also observe a weakening of the supervisory standards: supervisory action is dispensed with in line with a more generous interpretation of the norms. At times, amendments to the norms are proposed, such that in the future there will no longer be a need for the supervisory authorities to intervene (Hoffmann-Riem, 1989b; 1989c).

Conclusion: Unfinished Regulatory Business?

These doubts about the effectiveness of supervision should not be taken to imply that regulatory measures make no difference. If they were abandoned, broadcasters would very likely concern themselves even less with the values at stake, and a turbulent uncontrolled development might take place (as in Italy until recently). Nevertheless, supervision has been considerably less successful than had been hoped in most areas of broadcasting legislation. The regulatory and supervisory system is far removed from the 'effective supervision' called for by the Federal Constitutional Court, and a politically and legally workable alternative is not in sight. It is apparently difficult to ensure the protection of vulnerable values in the broadcasting sector through legal regulation and its control functions. Vulnerable values are to all appearances best protected when they are observed voluntarily; this is most likely the case when it is also in the interest of the broadcasting industry to observe them. But when conflicts of interest arise, the supervisory authorities are much like the tortoise that agreed to an unequal contest with the hare.

At the same time, this suggests that the protection of vulnerable values is best ensured when the broadcasting order makes provision for self-regulatory mechanisms, which allow them to be observed without much interference from external supervision. This presumes a broadcasting order with built-in, self-regulatory mechanisms. The market alone cannot ensure this. Of particular assistance would be a great number of 'guardians' of vulnerable values, including those regarded as trustees for society as a whole. The next step should be a media-policy discussion regarding how such a structure might look. This discussion has yet to take place.[2]

Notes

1. These authorities have enacted their own directives: Directives of the State Media Authorities for the Guarantee of Juvenile Protection (*Richtlinien der Landesmedienanstalten zur Gewahrleistung des Jugendschutzes*) of 26 September 1989. For public broadcasting, see also the Directives of the ARD for the Guarantee of Juvenile Protection (*ARD-Richtlinien zur Sicherung des Jugendschutzes*) of 22 June 1988; and Directives for the Programmes of Second German Television (ZDF) (*Richtlinien für die Sendungen des Zweiten Deutschen Fernsehens*) of 11 July 1963, *as amended* 17 March 1989.

2. See Chapter 14, however, for consideration of some of the issues and prospects concerned.

References

Bausch, Hans (1980) *Rundfunkpolitik nach 1945*, vol. I. Munich: dtv.
Berendes, Konrad (1973) *Die Staatsaufsicht über den Rundfunk*. Berlin: Duncker & Humblot.
Brockhorst-Reetz, Bettina (1989) *Repressive Maßnahmen zum Schutze der Jugend im Bereich der Medien Film, Video und Fernsehen*. Munich: C.H. Beck.
Bundesverfassungsgericht (1961) 'Judgment of 28 February 1961', in *Entscheidungen des Bundesverfassungsgerichts*, vol. XII (1962). Tübingen: Mohr. pp. 205–64.
Bundesverfassungsgericht (1971) 'Judgment of 27 July 1971', in *Entscheidungen des Bundesverfassungsgerichts*, vol. XXXI (1972). Tübingen: Mohr. pp. 314–57.
Bundesverfassungsgericht (1973) 'Judgment of 5 June 1973', in *Entscheidungen des Bundesverfassungsgerichts*, vol. XXXV (1973). Tübingen: Mohr. pp. 202–45.
Bundesverfassungsgericht (1981) 'Judgment of 16 June 1981', in *Entscheidungen des Bundesverfassungsgerichts*, vol. LVII (1982). Tübingen: Mohr. pp. 295–335.

Bundesverfassungsgericht (1986) 'Judgment of 4 November 1986', in *Entscheidungen des Bundesverfassungsgerichts*, vol. LXXIII (1987). Tübingen: Mohr. pp. 118–205.

Bundesverfassungsgericht (1987) 'Judgment of 24 March 1987', in *Entscheidungen des Bundesverfassungsgerichts*, vol. LXXIV (1987). Tübingen: Mohr. pp. 297–357.

Bundesverfassungsgericht (1990) 'Judgment of 29 May 1990', *Deutsches Verwaltungsblatt*, 105 (17): 933–6.

Bundesverfassungsgericht (1991) 'Judgment of 5 February 1991', in *Entscheidungen des Bundesverfassungsgerichts*, vol. LXXXIII (1991). Tübingen: Mohr. pp. 238–341.

Engels, Wolfram, Hamm, Walter, Issing, Otmar, Möschel, Wernhard, Sievert, Olaf and Willgerodt, Hans (Kronberger Kreis) (1989) *Mehr Markt in Hörfunk und Fernsehen*. Bad Homburg: Frankfurter Institut für wirtschaftspolitische Forschung e.V.

Faul, Erwin (1989) 'Die Fernsehprogramme im dualen Rundfunksystem', *Rundfunk und Fernsehen*, 37 (1): 25–46.

Gellner, Winand (1990) *Ordnungspolitik im Fernsehen: Bundesrepublik Deutschland und Großbritannien*. Frankfurt a.M.: Lang.

Gerber, Volker (1990) 'Das Rundfunksystem der Deutschen Demokratischen Republik', in Hans-Bredow-Institut (ed.), *Internationales Handbuch für Rundfunk und Fernsehen 1990/91*. Baden-Baden: Nomos Verlagsgesellschaft. pp. A92–107.

Hartstein, Reinhard, Ring, Wolf-Dieter and Kreile, Johannes (1990) *Kommentar zum Staatsvertrag der Länder zur Neuordnung des Rundfunkwesens (Rundfunkstaatsvertrag)*. Munich: Verlag für Verwaltungspraxis Franz Rehm.

Hege, Hans (1989) 'Jugendschutz im Rundfunk – aus der Sicht der Landesmedienanstalten', in Reinhold Kreile (ed.), *Medientage München '88*. Baden-Baden: Nomos Verlagsgesellschaft. pp. 30–8.

Hege, Hans (1990) 'Duales Rundfunksystem in einem vereinigten Deutschland', in DLM-Jahrbuch 89/90, *Privater Rundfunk in Deutschland*. Munich: R. Fischer. pp. 15–23.

Herrmann, Günter (1975) *Fernsehen und Hörfunk in der Verfassung der Bundesrepublik Deutschland*. Tübingen: Mohr.

Hesse, Albrecht (1990) *Rundfunkrecht*. Munich: Vahlen.

Hoffmann-Riem, Wolfgang (1979) *Rundfunkfreiheit durch Rundfunkorganisation: Anmerkungen zur Neufassung des Radio Bremen-Gesetzes*. Frankfurt a.M.: Alfred Metzner Verlag.

Hoffmann-Riem, Wolfgang (1989a) 'Kommentar zu Art. 5 Abs. 1, 2', in *Kommentar zum Grundgesetz für die Bundesrepublik Deutschland (Alternativkommentar)*, vol. I, 2nd edn. Neuwied: Luchterhand Verlag. (1st edn, 1984.)

Hoffmann-Riem, Wolfgang (1989b) *Rundfunkaufsicht, Bd. II: Rundfunkaufsicht im Ausland: Großbritannien, USA und Frankreich*. Düsseldorf: Presse- und Informationsamt der Landesregierung Nordrhein-Westfalen.

Hoffmann-Riem, Wolfgang (1989c) Möglichkeiten und Effektivität der Rundfunkaufsicht', in G.-M. Hellstern, W. Hoffmann-Riem, J. Reese and M.P. Ziethen (eds), *Rundfunkaufsicht, Bd. III: Rundfunkaufsicht in vergleichender Analyse*. Düsseldorf: Presse- und Informationsamt der Landesregierung Nordrhein-Westfalen. pp. 209–78.

Hoffman-Riem, Wolfgang (1990) *Erosionen des Rundfunkrechts: Tendenzen der Rundfunkrechtsentwicklung in Westeuropa*. Munich: C.H. Beck.

Humphreys, Peter J. (1990) *Media and Media Policy in West Germany: The Press and Broadcasting since 1945*. New York: Berg.

Jung, Heike and Müller-Dietz, Heinz (1981) 'Jugendschutz und die Neuen Medien', in Expertenkommission Neue Medien – EKM Baden-Württemberg, *Abschlußbericht*, vol. II. Stuttgart: Kohlhammer. pp. 133–86.

Kabbert, Rainer (1987) *Rundfunkkontrolle als Instrument der Kommunikationspolitik*. Nuremberg: Verlag der kommunikationswissenschaftlichen Forschungsvereinigung.

Krüger, Udo Michael (1988) 'Infos-Infotainment-Entertainment: Programmanalyse 1988', *Media Perspektiven*: 637–63.

Krüger, Udo Michael (1989) 'Konvergenz im dualen Fernsehsystem? Programmanalyse 1989', *Media Perspektiven*: 776–806.

Lerche, Peter (1979) 'Landesbericht Bundesrepublik Deutschland', in M. Bullinger and F. Kübler (eds), *Rundfunkorganisation und Kommunikationsfreiheit*. Baden-Baden: Nomos Verlagsgesellschaft. pp. 15–108.

Menningen, Walter (1981) 'Rundfunkarbeit als politisches Mandat', *Rundfunk und Fernsehen*, 29 (2–3): 185–99.

Mestmäcker, Ernst-Joachim (1988) *Offene Rundfunkordnung: Prinzipien für den Wettbewerb im grenzüberschreitenden Rundfunk*. Gütersloh: Verlag Bertelsmann Stiftung.

Montag, Helga (1978) *Privater oder öffentlich-rechtlicher Rundfunk?* Berlin: Spieß.

Ricker, Reinhart (1985) *Privatrundfunk-Gesetze im Bundesstaat: Zur Homogenität der Mediengesetze und Mediengesetzentwürfe*. Munich: C.H. Beck.

Ring, Wolf-Dieter (1990) *Medienrecht: Rundfunk, Neue Medien, Presse*. Munich: Verlag für Verwaltungspraxis Franz Rehm.

Scharf, Albert (1989) 'Jugendschutz im Rundfunk – in Deutschland und in Europa', in Reinhold Kreile (ed.), *Medientage München '88*. Baden-Baden: Nomos Verlagsgesellschaft. pp. 20–9.

Schatz, Heribert, Immer, Nikolaus and Marcinowski, Frank (1989) 'Der Viefalt eine Chance? Empirische Befunde ze einem zentralen Argument für die "Dualisierung" des Rundfunks in der Bundesrepublik Deutschland', *Rundfunk und Fernsehen*, 37 (1): 5–24.

Spieler, Ekkehard (1988) *Fusionskontrolle im Medienbereich*. Berlin: Duncker & Humblot.

Starck, Christian (1970) 'Rundfunkräte und Rundfunkfreiheit', *Zeitschrift für Rechtspolitik*, 3 (10): 217–20.

Stefen, Rudolf (1986) 'Zum Jugendmedienschutz', *Zeitschrift für Urheber- und Medienrecht*, 30 (3): 115–20.

Stock, Martin (1990) 'Konvergenzen im dualen Rundfunksystem?', *Media Perspektiven*: 745–9.

Thaenert, Wolfgang (1990) 'Programm- und Konzentrationskontrolle privater Rundfunkveranstalter', in DLM-Jahrbuch 89/90, *Privater Rundfunk in Deutschland*. Munich: R. Fischer. pp. 31–51.

Ziethen, Michael P. (1989) 'Rechtliche Spielräume der Lizensierung und Kontrolle: Ausgewählte Regelungsfelder', in G.-M. Hellstern, W. Hoffmann-Riem, J. Reese and M.P. Ziethen (eds), *Rundfunkaufsicht, Bd. III: Rundfunkaufsicht in vergleichender Analyse*. Düsseldorf: Presse- und Informationsamt der Landesregierung Nordrhein-Westfalen. pp. 59–161.

5

Broadcasting Regulation in Britain

Stephen Hearst

In Britain things proceed by precedent. An extended chain links prized qualities in the country's historically developed broadcasting services with the measures adopted to preserve those values that will be vulnerable in the multichannel television system of the 1990s.

Precursors

Two pieces of legislation, one passed in Victorian and the other in Edwardian Britain, constituted what the Government considered the appropriate forerunners for broadcasting. The first was the 1869 Telegraph Act, which granted exclusive rights to the Postmaster-General to transmit telegrams in Britain. The second was the Wireless Telegraphy Act of 1904, which brought wireless telegraphy under the control of the same Minister. It fell naturally to the Postmaster-General, therefore, to deal with broadcasting.

The 1904 Act was the first of its kind in the world, laying down that no person should establish a wireless telegraph station nor 'instal or work any apparatus for wireless telegraphy' without securing, as a necessary condition, a licence from the Postmaster-General. Thus was established the basis of British broadcasting regulation, the Act containing a further clause saying that 'every such licence shall be in such a form and for such a period as the Postmaster-General shall determine, and shall contain the terms, conditions and instructions, and subject to which the licence is granted'.

In other words, pragmatism decided that wireless broadcasting was an extension of wireless telegraphy. A way had been quickly found for a Government ministry to take political responsibility for a method to legalize an activity, the consequences of which were only dimly perceived by all those engaged in it. Above all, the idea of a licence to enable broadcasting to operate became rooted in fertile political soil.

On the other hand, very few people indeed had the faintest idea what broadcasting might mean or what it might do. The fears were many. Newspaper proprietors thought that broadcasting might usurp the functions of the press. News agencies dreaded rival means of news coverage. Publishers feared a diminution of reading habits. The Armed Forces were anxious about interference with their signals. In the event, none of these fears turned out to have any justification at all. And curiously very few fears indeed surfaced about political bias, let alone indoctrination.

BBC Foundations

The birth of British broadcasting, heralded by a licence to what in 1922 was called the British Broadcasting Company, was attended by two other factors which at the time and for many decades to come bore powerfully in all public broadcasting policy discussion. The first was British perception of American broadcasting practice. Right from the start British engineers, legislators and civil servants looked at American broadcasting practice, and what they found and continued to find well into the age of television was not to their taste. The tone for this virtually permanent disapproval was already set by the Postmaster-General in a reply to a Parliamentary Question in April 1922, years before what we now call public service broadcasting came of age. 'It would be impossible' he said:

> to have a large number of firms broadcasting. It would result only in the sort of chaos, only in a much more exaggerated form, than that which arises in the United States, and which had compelled the United States, or the Department over which Mr Hoover presides and which is responsible for broadcasting, to do what we are now doing at the beginning, that is, to lay down very drastic regulations indeed for the control of wireless broadcasting.

The contrast between practice on the two sides of the Atlantic was to become even sharper. Nothing underlines this contrast more pertinently than the fact that international European wavelength regulation, which involved dozens of countries, preceded the United States Radio Act of 1927 which brought the States' first regulatory authority, the Federal Radio Commission, into being. Nowadays it is fashionable to describe the tight British regulatory system as being largely due to spectrum scarcity while British criticism of American practice is overlooked.

The second factor which profoundly influenced Britain's course was distrust of what the British opinion-forming classes called 'commercialism'. Even the manufacturers of broadcasting equipment, who were each shareholders in the British Broadcasting

Company, expected their profits to come from the sale of receivers, not in any shape and form from the programmes.

The brief pioneer existence of the British Broadcasting Company from 1922 to 1926 was towered over (the verb is no exaggeration) by its Scottish General Manager, later the first Director-General of the British Broadcasting Corporation, John Reith. He combined organizational and creative faculties with so stern a religious outlook on life that what is now called 'the high moral ground' was constantly occupied, and seen and heard to be occupied, by the broadcasters themselves.

Such was the development of broadcasting that the British Government only four years from its birth appointed a committee, the Crawford Committee (1926), to make recommendations on its future. Reith had increasingly come to the view that broadcasting in Britain ought to be treated as a public service, that it must not be used for entertainment purposes only. He refused to give evidence on behalf of the British Broadcasting Company, as constituting an interest in the preservation of its own existence, and wrote a personal memorandum which contains a memorable sentence that was to echo down the century, although with diminishing strength: 'He who prides himself in giving what he thinks the public wants is often creating a fictitious demand for lower standards which he will then satisfy' (cited in Briggs, 1961: 334).

The Post Office was in agreement with Reith's position. And in 1926, the Crawford Committee unanimously agreed that 'the United States system of uncontrolled transmission and reception is unsuited to Britain', and that British broadcasting must accordingly remain a monopoly – in other words, that the whole organization should be controlled by a single authority!

The British Broadcasting Corporation accordingly replaced the Company at the start of 1927, operating under a Royal Charter which was to last initially for ten years. The Charter can be described as an enabling, rather than regulatory, document and has not been greatly changed in any of its later renewals. The Charter, which is granted from the Crown, was accompanied by a Licence from the Postmaster-General. The provisions of the Licence gave, and still give, wide powers to the Government, which, however, it has seldom used.[1] Broadcasting could, for example, be taken over in an emergency. The responsible Minister – formerly the Postmaster-General, then briefly the holder of a short-lived post as Minister of Posts and Telecommunications, now the Home Secretary – can, as a further example, require a programme not to be broadcast. The Corporation is precluded from broadcasting its own views on matters of public policy. In relatively recent times, that last embargo has ceased to apply to broadcasting issues which may also be matters of public policy and while, originally, the BBC could not broadcast any political, industrial or religious controversy, that interdict lasted a bare two years.

Overall, it was to be the BBC's job to inform, educate and entertain. No shorter or more literal injunction was ever issued to a broadcasting organization. The fact that the Corporation was financed by a licence fee, collected annually through the Post Office, has persuaded many American observers that the BBC is a Government institution which could not be said to be truly independent. There is, in truth, a subtle relationship which depends more on the BBC's Governors' wise exercise of their temporary authority and on Ministers' restraint than on the precise letters of agreement that are in force. In the sixty-odd years of its existence as a public corporation there have been celebrated moments of defiance of Government as well as other less glorious occasions left to historical research to remember (Briggs, 1979). In general, the most constricting aspect in the relationship between successive Governments and the BBC has been the power of Government to decide what the licence fee should be and thereby to keep a mighty say over its financial well-being. The other prominent power, to appoint the Governors of the BBC (who in law are the BBC), has over the years been largely exercised in a non-partisan spirit by Governments both Conservative and Labour. They are 'the trustees of the national interest' (Crawford Committee, 1926). It has also become a wise parliamentary convention for government spokespersons to deflect criticism of the BBC and of any particular programme by saying that the matter under discussion was one for the Governors of the BBC to look over or to decide on.

Such was the regard for the BBC and its Director-General that the BBC in its submission to the next broadcasting enquiry, the Ullswater Committee of 1936, dared to claim that its programme policy had been shaped from the outset 'by the conviction that listeners would come to appreciate that which at first might appear uninteresting or even alarming'. The Corporation had 'aimed at providing a service somewhat ahead of what the public could demand were it possible for such a demand to be made articulate and intelligible'. Such language was, of course, made possible by what John Reith called the 'brute force of monopoly', a state of affairs, as later turned out, that stuck in at least some political throats. The Ullswater Committee (1936) recommended the extension of the BBC Charter for another ten years and largely endorsed the work of the Corporation. In the same year as the Ullswater Committee reported, the first public television service was launched by the BBC. However small the tent pegs of public broadcasting regulation were at the time, and however proud and confident a 'tent' they tied down, it is worth remembering that one is talking only of one domestic and one overseas radio service, plus a fledgeling television service.

That television service owed its birth to the recommendations of the Selsdon Report of 1935 that the BBC should be entrusted with its operation and that the running costs should be settled between HM Treasury and the BBC. In actual fact, the radio licence, overburdened as it was, had to be 'tapped'. In terms of regulation, nothing new needed to be done. The same BBC, the same Board of Governors, above all the same John Reith, were in charge. Thus the most potent medium of communication yet devised by man started its life in Britain. Four years later, the service was switched off without announcement. The Second World War had begun.

John Reith left the BBC in 1938 for Imperial Airways. If his name crops up so frequently, it is because no other individual throughout this century was ever again to play so dominant and creative a part in shaping broadcasting policy. There might have been a host of other regulatory provisions on the statute book but for him. He set the tone, he initiated virtually every ethical or moral debate, and his name is still being evoked sixty years later when the purposes and aims of broadcasting are being detailed.

Originally, the Government had planned to take the BBC over in wartime, as the Licence permitted. That this was not done was a tribute to the position the BBC had acquired in national life. The BBC carried on with its domestic and foreign radio services. There was no new broadcasting legislation, but an undated BBC document C which laid down detailed instructions to BBC engineers and programme staff as to how to carry out their duties in wartime. The Second World War helped to make broadcasting a major influence in the social, cultural and political affairs of the nation. The BBC emerged from it immensely strengthened both at home and abroad. Almost within a year, it launched a third radio network, the Third Programme, which, despite its minute audience, exerted a considerable upward pressure in raising broadcasting standards and widening cultural choice. The Television Service resumed its activities in the autumn of 1946.

If radio is frequently quoted here, it is because usually too little attention is paid to its subtle influence on the television domain. For instance, virtually every major television playwright (Harold Pinter, Peter Nichols, Tom Stoppard, etc.) started in radio, so that what has become the true national theatre, television drama, would have been unthinkable without the hundreds of scripts and productions of radio drama. British broadcasting had won national trust, and its emergence as an interesting and worthwhile profession attracted some of the best minds and talents in the country. The gradual dissolution of the British Empire had two distinct knock-on effects on broadcasting: first, to draw talent, particularly from the Dominions, to London, and second, to persuade hundreds of university graduates, who in an earlier age would have joined the Foreign or Colonial services, to take up broadcasting, and in the 1950s particularly television broadcasting, as a career. The cultural consequence of this type of recruiting over some twenty years was to make British television into the Fourth Estate, a position the British press with its large tabloid production never achieved. The continued performance of the television profession made it a formidable lobby, both in the sphere of politics when it came to repeated broadcasting legislation and on public opinion, and helps to explain why even today, at a time of technological pluralism and under a Government persuaded of the sovereign virtues of the marketplace, regulation has not been wholly discarded. The long shadow of John Reith has not departed from the British broadcasting scene.

The Public Service Duopoly

The Report of the Beveridge Committee in 1951 recommended, after intense investigation, the maintenance of the BBC monopoly. The dissenting opinion in a minority report of the Conservative politician, later Foreign Secretary, Selwyn Lloyd, was, however, to have far-reaching consequences. The same year saw the advent of a Tory Government under Winston Churchill and a brief White Paper in 1952 forecast the introduction of commercial television. A great deal of national controversy raged over the introduction of a competitive, commercial television network before the Independent Television Act of 1954 reached the statute book. The Labour Opposition and influential Conservatives pointed to America, as their forerunners had some thirty years before, and forecast cultural disaster (Wilson, 1961). Appeals to the effectiveness of competition and distrust of the brute force of monopoly nevertheless prevailed, and, for the next thirty-five years, British broadcasting became a duopoly.

The old mistrust of commercialism ensured that the Independent Television Act of 1954 was drafted with great rigour. The powers of regulation given to a newly created Independent Television Authority were extensive. Nothing of the sort was ever vouchsafed to America's Federal Communications Commission. Advertisers were to have no say in programme content; no religious service nor any propaganda relating to matters of a religious nature was to be included in any programme, thus preventing the weekly appearance of American Sunday mornings on this side of the Atlantic. Programme companies were to be chosen by the Authority, and their contracts could be non-renewable on inadequate programme performance. This was in fact done subsequently and put the programme companies on their mettle. A further provision required 'proper proportions' of programmes to be of British origin, thus preventing any predominance of bought-in American programmes. In actual fact, the 'quota' for such purchases settled down to something like 14 per cent, a figure to which the BBC also approximated by voluntary agreement. Nothing was to be 'included in the programmes which offends against good taste and decency or is likely to encourage or incite to crime or to lead to disorder or to be offensive to public feeling'. Some years later, the BBC indicated its voluntary compliance with these principles of good behaviour.

Nearly forty years later, it is possible to say that the severity of this Act, coupled with the crucial fact that the competition between the BBC and the new commercial system was confined to programmes and did not, as in the United States, extend to revenue (since the BBC remained financed by a continued radio and television licence), resulted in a duopoly that produced programmes of high quality and prevented Gresham's Law, the bad driving out the good, from applying to British broadcasting. The new competition did the BBC Television Service a power of good. Independent Television News, for example, pioneered and for some time produced a more professional service than its rival, and the competition for excellence has made both television services the principal news sources of the British public.

In neither news services nor current affairs programmes nor indeed religious programmes did market pressures ever play a predominant part. To a great extent, the requirement by the Independent Television Authority that programme companies had to place such programmes in prime time prevented British television screens being handed over, lock, stock and barrel, to the sole purposes of entertainment. The BBC 're-arranged' its priorities as regards broadcasting information, education and entertainment, while the new Independent Television service, staffed as it had to be to some extent by people who came from and were trained by the BBC, always kept its eye on its formidable competitor, taking good care not to imitate either the worst excesses of American television or the unashamed voyeurism of the British tabloid press.

The growing maturity of British television coincided with some of the most fundamental changes in the thoughts and feelings of our society in modern times. The dropping of two atomic bombs in August 1945 signified that mankind had discovered a means of ending its own existence. The discovery of physical and chemical contraception meant not only that we could in future control our rate of reproduction, but also that the female sex acquired a freedom in sexual mores previously denied to it. This new sexual freedom was to lead to strongly contrasting views as to what constitutes public and private decency. Thirdly, the frequency of travel outside national borders for business and pleasure greatly increased. All these partly visible, partly invisible changes have affected society's perceptions of matters of taste and decency.

British television never divided its public in terms of class. This particular division remains a characteristic of the British press, of British publishing and of British theatre-going. Instead, British television tended to divide its viewers in terms of generations. For example, men and women, during or after the Second World War, took a drastically different view of sexuality from that of their parents. And since television tends to be written and produced by younger rather than older people, a conflict in perception was bound to exist – although this is a simplified version of a more complex process – between the assumptions of young producers and writers and older viewers. No amount of regulation could either foresee and account for this subtle, if deeply disturbing, clash which to a greater and lesser extent involved every family in the land. All real argument, said John Maynard Keynes, is about premises not conclusions.

The Television Act of 1963 extended the life of the Independent Television Authority until 1976, with further extensions eventually extending its life until 1982. The Act charged the Authority to 'draw up, and from time to time review, a code giving guidance as to the rules to be observed in regard to the showing of violence, particularly when large numbers of children and young persons may be expected to be watching the programmes'. Public debate on television violence has not diminished from that day to this. What is seldom admitted by politicians is that considerable proportions of the public are attracted by violent programmes. One needs only to look at the titles of available videos in virtually every town and village for convincing evidence. In consequence, British television executives have in essence compromised in letting on to the public screens what in their eyes constitutes a reasonable, but not excessive, amount of violence consonant with public regulation and the narrative logic of any programme in question. What has never been established, even in extensive research which now occupies entire sections of libraries, is whether this television violence merely reflects violence in society, thus holding up a mirror to it, or has imitative let alone enhancing potencies (Cumberbatch and Howitt, 1989).

The Pilkington Committee, reporting in 1962, reached conclusions which were critical of the ITV network programmes and recommended the award of a second television network to the BBC. BBC 2, as it was called, opened in 1964 and enabled the BBC to widen programme choice as well as to include material which in the nature of things was bound to prove more controversial.

A similar public reaction could be observed when a second television channel, named Channel 4, was allocated to the Independent Broadcasting Authority – renamed when commercial radio was added to the remit of the Independent Television Authority at the start of the 1970s. It opened at the end of 1982.

During the 1960s and 1970s a number of rules, which in practice amounted to self-regulation, were added to the code of practice, now partly written, partly unwritten, to which the broadcasters sought to conform. An example would be the so-called 'watershed' rule under which programmes unsuitable for children were not to be broadcast before 9:00 p.m. Another was the need for upward referral to director of programmes level of scripts containing either foul language or language that included so-called four-letter words. This particular directive was a response by broadcasters to vociferous public complaints which consistently concentrated on language used in television plays rather more than on any visual transgression which viewers might deem an outrage to their feelings of what constitutes decency. The broadcasters' defence that any foul or explicit language was no more than a truthful account of what people said to each other in real life never cut any ice with large sections of the British public, which prefers to preach what it does not itself practice.

Once the postwar generation of broadcasters replaced its parents in the driving seats of editorial broadcasting policy, the habitual tensions between Britain's political and televisual constituency sharpened. The recommendations of the intellectually towering, but, as it turned out, politically ineffective Annan Report of 1977 were transformed almost beyond recognition by the Thatcher Government of 1979 into the Broadcasting Act of 1980, which established both Channel 4, a Welsh Fourth Channel and a Broadcasting Complaints Commission (which was to deal with issues of privacy and fairness in programmes). Inevitably, the remit of Channel 4, which stressed its service for minorities, made it certain that a few of its programmes would jar the sensibilities of people whose codes of morality and conduct were Manichaean. Television programmes probed the affairs of state and home; increasingly they found them wanting. At the same time, the hold the broadcasting constituency had and still has over the leisure pursuits of the British people continued unabated: television viewing is by far its preferred leisure activity.

The Market Shake-up

The late 1980s were dominated by the determination of the Conservative Government to inject more competition and market discipline into British broadcasting. A first step was the appointment of a Committee to review BBC finance, chaired by a liberal economist, Professor Alan Peacock. Although it counselled against advertising on BBC channels, its Report castigated the existing system as a cosy and overly 'comfortable duopoly'; questioned the professionals' pride in their television record; proposed consumer sovereignty as the ultimate criterion of good broadcasting; and concluded that the fundamental aim of broadcasting should be to increase through competition 'the freedom of choice of the consumer and the opportunities available to programme-makers to offer alternative wares to the public' (1986: 125).

In a White Paper founded on this rationale, the Government agreed that 'we should move away from a highly regulated television duopoly toward a more competitive future, for the benefit of the viewer' (Home Office, 1988: 11). It argued that with the emergence of new terrestrial, cable and satellite services, 'viewer choice, rather than regulatory imposition, can and should increasingly be relied upon to secure the programmes which viewers want' (5). Its 'radical' proposals were nevertheless allied with what it called 'strong elements of continuity' (4). The BBC would still be 'the cornerstone' of public service broadcasting, financed in the short term by the licence fee (which could eventually be phased out, however, and be replaced by subscription income). In the Independent television sector, safeguards of the variety, range and quality of programme services would also be needed. In December 1989, the Government accordingly tabled a Broadcasting Bill, which, after close parliamentary scrutiny, solid opposition from a majority of the broadcasting professionals and alternative softening and toughening of provisions, became the Broadcasting Act of 1990.

The Act dealt almost entirely with the commercial sector of British broadcasting. (In early 1991 the BBC was granted a licence fee increase 3 per cent lower than the inflation rate but was told it would be pegged to the retail price index through to the expiry date of its present Charter in 1996.) It replaced the Independent Broadcasting Authority with an Independent Television Commission (ITC), which was to enfranchise commercial television companies by a process of first tendering for and then auctioning the eventual licences. A relatively novel term made its appearance in broadcasting parlance, the 'quality threshold', which all applying companies would have to cross before being allowed entry to the auction itself, in which the highest monetary bidder would normally be the winner. Considerable political and professional pressure, however, led to a final draft allowing the ITC to award a franchise in 'exceptional circumstances' to a prospective applicant with a lower bid, if it considered that the quality of its proposed service was 'exceptionally high' and also 'substantially higher' than that of the highest bidder.

One thread of continuity with the less commercial past was the retention of strict controls on advertising. Commercials are still limited to an average of seven minutes per hour and may not exceed seven and a half minutes in any single hour (though the ITC is free to vary this). The Act specifically bans political advertising on television and radio. Advertising in and around children's programmes is closely controlled – with commercials for programme-based toys, for example, disallowed for periods of two hours either side of the programme concerned. Although a former ban on sponsorship has been lifted, the ITC has spelled out a detailed set of rules intended to safeguard the editorial integrity of programme content.

The focal point of the broadcasting debate, both inside and outside Parliament, however, was what the quality threshold should require of applicants for the 15 regional franchises of Channel 3. The final wording of the Act specified that licensees must provide:

1 National and international news and current affairs programming 'of high quality', broadcast at intervals throughout the day and 'in particular at peak viewing times'.
2 A suitable range of regional programmes.
3 A 'sufficient amount of time' for religious and children's programmes.
4 A service that appeals 'to a wide variety of tastes and interests'.
5 A 'sufficient amount of time' for 'programmes that are of high quality'.

Before it disappeared the old IBA and the professional lobby, the Campaign for Quality Broadcasting, had pressed the Government to give 'quality' a central role in the franchising process. This may explain why the ITC ('son of IBA'!) took the quality threshold so seriously, elaborating it in remarkably close detail in an *Invitation to Apply for Regional Channel 3 Licences*, issued in February 1981.

According to that document, to qualify to submit a monetary bid, applicants had to promise to supply the following:

1 A national and international news service, consisting of at least three programmes: 20 minutes at lunchtime, 15 minutes in the early evening and 30 minutes in peak time.
2 At least 90 minutes per week of high-quality current affairs programmes, containing 'explanation and analysis of current events and issues'.
3 At least two hours a week of religious programmes.
4 A 'strong regional service', including high quality news 'and a suitable range of other material, for example, social action programmes reflecting social need or promoting individual or community action'.
5 At least 10 hours a week of children's television, including 'a range of entertainment, drama and information programmes'.

That was not all. There were also more general criteria of diversity and quality to satisfy.

The ITC would 'have regard' to 'the present ITV schedule' as a diversity benchmark. It also obliged applicants to spell out in hours and minutes how much programming it would offer per week in each of nine categories. They included drama (broken down into single plays, anthologies, feature films, dramatic series and serials), entertainment, sports, news, other factual programmes, education (including adult education and social action), religion, the arts and children's programming.

Over 'quality programmes' the ITC waxed more philosophical, acknowledging that they could not be reduced to a single formula. They could be programmes of a 'special one-off character', programmes of 'marked creative imagination' or programmes of 'exceptionally high production standards'. But they were not to be equated solely with minority interests, since 'it is important that programmes of wide audience appeal should also be of high quality'. The ITC even invited applicants to fly their own philosophical kites and to explain how they proposed 'to secure a range of high-quality programmes and to encourage and sustain the professionalism and creative talent needed for this'.

The British political system has thus concentrated on programme 'diversity' and 'quality' as the core vulnerable values that will need some protection in the television system of the 1990s. Anyone adopting a relativist position ('who is to say what is quality?') will be dissatisfied with these terms, but since they are firmly embedded in British consciousness about broadcasting and in the Act, they cannot be wished away nor should they be. It is better to aim high and fail than to aim low and hit your target.

Nevertheless, the prospects for regulatory success (or failure) were intriguingly poised. On the one hand, the ITC had done its best to tie the applicants to a demanding set of conditions. What successful applicants proposed would be translated into binding obligations in their franchise contracts. The ITC also declared its intention to 'monitor' successful applicants' 'performance in relation to these licence conditions over the term of the licence'. It should be able to apply a range of sanctions against non-compliance, including reprimands, fines, reduction of the licence period and, ultimately, revocation of the licence.

On the other hand, many financial and competitive realities could stand in the way of effective enforcement.

First, the auction winners' bid could take huge sums of money out of the television system that would have otherwise been available for investment in programming.

Second, from 1993, competition for advertising revenue will become unprecedentedly keen, increasing pressure on all to channel their resources to mass appeal programmes. This is because the Broadcasting Act makes Channel 4 responsible for the sale of its own advertising (to be rescued by its Channel 3 competitors if this falls below a defined minimum) and authorizes creation of another national television channel (Channel 5), to be financed by advertising and to be franchised by the same licensing procedures as Channel 3. This means that, for the first time in British broadcasting history, three terrestrial commercial television channels will compete for revenue from a single source, advertising.

Third, under the 1990 Act the discretion of the ITC to award franchises to more public-spirited companies was decidedly limited. If it exercised its 'exceptional circumstances' option on behalf of more than one or two qualitatively superior companies, its decisions (which may be challenged in the courts) could hardly stand up as 'exceptional'. After 1994, it will lack power to protect successful licensees from take-over bids by other companies. And although the franchises are supposed to run for ten years from 1 January 1993, in practice they could prove perpetual, since, according to the Act, the ITC must grant a licensee's request for renewal unless it is satisfied that it cannot any longer provide a service in line with the licensing conditions.

Fourth, since the Act obliges the ITC to award franchises separately for each regional area, it could not take account of the needs of the ITV service as a whole. Of the 40 companies that applied for franchises in mid-1991, all the *incumbents* proposed to be full-service broadcasters (making most of their programmes in-house), while all the *challengers* proposed to function chiefly as publishers (making only their own regional news programmes but commissioning everything else from independent producers). Since highest bids would prevail, however, the ITC could not try to fashion a system with an optimal mix of these two distinctly different kinds of providers.

Fifth, once the new system is up and running, the seeming subjectivity of appeals to quality could count for little in the face of the seeming objectivity of market forces. The ITC might hesitate to inflict sanctions on licensees for failing to comply with conditions, the exact implications of which could seem endlessly open to argument – with the franchise holder, inside the Commission, and prospectively in the courts.

If the free market ideology behind the 1990 Act was deregulatory in intent, other enactments moved in the opposite direction. These had to do with standards of taste and decency, as well as with public morality itself. Whereas broadcasting had hitherto been exempt from the provisions of the British Obscene Publications Act, under which any aggrieved individual could sue a writer or theatre producer if in his opinion a piece of fiction or drama offended against public decency, broadcasting was now brought under that Act. It was no longer left only to the Governors of the BBC or the Board of the ITC to seek to safeguard the public good. Nor was this all. The Broadcasting Act 1990 not only maintained the Broadcasting Complaints Commission, to whose jurisdiction members of the public can appeal if they feel themselves wronged in broadcast programmes; it also established a statutory Broadcasting Standards Council. The Council's remit covers the portrayal of sex and violence and standards of taste and decency in general. The Act stipulated also that the Council was to draw up a Code of Practice, in the light of which viewers' complaints could be considered.

What to Make of It All?

A dispassionate observer must have some difficulty in envisaging the new marketplace in the making: in one corner, an auction for stall holders, in another, scrutineers of conduct and of the beneficence or malignity of the goods on sale, and in a third, the judge or magistrate waiting to deal out condign punishment for miserable offenders.

There are now three constituencies in the broadcasting affairs of the United Kingdom, that of the broadcasters, of the politicans, and of the general public. Each holds a different opinion on what is now broadcast and likely to appear on our screens in the future. A sizeable majority of broadcasters opposed the deregulatory policy now in place on the supposition that it is likely to lower broadcasting standards and may transfer programme decisions from broadcasters to businessmen. They fear that, in the private sector, competition for advertising revenue is bound to produce some of the cultural television artifacts now evident in the British tabloid papers; and they hold their breath over the future of the licence fee in particular and the BBC in general. To them, arguing of course on their own behalf, the present programmes on offer on four television channels are 'the least worst in the world'. Finally, they regard a good deal of regulation as a *sine qua non* for wide programme choice whilst deeply distrusting the extension of the Obscene Publications Act to broadcasting.

The Conservative majority of Britain's political constituency sees British television in the hands of unselected young, often Oxbridge-educated, producers, whose critical stances disseminated to millions of viewers put items on the national political agenda whose proper place for discussion, they believe, should be Whitehall and Westminster. Large numbers of Conservative Members of Parliament are convinced that most television producers stand to the left of the political spectrum and that their instinctive attitudes to industrial regeneration, to British policy in Northern Ireland, to judicial fairness and, of course, to traditional and patriotic values are suspect. They pin their hopes not only on the working of the market, which they believe will at last give the public what it wants, but also on the effects of cable and satellite technology, which, it is hoped, will fragment audiences and make it harder for television producers to influence the political agenda.

Thirdly, there is the British public, over eighteen million licence holders, whose audience reactions, researched programme by programme for over half a century, suggest a high degree of satisfaction with present programmes. Well over half of those licence holders also have video-recorders in their homes and record programmes to view when it suits them and to buy or hire video-works in local shops and libraries. The slow growth of cable and satellite subscription, in contrast to that of the United States, offers additional

evidence that the heady promises of a continued television hardware and software bonanza leaves John Bull, citizen, largely
unimpressed. He or she, however, is also apathetic towards the
formation of broadcasting policy. In the entire history of British
broadcasting there is little evidence that the public at large have
played any noticeable part in policy discussions: it has reserved its
often passionate interest for the resulting programmes. Broadcasting structure has been largely left to interested parties, to the
politicians and to the watchdog role of the 'Great and the Good' in
British society.

Nor is there any great secret about the prerequisites of quality
broadcasting:

1   There must be security of funding for at least three years ahead,
    since it takes that amount of time to produce major drama or
    documentary or arts programme series.
2   There must be a critical mass of talent, since television is a
    collective enterprise. Absence of such a critical mass, largely in
    one place, renders *sustained* quality broadcasting virtually
    impossible to produce. This is why small countries need to
    import a large amount of foreign programmes to maintain high
    standards.
3   Programme initiatives must come from the people making
    programmes, not agents for whom programmes are means to
    other ends.

In television broadcasting you can appeal with equal success to
the best as to the worst in human nature. Appealing to the best
takes longer. Appealing to the worst is easier and cheaper. Over the
last seven decades, regulation coupled with professional pride has
kept news and news gathering, together with a large amount of
current affairs programmes, away from marketplace pressures.
Competition has thus far been, but will be no longer, for audiences
only, not for broadcasting revenue. Once competing television
organizations aim for the same pot of gold, economic pressure
makes it much harder for minority programmes and interests to
survive, even for the weakened regulators to maintain the rigour of
their supervising hold. Moreover, security of funding disappears.
This lack of financial security explains the failure of American
television to match the excellence of European television output in
major series such as the French *Molière* or the British cycle of
Shakespeare's plays.

Drastic changes in the postwar world have created fissures
between generations which throw up deep differences in matters of

taste and decency between the under-thirties and over-fifties. Public complaint has largely centred on language and only very rarely made itself manifest over the public television display of sex and violence. In general, such complaints have seldom exceeded 5 per cent of the viewing public. Since both legislation and viewing public tend to be dominated by an older generation, the regulatory process in Britain has on the whole erred on the side of caution. Now we see a change from general to specific prescription over what broadcasters must and must not do. A further new clause in the 1990 Broadcasting Act instructs the Independent Television Commission to define 'due impartiality' in their Code of Practice. One must pity the drafters of this code and envy the lawyers for the opportunities that will open up for them. The blame sometimes heaped upon television for causing various ills in society is part of the price a free society pays for free expression on its most influential medium. The explosion of new outlets – satellite, cable, new terrestrial channels, video-works, together with the deregulated trend of new broadcasting legislation – is bound to throw up new and unexpected problems. May you live in interesting times, curse the Chinese. We are so cursed.

Note

1. A late 1980s exception is a Government ban on soundbites from IRA spokespersons in radio and television programmes.

References

Annan Committee (1977) *Report of the Committee on the Future of Broadcasting.* Cmnd 6753. London: HMSO.

Beveridge Committee (1951) *Report of the Broadcasting Committee, 1949.* Cmnd 8116. London: HMSO.

Briggs, Asa (1961) *The History of Broadcasting in the United Kingdom: The Birth of Broadcasting*, vol. 1. Oxford: Oxford University Press.

Briggs, Asa (1979) *Governing the BBC.* London: British Broadcasting Corporation.

Crawford Committee (1926) *Report of the Broadcasting Committee.* Cmnd 2599. London: HMSO.

Cumberbatch, Guy and Howitt, Dennis (1989) *A Measure of Uncertainty: The Effects of the Mass Media.* London and Paris: John Libbey.

Home Office (1988) *Broadcasting in the '90s: Competition, Choice and Quality.* Cmnd 517. London: HMSO.

Peacock Committee (1986) *Report of the Committee on Financing the BBC.* Cmnd 9824. London: HMSO.

Pilkington Committee (1962) *Report of the Committee on Broadcasting, 1960.* Cmnd 1753. London: HMSO.

Selsdon Committee (1935) *Report of the Television Committee*. Cmnd 4798. London: HMSO.

Ullswater Committee (1936) *Report of the Broadcasting Committee*. Cmnd 5091. London: HMSO.

Wilson, H.H. (1961) *Pressure Group*. London: Secker and Warburg.

6

Is there a Question of Vulnerable Values in Italy?

Gianpietro Mazzoleni

Introduction: The Systemic Context

To understand how Italians approach issues of vulnerable values in multichannel television, it is necessary to take account of three systemic factors that have greatly influenced their attitudes to broadcasting in recent years.

The recent history of Italian broadcasting

The first factor is the unique direction that the country's television system has followed since the mid-1970s.

During this period, Italian broadcasting has been dominated by a series of events that have radically transformed the traditional scenery: the rise of private stations; the formation of large commercial networks; the fierce competition between the latter and the public service broadcaster, Radiotelevisione Italiana (RAI); and the increasing commercialization, as a result, of the entire broadcasting system. A peculiar feature of these developments is that they took place in conditions of legislative anarchy. The political forces were at first taken by surprise. As they tried, half-heartedly, to react, they were overwhelmed by the impetus of the phenomena. Because the issue of broadcasting regulation was a source of continual discord among the Government coalition parties, a protracted period of policy stalemate ensued. The inability of the policy makers to reach a compromise on the keenest points of dispute allowed the main players in the broadcasting arena to set their own rules of the game for many years and the broadcasting system to evolve into a duopoly, half dominated by the public company (RAI) and half by a thrusting private entrepreneur (Berlusconi). When, after many dramatic clashes, Parliament on 6 August 1990 at last passed a new Broadcasting Act, it could not avoid confirming this partitioning.

The tug of war between all the interested parties over broadcasting issues centred mostly on *political* and *economic* aspects. On the one side, the political parties, which had traditionally controlled the system through RAI, aimed to extend their control over the new channels. Information was the strategic resource at stake in this struggle. On the other side, the private broadcasters, chiefly looking for increased financial opportunities and rewards, pushed for as much market freedom as possible. At stake in this part of the battle was control of the strategic resource of the advertising cake (including RAI's interest in securing its share).

It is true that *cultural* issues – over the quality of programming, levels of domestic production and the like – were at times also a focus of sharp controversy, particularly between the opposition parties and the majority coalition. The Communist Party especially was distinctive for its strong stand in defence of the public service philosophy (emphasizing information, education, pluralism, levels of domestic/European production, culture as opposed to commercial/mass audience programming, etc.). The other parties seemed more absorbed in the political and economic facets of the broadcasting problem and rarely exhibited interest in the cultural ones. Even when cultural themes dominated the political debate, they were often exploited instrumentally for other, largely unconfessed, partisan purposes. This was most evidently the case in the conflict over the norms proposed for regulating commercial breaks in feature films shown on television (discussed below).

Italians were particularly ambivalent over issues of commercialization, realizing, on the one hand, that it had come to stay, but aware, on the other hand, of some of its more crass excesses. The explosion of private broadcasting had precipitated a revolution in the traditional, public way of making television. RAI, which derives its income from household licence fees and the sale of commercials, had to adjust to the new commercial outlook in order to survive. This mutation by the public company did not occur without pain, neither in the organization itself nor in the political establishment. It had been foreshadowed, however, by certain trends in RAI's earlier history.

For two decades the public company had been the major producer and dispenser of cultural fare for the entire national audience. Its public image was identified with that of a 'mother' ('mamma RAI'), nurturing generations of Italians and enhancing their civic education. It was even said that Italian national unity owed more to television than to the nineteenth-century Independence Wars! Public television undoubtedly helped to consolidate the Italian language as the national idiom. This pedagogic function was largely intentional, as RAI's top officials reflected the prevailing conservative ethos of Governments of the period. Their ideological outlook encouraged these executives (incidentally, one RAI President ended up as a monk in a Trappist abbey!) to regard television as a tool more for instructing than for entertaining the public. This philosophy served as an 'imprint' in the history of RAI-dominated television, and traces of its influence can still be found in some current decisions. The first blow to such a style was struck by the 1975 Reform that opened control over RAI to a plurality of political forces, supplementing the Christian Democratic influence with lay and democratic socialist elements that gradually modernized the public company, even while defending and strengthening its public service status. But that status was no longer identified *tout court* as a synonym for more education and culture. The private television revolution was around the corner in the mid-1970s. The decline of RAI's cultural 'motherhood' had paved the way for the new commercial vogue that demanded more entertainment for the sake of it, more channels, a broader and richer programme provision.

Complex cultural formations

A second systemic factor can be found in the peculiar cultural pattern of Italian sociopolitical life.

The common impression that Italy is a Catholic country is nothing more than a stereotype – equivocal and potentially misleading. The fact that 90 per cent of the Italian population are registered in the Roman Catholic Church might be taken to suggest that the Italian polity is informed by religious principles and that the country is full of faithful churchgoers. But the first part of this assumption is at best only partially correct and the second is even further from the truth.

In Italy, the predominant cultural outlook seems more inspired by non-confessional or lay principles than by strictly Catholic conceptions. This arises from complex historical roots: the long domination by the Pope of Rome over a considerable part of the country's territory was dismantled in 1870 by masonic and nationalist forces that imposed a liberal state regime which still underpins the postwar republican Constitution. The presence of a powerful Communist Party has been another secularizing influence in the postwar era, exposing the life style of many Italians to various tenets of Marxist ideology and ethics.

Of course the Catholic political forces (working inside the Christian Democratic Party) gained power at the fall of Fascism and have taken part in all Government coalitions ever since, usually leading them. Despite this dominant status, in its legislative programmes the Christian Democratic Party usually refrained from a crude religious doctrinalism, thanks also to the surveillance of the other coalition parties of different (and mostly colliding) ideological traditions. On the few occasions that the Catholics tried to impose their religious world-view on the country, such as in the referenda on divorce and abortion, they suffered searing defeats.

Those two poll tests are often interpreted by analysts as evidence of the crisis of the Catholic and confessional influence over Italian culture. However, the Communist/Marxist cultural weight is also declining, both for external reasons (the crumbling of the Communist bloc in Eastern Europe) and for internal ones, principally the abandonment by many Italians of collectivist beliefs and austere practices in favour of more utilitarian, affluent and individualistic attitudes.

This is not to characterize the Catholic and Communist cultures as marginal or uninfluential: they maintain a series of strongholds in several vital ganglia of the country, such as the education system, the cultural institutions and of course the political system. From a sociological point of view, however, they are now but sub-cultures, sharing influence between themselves in the larger national culture and competing with other sub-cultures.

In short, Italian culture harbours several perspectives for identifying 'vulnerable values' in how television is organized, each inspired by a distinctive world-view and ethical orientation. Cultural pluralism mingles with moral relativism in modern Italian society.

Laissez-faire morality

The third systemic factor that influences the attitudes of Italian politicians and audiences toward regulatory needs in broadcast programming is closely tied to the previous one. It is the typical indulgence of Italians toward certain kinds of social and individual deviance from accepted moral standards. This widespread tendency follows different contours, depending on the nature of the case. It may take the form of a ready tolerance of pornographic films; disregard of instances of coarse language in television programmes; non-prosecution by police or judges of minor offences against public decency and the like. A scathing portrait of this Italian idiosyncrasy was painted by Sabino Acquaviva, a leading sociologist, in an article that appeared in *Il Corriere della Sera* (17 August 1990):

> We [Italians] are Catholic but with scepticism. We are for a rigorous sexual morality, but we mostly pay lip service to it. We demand an incorruptible political and bureaucratic class but with reservations, especially when we are personally involved. We are for the country, but only if she does not cost us dear, and thus we find ways to not sacrifice ourselves for her . . . . In sum, this is the society of compromise, of but, who-knows, shall-see, of doing and undoing, of saying and not-saying, of

standing for one thing and for its opposite at the same time, of going with the Saints as well as with the Devil.

Acquaviva does not maintain that Italians are necessarily any less moral than the peoples of other Western countries. Nevertheless, a laissez-faire philosophy toward moral conduct undoubtedly has more adherents in Italy than elsewhere. The history of the country's broadcasting revolution is of course one expression of this tendency.

Another Italian sociologist, Giovanni Bechelloni, traces such an outlook back to the previously mentioned historico-cultural precedents:

> The presence of a strong Catholic tradition, anchored to the visibility of a Church that by definition was depository of all matters tied with morals and ethics, and the weakness of a normative pole within civil society, have subtracted from public discussion and thus from consensual regulation important issues concerning the ethical conduct of business, of the professions, of public administration and of politics. (1989: 253)

Relative neglect of broadcasting issues
Partisan priorities in broadcasting regulation, cultural syncretism in societal matters and moral permissivism in day-to-day affairs challenge the very possibility of coherently posing issues about vulnerable values in the Italian television system. Are there any values worth safeguarding by law? If yes, which ones? On which bases are they defined as values and deemed endangered? From a confessional standpoint, or rather from a pluralist, lay perspective? Should freedom of expression and the responsibility of adult people be penalized by or privileged over restrictive and paternalist measures?

These are hardly idle questions, at least in the cultural context of a country like Italy. Nevertheless, they have rarely been addressed in sustained public debate, for the simple reason that they do not have univocal answers and are potential objects of sharp ideological and political conflict among the different components of Italian society. No one wishes to open old wounds for the sake of a handful of cultural values. Fifteen years of wavering over whether and how to legislate on broadcasting have shown beyond doubt that policy makers need more politically succulent issues to be drawn into hand-to-hand combat.

A Set of 'Second-Rank' Values

Having emphasized the normally subordinate standing of cultural and ethical issues in the agendas of Italian publics and policy makers, we can now turn to the task of identifying those values that have nevertheless surfaced in Italian debate and broadcasting law as deserving some protection at this time. The criteria used to determine the most significant concerns are: (a) the adoption of any definite regulatory safeguard (for example, in the 1990 Broadcasting Act); (b) the volume of 'noise' they have generated in media coverage.

Combination of these two parameters yields the following set of preoccupations (in descending order of importance):

1 The integrity of creative production.
2 Respect for human dignity.
3 The advertising of harmful products: tobacco, alcohol and drugs.
4 Levels of domestic television production.
5 Portrayals of sex and violence.

Items 1 and 4 in this list refer to the 'quality' of programme content, reflecting a *cultural* set of values that have stirred a certain amount of concern in political and professional circles and led to some safeguards in the 1990 Broadcasting Act. The other items focus on *moral* standards, which have traditionally been an object of regulation in both broadcasting law and the penal law generally.

Integrity of creative production
Of the five listed topics, this was undoubtedly the most heated and controversial in the year preceding passage of the Broadcasting Act by Parliament. In fact, it became a thorny problem soon after the establishment of commercial networks and the insertion of frequent advertising breaks into feature films on television. A number of influential directors (like Fellini and Zeffirelli) criticized the practice, labelling it 'a barbaric action' and an outrage against works of art (Mazzoleni, 1991). The Communist Party took up the artists' cause and staged a decade-long campaign to safeguard the integrity of feature films screened on television. The climax was reached in March 1990 when a majority of Senators, composed of Communists and a number of dissident Christian Democrats, passed an amendment to the draft broadcasting bill (unexpectedly defeating the Government coalition) which would allow 'advertising spots *only* in breaks foreseen by the authors themselves in their dramatic, lyrical and musical works and *only* in the interval between the first and second halves of feature films'.

This immediately provoked an outcry of protest from large and small private broadcasters as well as advertisers' associations. They denounced it as a tremendous blow to the survival of commercial broadcasting: the networks would lose billions of liras; small stations would be deprived of much of their income; and the advertising industry would face serious difficulty.

The Government coalition parties committed themselves to reform the amendment when the draft bill was sent to the Chamber of Deputies for discussion. The resulting debate in July 1990 was so incandescent that the Andreotti Government came close to resignation on the issue. The Christian Democratic Party split into two factions: one in favour of the limitation on breaks (the Left, led by former Party leader, De Mita); the other backing the Government against it (the Centre-Right). Five Ministers associated with the Left left the Government in an attempt to coerce the pro-advertising faction into accepting their position, but were immediately replaced by the Prime Minister, who refused to contemplate a political stalemate. In the end, a compromise was worked out that enabled the Left to vote with the rest of the Party in favour of the new negotiated position.

This story (drastically abridged for non-Italian readers) may at first appear exemplary: a genuine battle on behalf of a lofty goal, the integrity of artistic creativity. According to some political analysts, however, even this dramatic confrontation had less to do with vulnerable cultural values than with factional manoeuvring inside the Christian Democratic Party.

Whatever the motives, the pay-off of all this drum-beating was the following provisions of the Broadcasting Act:

par. 3, art. 8
In relation to the EC ruling (89/552/EC), commercial breaks in transmissions of feature films, dramatic, lyrical and musical works are allowed in the traditional intervals made in cinematic and operatic theatres. For parts lasting over 45 minutes, one additional break is permitted. A further advertising break may be introduced in parts exceeding 20 minutes beyond the initial 45 minutes.

par. 4, art. 8
The Guarantor [see Conclusion for comment on the role of this institution in Italian broadcasting], after receiving advice from a committee of five members, chosen as professionals of acknowledged competence, will determine the works of high artistic value and decide which programmes of an educational and religious nature may not be interrupted by commercial breaks.

Underlying this specific issue was a broader anti-commercial theme in the Italian broadcasting debate, namely, a tendency to regard advertising pressures as inimical to programme quality and range. In the Italian intellectual class especially, warnings of a contamination of informational resources for the public sphere by encroaching advertising influences have repeatedly been sounded. The vogue for market solutions and deregulation that spread throughout the Western world in the 1980s was seen as threatening to absorb all the major news media – the private television and radio stations, the daily and periodical press, even public broadcasting – into the commercial philosophy. Demands consequently ensued from diverse political and progressive-minded circles for policy makers to introduce measures to curb the tendency for informational provision, a critical function in the democratic process, to be impoverished, trivialized and subordinated to the marketplace.

This ferment may help to explain several other provisions of advertising control in the 1990 Broadcasting Act, notably:

> *par. 11, art. 8*
> Any clauses of advertising contracts that deal with the scheduling of non-advertising programmes are null and void.
>
> *par. 13, art. 8*
> Sponsored programmes must conform to the following conditions:
> (a) the content and scheduling of a sponsored transmission may never be influenced by the sponsor in a way that is prejudicial to the private and public broadcasters' responsibility and autonomy;
> (b) sponsored programmes shall be clearly recognizable as such and shall exhibit the name or logo of the sponsor at the beginning and the end of the transmission.

Other interests have also taken non-legislative steps to control advertising, such as: (a) a protocol on transparency (discouraging concealed or deceptive advertising) signed in 1988 by representative bodies of journalists, advertisers, advertising agencies and public relations firms; (b) codes of practice adopted by a number of newspapers; (c) a blueprint for a code of practice proposed by a progressive group inside the National Press Federation (the journalists' trade union). All these self-regulatory measures oblige the signatories to respect the autonomy and professionalism of the media workers concerned.

Respect for human dignity
Under this umbrella may be gathered a number of concerns about standards of taste, decency and propriety, including respect for individuals' privacy and reputation, the welfare of juveniles and avoidance of offence to religious sensibilities.

When television was the monopoly of RAI, controls over taste and decency in programmes were very strict, at times so exaggerated as to court ridicule. Nowadays, however, conventions have changed, channels have multiplied, authors have become more daring, and live transmissions have increased in number, all making vigilance more difficult.

Italian attitudes on these matters are rather mixed at present. On the one hand, there has been no major recent scandal, capable of stirring up a wave of enraged opinion in large sectors of the national audience. The above-noted easy-going outlook of Italians may also have served to dampen the potential explosiveness of certain practices. On the other hand, there has been a long series of minor episodes of alleged programming offences that have enlivened the public debate: a few curses and foul words uttered by showmen; some insults against public figures, including politicians; the occasional seeming exploitation of popular gullibility. What more recently triggered a significant volume of controversy was the emergence of a genre of so-called 'truth-television' – programmes, mostly produced by RAI, that many regard as excessively intrusive into the privacy of individuals. These programmes, defended by their makers as innovative and intelligent, are true-to-life chronicles of trials, arrests of presumed criminals, and enquiries into the whereabouts of missing persons. Although the producers' intentions are far from being offensive to people's rights, according to critics the result is often just that. In addition, the depicted persons are often least capable of taking legal action to defend their privacy or reputations. This explains much of the criticism levelled against 'truth-television' (not unlike what Americans call 'tabloid television').

Italian legislators have not been keen to develop an elaborate framework of protective norms specifically for broadcasting in this area, either because relevant provisions already exist in the Penal Code and in the 1948 law on libel, or because matters of taste are thought to be too subjective for regulation by detailed, stable and judicable norms.

Nevertheless, concerns about the vulnerability of such values in more competitive broadcasting conditions are probably responsible for the following provisions in the 1990 Act:

par. 1, art. 8
Broadcast commercials shall not violate individual dignity, shall not be based on racial, sexual or ethnic discrimination, shall not offend religious or moral sensibility, shall not encourage conduct deleterious to health, security and the environment, shall not be morally or physically injurious to minors . . .

pars 2, 3, 4, art. 10
Anyone deeming to have received moral and material offence from the slanderous content of broadcast programmes has a right to secure redress

from the transmitting organization . . . . In the event of denial, he can appeal to the Guarantor . . . who shall rule within five days . . .

par. 9, art. 15
The transmission of cryptic or subliminal messages is forbidden.

In addition, the well-being of children has been a source of concern to parents' and viewers' associations and to numerous civic groups of otherwise divergent political outlooks. Many of their worries have focused on portrayals of sexual conduct (see below), but with the increasing commercialization of television, the advertising sphere has also attracted scrutiny. In fact, some 100,000 parents signed a petition for a ban on commercials in children's programming, which was presented to the authorities in early 1990. An amendment to the draft broadcasting bill in favour of such a ban, proposed by the Left, was immediately accepted by the Government and was added to par. 1, art. 8 in the following terms: 'Commercial breaks in children's programmes are forbidden.'

Advertising of harmful products: tobacco, alcohol,
drugs
This is a traditional area of normative policing by law-makers in many countries. Italy is no exception. Cigarette advertising has always been prohibited. But tobacco companies have long since devised clever ways of circumventing the law by supporting various events and activities under their logos, many of them covered on television. For years consumers' associations and medical organizations have denounced such practices without winning any intervention from Parliament.

The Broadcasting Act does not address this issue specifically. However, the following clause does partially reflect such concerns:

par. 2, art. 8
The broadcasting of advertisements for drugs and medical care available only through medical prescription is forbidden . . . . Broadcast programmes may not be sponsored by firms producing or selling cigarettes and other tobacco-related goods, or drugs, or by organizations offering medical care available only through medical prescription.

As for alcohol, the only limitation on its advertising applies to RAI. The public company may not run commercials for alcoholic beverages containing more than 21 per cent volume before 8.30 p.m. Although the commercial networks are exempt from this provision, some restrictions do appear in a Code of Practice adopted by the Italian advertising agencies. This states, for example, that advertisements should not encourage immoderate or uncontrolled consumption; should not show situations of alcohol addiction; should not encourage drinking by minors; should not associate drinking with car driving; nor identify it with physical fitness or mental brilliance.

Levels of domestic television production
One of the fiercest charges directed against commercial broadcasting by the Italian Left is that the private networks have served as instruments of a cultural 'neo-colonization' of the Italian broadcasting market on behalf of Hollywood. It is significant in this connection that the Italian Communist Party praised the policies of former French Minister of Culture, Socialist Jack Lang, to limit imports of American films.

The ground of Communist hostility toward the commercial networks was the observation that a major proportion of the programmes carried by their stations were not bought in the domestic marketplace. Moreover, RAI had also started to follow their lead, jeopardizing the previous attainment of high levels of self-production.

The trend was regarded as a calamity for the export/import balance, for the domestic production industry and for the quality of Italy's television offer as a whole. Accordingly, the Party – backed by many cultural bodies and progressive intellectuals – put forward proposals for quotas on imported programming. In contrast, the other parties did not exhibit as much concern over this issue, limiting themselves to bland references to the cultural risks involved.

However, the Left's initiative did have some influence on policy. The transitional Law of 1985 included the following article: 'Television stations shall reserve at least 25 per cent of their scheduled films for works produced in Italy or EC countries. This percentage shall be raised to 40 per cent beginning 1 July 1986.'

Due to a series of political circumstances, this provision was never enforced, but the debate that it precipitated helped to increase sensitivity to the issue. The commercial networks felt obliged to spend more on home-produced programming. Statistical evidence shows that by 1988 23 per cent of private channel output was domestically produced. The public company also mended its previous policies, stablizing its ratio of domestic programming at around 73 per cent (RAI, 1988).

Such heightened attention to the value of a strong domestic production industry was also reflected in the following provisions in the Broadcasting Act:

par. 4, art. 20
The licensees of private broadcasting stations shall keep a special register on which they must file every week data concerning the origins and particulars of self-production of the broadcast programmes.

par. 1, art. 26
Starting from the date of validity of this Act, the public broadcasting company and the commercial networks, according to art. 6 of the EC ruling of 3 October 1989 (89/552/EC), shall reserve its investment in domestic and European production, acquisitions and works in the following degree: no less than 40 per cent in the first three years, no less than 51 per cent in subsequent years.

par. 3, art. 26
To works made in Italy shall be reserved no less than 50 per cent of the transmission time devoted to European production. Among feature films within this percentage, a minimum of one fifth should have been produced in the last five years.

Parallel with such concerns about domestic programme production has been a periodic airing in the Italian media of anxieties about the maintenance of cultural programming specifically. These have mainly been voiced by liberal intellectuals and politicians. They have often criticized the process of commercialization and 'vulgarization' that Italian television has gone through in the past decade. By way of remedy, they demand a substantial commitment to cultural programming, particularly by the public broadcaster.

In early 1990 an influential group of intellectuals issued a *Manifesto for the Safeguarding of Endangered Cultural Television Species*, a provocative document which was intended to put pressure on legislators on the eve of the parliamentary debate over the Broadcasting Act. An indication of their point of view is given in the following passages from the Manifesto:

> He who uses the sole criterion of audience ratings to discriminate against culture in television, arguing that it interests only the few, is acting in bad faith. It is easy to demonstrate that there exists room and a public for intelligent television. The only problem is that it is more difficult to make it.

> Television is not a school: the educational tone drives the public away. But culture in television can be offered as an intelligent form of amusement.

These expressions of concern elicited little response from Italian law makers. No clause in the Broadcasting Act insists on the provision of cultural programmes. The success of RAI-TRE, the third public channel, in providing an impressive amount of programming for cultural minorities, may have reassured the political parties about the survival of a strong cultural pole in the public television sector at least. Nevertheless, the obligation imposed by the Act on all commercial channels to produce a daily newscast goes some way toward ensuring at least a minimal presence of serious content in what are otherwise predominantly all-entertainment outlets:

> *par. 6, art. 20*
> Commercial nation-wide networks are obliged to broadcast daily newscasts.

Portrayals of sex and violence
This issue indeed occupies the last and least place in the rank order of vulnerable values in the minds of Italian legislators and members of the public. Some of the explanation for this low priority has already been given. In addition, so far as sexual matters are concerned, no roaring scandal has recently set off any major popular alarms. The only significantly critical stands are those taken by certain religious groups that tend to manifest anxiety over possible effects on the moral outlook of the younger generation. But the announcement by a private company that it would open a pornographic Pay-TV channel aroused more humorous comments than disapprobations. Similarly, the regular scheduling of a strip-tease show on a commercial network has been the target of only mild criticism – while scoring quite high audience ratings. In the mid-1980s even RAI dared to portray nudity on its channels – and no top executive lost his job over it!

Over violence in programmes there obtains a somewhat broader concern among religious and secular groups alike. But its intensity is far from sufficient to pierce the public's characteristic indifference. Again, all public and private channels usually refrain from scheduling programmes portraying extreme violence and brutality. But as a matter of course many films, serials and cartoons are based on violent stories, and it is obviously impossible to strike them all from the screens. If agreement on diagnosis of the phenomenon is wide, it is not so with prescription: measures of censorship, for example, are rejected in non-Catholic political and cultural circles.

Censorship continues nevertheless to be the classic tool of the state for repressing major deviations from public decency in films and drama. A national board of the Ministry of Spectacle is in charge of judging the works destined for television and movie theatres and classifying them as 'for all', 'forbidden to under 14' or 'forbidden to under 18'. In addition, the Penal Code prohibits obscene displays. The relevant clauses of the Broadcasting Act consequently rely on those norms, the only additions having to do with scheduling:

par. 10, art. 15
Television channels shall not broadcast programmes that may damage the psychological and moral development of minors, that portray scenes of gratuitous violence or pornography, or that induce racial, sexual, religious or ethnic intolerance.

par. 11, art. 15
The transmission of films or dramatic works lacking the necessary permit from the Board of Censorship or classified as 'forbidden to under 18' is prohibited.

par. 12, art. 15
In the event of violation of the foregoing norm, the station concerned shall be closed.

par. 1, art. 30
In the event that radio and television broadcasts are judged to be obscene, the licensee will be punished by the penalties specified in art. 528 of the Penal Code.

Concluding Remarks: Problematics of Enforcement

On the whole, firm, clear and coherently considered policies do not appear to have been developed for the preservation of 'vulnerable values' in Italian television. The legislators, political parties and sundry religious and lay groups have voiced or responded to a scattered cluster of concerns. If anything links them it is perhaps reservations about the excesses of commercialism bred by the 15-year experience of unrestrained, Berlusconi-led and advertising-financed broadcasting. But the protective provisions that have emerged are scant and dispersed. This is undoubtedly consistent with the systemic preconditions influencing Italian approaches to issues of culture and morality that were outlined in the introduction to this chapter.

Another sign of such minimal concern has been limited attention to enforcement machinery.

RAI is supervised by a Parliamentary Commission composed of 40 representatives of all parliamentary parties. On the face of it this has many duties: to issue programming guidelines, monitor output and appoint a Board of Administration with programme policy responsiblities, including approval of the Director-General's annual scheduling proposals. Its effectiveness is doubly constrained, however – first, because its composition mirrors that politico-cultural patchwork that has thwarted consensus formation over broadcasting for so many years; and second, because the legitimacy of such a seemingly direct political control over broadcast expression is at least open to question. At any rate, once RAI's audience share and advertising income were challenged by the surge of the three rival and unregulated commercial channels, the organization was left more or less free to decide how to fight back, which, in the first instance it did by to some degree pitting like against like, whilst striving to maintain a presence in journalistic, cultural and scientific programming.

The slackness of control is particularly noticeable, however, on the private side of the television duopoly. Responsibility for enforcing the relevant provisions of the 1990 Broadcasting Act has been put in the hands of the so-called Guarantor, an office that was first created in 1981 to supervise a recently passed law on the Reform of Publishing Activities (dealing, for example, with questions of media ownership and control). The Guarantor is a single person, appointed by the Chairmen of the two chambers of the Italian Parliament. Even though the present holder of the position is a quite active Magistrate, who can be expected to do his best to watch over implementation of the new law, he has wide-ranging duties (including many not concerned with broadcasting); his resources and staff are limited; and his powers of enforcement are not all clear and impressive. His energies will very likely be directed to a few particularly sensitive areas – such as ownership and advertising control – leaving more 'cultural' matters to fend largely for themselves. Moreover, the Broadcasting Act has delayed the deadline for complying with certain rules, giving scope and time for the would-be targets of regulation to figure out ways of doing what they want without violating the strict letter of the law. No wonder that in the months since the passage of the Act critics have voiced scepticism over its likely effectiveness.

This analysis suggests that the most suitable approach to the defence of vulnerable values in Italian television may be through self-regulating codes of practice among broadcasting professionals and the vigilance and intervention of concerned voluntary organizations. Several pressure groups, tied to religious or cultural interests, already operate in the broadcasting field. These include Aiart (a Catholic association of viewers and listeners), Sidef (a family organization), Diesse and Age (parents' and teachers' associations), the League for Children's Rights in Communication, a League for Defence against Television Intrusion, and several others. All in their own ways intend to try to keep public attention alive on the most significant issues that developments in television programming raise, particularly with regard to children's viewing. They have been quite active in laying down guidelines for family viewing, educating viewers in critical consumption, alerting parents to the hazards of television for children, etc.

Normally such bodies have exerted little influence on legislators, even on those of like-minded political persuasion. Nevertheless, they scored a success in the very last moments of the parliamentary debate on the Broadcasting Act. An amendment proposed by a Deputy close to one of these bodies passed almost unnoticed. This authorized the creation of an advisory body to the Guarantor, to be known as the National Council of Viewers.

The terms of reference of this Council, promptly issued by the Guarantor, state that its purposes are to safeguard in the broadcasting sector 'human dignity, pluralism, fairness, openness to diversity of opinions and to all political, social, cultural and religious standpoints'. The members, appointed by the Guarantor, are to be chosen from representatives of the private associations of television viewers.

It is too early to assess how influential the Council may be and what directions it will follow. There is a risk that, within the new body, the spokespersons of the diverse sub-cultures will engage in the same tug of war as in the society at large with stalemate the chief outcome once again. The lay forces in particular are inclined to resist rules limiting free expression and choice. In fact, they publicized such views several times during the parliamentary battle over the Broadcasting Act. An example is the reaction by an influential columnist of *Il Corriere della Sera* to Christian Democratic bids for stricter norms: 'To assume an absolute passivity of the viewers, an almost total incapacity to select the messages received through television, elevates to a dogma the confessional itch of those who take society to be only a flock of defenceless lambs or a herd of sinners' (30 July 1990). The same stand was voiced by a popular entertainer, commenting on the problem of vulgarity in television: 'Between prior censorship of programmes and the risk of bumping into indecencies, I see the latter as the least danger. The boss is in any case the spectator; he holds in his hands the omnipotent remote control that enables him to zap "video – stupidity"' (*Il Sole 24 Ore*, 9 April 1990). Thus, certain lay circles favour a strictly limited number of legal restrictions and more reliance on self-regulation and Codes of Practice by the broadcasting organizations.

In conclusion, no matter the approaches taken by the Parliamentary Commission, the Guarantor, and his National Council of Viewers, it is safe to assume that in Italy the realm of broadcasting will by no means be regulated with the elaborate scrupulosity of, say, the Independent Television Commission under the British Broadcasting Act of 1990, or of the Code of Practice of that country's Broadcasting Standards Council. Much will be left to the common sense, to the good taste and to the moral balance of the professionals and the viewers. On this more than on enforcement may depend the effectiveness of value-protective measures.

References

Bechelloni, Giovanni (1989) 'Questioni di etica professionale', in G. Faustini (ed.), *Studiare da giornalista. Radio e televisione. Pubblicità.* Rome: OG. pp. 253–9.

Mazzoleni, Gianpietro (1991) 'Broadcasting in Italy', in Jay G. Blumler and T.J. Nossiter (eds), *Broadcasting Finance in Transition: A Comparative Handbook.* New York and Oxford: Oxford University Press. pp. 214–34.

RAI (1988) *Informazione Radio TV.* Turin: Radiotelevisione Italiana.

7

The Netherlands: Freedom and Diversity under Multichannel Conditions

Denis McQuail

The Dutch situation calls for simultaneous attention to underlying values of the broadcasting system and to the structures which have been developed for implementing and safeguarding those values. The *forms* of implementation themselves embody key values. Despite several major moments of upheaval and change in the history of Dutch broadcasting after its prewar establishment, there has been a fair degree of continuity of principles of organization and control, rather more continuity, perhaps, than in the specific content of the values which are advanced or protected. Most briefly put, this means that the principles of freedom and self-regulation on the one hand and of diversity of expression on the other are more important in the Netherlands than what either the practice of freedom or the protection of diversity might actually lead to in broadcasting 'performance' – or in programming terms.

Historical Excursion

The Dutch system cannot be understood without reference to its history and to the basic principle of the 'pillarization' of its society, according to which the social structure was vertically stratified along lines of religious (especially Catholic or Protestant) or non-religious (especially socialist/humanist or liberal) groupings or communities, rather than horizontally by social class or occupation. In varying degrees, homogeneous social and cultural environments of residence, education, religion, ideology and even work were determined by membership of different formations. This particular form of social organization evolved during the later nineteenth and early twentieth centuries as a way of resolving potentially deep social conflicts within the national society, and strongly influenced institution-building during this period – in politics and education but also in relation to radio broadcasting during the 1920s.

A series of incremental decisions taken during the 1920s had laid the foundations (Radio Decree of 1930) for the broadcasting system of the 1990s. The essential feature was the allocation of radio air time to four main voluntary associations having some clear allegiance to, respectively, the Roman Catholic Church (KRO), the Socialist Party (VARA) and the Protestant Christian denomination (NCRV), or with no such allegiance and a commitment only to providing general (and non-ideological) radio programming (AVRO). The last was, de facto, politically liberal. A fifth (liberal-protestant) association (VPRO) also existed from 1925, albeit with a more limited scope. Air time was divided up on a basis proportional to the number of 'members' of each association, who also paid for the radio services with their subscriptions. A minority share of time was also reserved for some central or common services. Central control was in some degree retained by a Radio Control Commission. Under the same names, the successors to these five bodies, plus three new ones and the NOS (Netherlands Broadcasting Foundation, a provider of certain central services), still dominate the television broadcasting scene and share the air time, according to much the same principles.

This potted history is essential to understanding the policy response to current challenges. In the intervening years, the system has been shaken up three times – once by the war, then by two major legislative events (the Broadcasting Law of 1967 and the Media Law of 1987). Now, in terms of its purpose and form of organization, it is being shaken up again by heavy commercial competition within what is still a firmly public and non-commercial system. Some initial lessons may be derived from the origins of the broadcasting system: that division was preferable to unity; that belief and ideology were recognized as important principles of quality of service offered as well as being guides to allocation; and that voluntary self-control was relied on more than strong centralized control (although the latter was exerted to some extent by way of the Radio Control Commission). It may also be suspected that an early political expediency or necessity (dividing up access) was later elevated into a fundamental principle which may have outlived the particular circumstances of its origin.

When the system was being reconstructed after the war (during which the occupier had turned it into a centralized system financed by a licence), the virtues of the prewar arrangements seemed to glow with a new light, especially: the diversity based on traditional cultural values; the self-management and freedom; the decentralization of form. The elements of control and censorship (especially in relation to political or international controversy) which had existed before the war were not restored. The main prewar regulation, dating from 1933, forbade any messages which might 'undermine religion, morality or national authority'. Even political messages were required to be strictly factual or informative about positions. This kind of control had been misused during the war and was deeply unpopular.

Postwar voices asking for more efficiency and coherence, more professionalism, more national unity, less ideological or confessional emphasis and more openness to change were not strong enough to have much effect in producing a fundamentally new system. However, the arrival of television, with its greater financial and organizational demands, its openness to international influences, the cross-border 'threats' from neighbouring broadcasting systems (especially from Germany), in the end forced a thorough reorganization and a rethinking and restatement of basic principles. This resulted in the Broadcasting Law of 1967/9, where we find the first clear statement of the principles and values of the television system, previously governed by a series of administrative decisions.

A major factor which also contributed to change during the 1960s was the very marked social–cultural upheaval, especially amongst the young, which changed a traditional and rather culturally conservative society (compared to most of its European neighbours) into a standard bearer of change and political progress. While these changes were independent of television, it seems that they were reflected and magnified by way of the new mass medium, which effectively crossed the frontiers of the old vertical 'pillars' (Wigbold, 1979). The popularity and scarcity of television (only one channel until 1964) turned it more effectively than in the case of radio into a national medium, whatever the theory.

One of the peculiarities of the previous regime was that the enforcement of 'standards' in programme content, in relation to politics, religion, morality, or culture, was largely left in the hands of the broadcasting associations, most of which were normative in essence and all of which had statutes which indicated various 'ideal' goals and purposes. In the case of the Catholic and Protestant bodies, specifically religious aims were adopted, and matters of morals were automatically covered. These circumstances helped to maintain control but not always political order. Accountability to members still persists and is one reason why there is no explicit law making about violence, sex and related matters of taste and decency on television (see below). The explicit legal controls that once existed have gradually been weakened. The early regulation mentioned above was abandoned after the war and was replaced by a prohibition on broadcasts which give rise to danger for the security of the state, public order or good morals (but removed from the former broadcasting law in 1978). This phrase appears in similar form in Article 10 of the European Treaty. In part, the current rather permissive (or unrestrictive) regime owes its existence to a condition of rather strict control in the past (even if this was exercised by community and religion rather than by a secular state).

Principles and Values of the Public Broadcasting System

In the light of these preliminary remarks we can look at the main values and expectations which characterize the television system as these were incorporated into the broadcasting legislation of 1967/9. For the most part the same principles have been taken over by the new Media Law (1987), sometimes specified more clearly and pointedly, sometimes supplemented or modified to take account of new circumstances (see below). The main principles of system and performance, and thus the main values which might be held to be vulnerable, are as follows:

Independence in organization and autonomy in
programme decision making
This is mainly secured by the procedure according to which air time is allocated to approved organizations that are independent of each other, accountable to their own memberships according to their own statutes, and financed by a grant from central funds (licence plus advertising revenue). Although there are some overall rules about the *balance* of service offered and some other matters (see below), Article 10 of the 1967 Broadcasting Law and Article 48 of the new Media Law state that the approved associations are free to determine the form and content of their broadcasts autonomously. Radio and television are also protected from advance censorship, along with the press, in the constitutional guarantee of Freedom of Expression. The 1987 Media Law contains no clause requiring respect for public order and good morals, as was the case in the original 1967 Law. There is, consequently, no specific legal control over matters of sex, violence, taste, decency, etc. in the content of television.

Autonomy also extends to the right of broadcasting organizations to provide partisan, or 'unbalanced', political or ideological content on matters of current controversy. There is even a positive expectation that such content will be provided from time to time. There are some 'natural' checks and balances on how political freedom will be used, arising especially from the 'professionalism' of broadcasters, in which objectivity is often one component, and from the perceived expectations of the audience. The system is also structured so that there is a good chance that 'bias' from one perspective will be matched by an opposed 'bias'.

The freedom to be partisan does not, in practice, extend to the NOS, the foundation which has about 20 per cent of air time and whose task is to serve needs which are not likely to be, or are not easily, met by the other organizations. This includes programming for certain minorities, but also nearly all regular television news and a considerable number of documentaries. While there is no formal regulation of NOS programme and editorial policy, the structure of the NOS and its general task and tradition lead it to provide a very impartial and neutral news coverage. In general, balance in information is valued as much as autonomy, but it is achieved in other ways than by prescription. The allocation of access to associations with different outlooks and priorities is seen as the best way to achieve this value.

Pluriformity of structure and diversity of content
This is often held to be the most distinctive and most fundamental value upheld by the system, for the specific Dutch reasons mentioned at the outset, but now also because of a wider and more general valuation of the principle of democratic pluralism. Implementation of the diversity value is mainly a matter of structure and organization, but it is best understood by reference to the relevant article of the law which states the main criteria that an organization has to meet in order to qualify for an allocation of air time. According to Article 14, 1, c of the 1987 Law (not much changed since the 1920s in form of words), a broadcasting association: 'should aim, as laid down in its statutes, to represent some clearly stated societal, cultural, religious or philosophical stream and to direct itself in its programming to the satisfaction of some actively present social, cultural, religious or philosophical needs'. New applicants for broadcasting time are required to show evidence of performance such that programme contents and manner of presentation are sufficiently different from programmes of other organizations that they will provide a definite increase in the diversity of the broadcasting system.

It is nowhere made precisely clear what diversity consists of, but the general principle is to leave this to programme providers to work out for themselves, with reference to their own stated goals and their target audiences, especially their 'members'. The actual share of air time is related, in a progressive way, to the number of 'members' which have been recruited, so there is some measure of competition for audiences of a kind which is supposed to increase diversity.

The original version of diversity was that of the historical, religious and political differences referred to, although there is now some doubt as to whether this is a very relevant basis for a modern pluralistic society. Nevertheless, the *idea* does mainly relate to an '*external*' and *exclusive* diversity, in which different 'voices' and outlooks have their own separate channels, rather than to the more commonly encountered '*internal*' diversity, according to which all tastes are catered for by channels serving large, heterogeneous audiences. This feature might very well be counted as one of the most 'vulnerable' values which is still formally protected by the system, but which is not very much in tune with current realities of society or the media marketplace.

Another expression of the diversity of the system is the provision in law for giving access to a numerous (about thirty) and changing set of 'small broadcasters', bodies which represent some particular social group or cause but which do not claim the status of a general provider of programmes. These include religious, cultural and humanistic groups, but also the political parties, which each receive an equal allocation of air time in and between election times. Such access for small senders can be used for informational or propagative purposes. The 1987 Law indicates a guideline figure of 15 per cent of total air time as appropriate to reserve for such access purposes. This is about twice the amount of time that is reserved for commercial advertising. (See Geersing, 1989, and Wieten, 1979, for further discussion of pluralism as a Dutch broadcasting value.)

Openness

The system is claimed to have a special virtue of *openness* (thus of an open form of diversity). This is particularly an outcome of the social upheavals of the 1960s and a response to the long years of dominance by the initial, established 'confessional' bodies. Effect is given to the principle in law by provision for aspiring new broadcasting bodies to claim a share of available air time, as long as they can show that they have a minimum number of 'members' and fulfil the qualifications mentioned above (Article 14 of the 1987 Law). Under these arrangements, three new bodies have entered the system since 1967, one an Evangelical group (EO), another a general television provider (TROS) which is politically liberal, and a third more oriented to youth and popular culture (VOO).

Non-commercialism
This principle has been especially prominent in the system since the moment when it actually became somewhat more commercial – under the 1967 Law, which introduced an element of commercial funding by way of strictly controlled advertising. In part, the emphasis on non-commercialism in the regulations was the result of wishing to satisfy the political opponents of this change, but it also reflected a strong fear that certain religious or ethical values, and thus the foundation of the whole system, might be threatened by submission to consumerism and commercial goals. Behind the opposition to commerce there are mixed elements of puritanism, high mindedness, left-wing politics, conservatism, protectionism for the commercial press and pragmatic assessment of the vulnerability of the whole regulatory structure if consumer-market forces were allowed free rein.

It is hard, certainly for an outsider, to disentangle the relative strength of the motives for opposing commercialism, but the overall rationale is probably not so different than is found in Britain for maintaining the non-commerciality of the BBC. The expression of non-commercialism in regulation also follows familiar lines. The most fundamental regulatory requirement is that a broadcasting organization, in order to qualify for access, has to have broadcasting as its chief aim and is forbidden to assist in making profits for third parties (Article 55, 1987 Law). Flowing from these provisions are detailed regulations in the Media Law forbidding indirect forms of advertising or sponsoring and for minimizing the appearance on the screen of identifiable commercial products, brand names or pictures of advertisements. These matters are pursued from time to time very strenuously, with financial penalties or witholding of air time threatened or applied.

The contrast with the lack of any comparable prosecution by the authorities in matters to do with sex, violence, decency or political controversy is quite striking. The advertising that is allowed (it accounts for more than a third of the public broadcasting system's income) is confined to certain times, administered through a public foundation (STER), forbidden on Sundays and subject to strict codes designed to protect consumers. Strong efforts are made to separate advertising from programme content.

Other public service values
While the items discussed are the four most distinctive features of the broadcasting value system in the Netherlands, they do not exhaust the range of relevant (and also vulnerable) values, many of which are familiar in other public service systems. Most significant

of these are those of: *universal provision*; stimulation and protection for *culture* and for *education*; advancing the *national* interest in cultural and other matters; and maintaining standards of taste, quality and decency. Certain widely held principles of public service have already been covered by the four values described at the outset – especially the need to provide for minorities, to limit the influence of commerce and self-interested third parties, and to encourage diversity and balance.

The television system provides the whole country with three full channels by way of terrestrial transmitters, and the law requires all cable systems to carry these channels. Universalism is also achieved in programme content by two measures: first, by way of the provisions concerning diversity of purpose and openness of access which should ensure a representation of all interests; second, by a key clause in the law which requires each of the eight main associations to provide a full range of programming spread over the time which they have been allocated, so as to ensure a balance of content over the course of a particular day or week, thus providing for varied tastes. The law (Article 50, 1987) mentions four main categories of programme which have to be covered: culture; information; education; and entertainment. Minimum percentage figures for the shares of information and culture are set by the Ministry responsible for broadcasting (Health, Welfare and Culture).

Cultural and educational provision is also secured as a matter of the general public interest by a number of other measures. Most important are probably the requirements just mentioned – that all broadcasters give a minimum (and significant) share of their time to culture and entertainment. What counts as 'culture' is also defined with some care, according to the EBU 'Escort' programme category system. These provisions are enforced on the basis of systematic monitoring carried out by the NOS research department. It is clear from the results of such monitoring that the system has, until now, consistently fulfilled its broad obligations in these matters, although there are some differences between different broadcasting organizations.

In addition, the law provides for a separate educational broadcasting foundation. The NOS, which is the largest single broadcaster in terms of time allocation, has special tasks in the field of culture and information. The law states that at least 20 per cent of its programming should have a cultural character. In the matter of service to the national language and culture, there is less specific emphasis and seemingly less concern about this as a value. It may not have been considered very vulnerable in the past, and the system was traditionally highly self-protective, without there being a need for very specific regulations. Again, it was the allocation of time to associations that were themselves embedded in the national culture which was the best guarantee of safety in this respect.

Changing times and the influence of European regulation have nevertheless demanded more specific measures. Indicative are two provisions in the 1987 Law – one obliging broadcasting associations to produce a minimum of 50 per cent of their own content (it has normally been higher); another requiring the newly legalized subscription services on cable television to contain a minimum proportion of Dutch national content. There were also signs in the 1980s, however, of an increasing awareness of the problems posed by trying to provide a full range of programming within the boundaries of the national culture, on the basis of a rather limited market and with a minority language (hence dependence on foreign imports).

Of the final set of items within the scope of the public service concept, there is little to say, for reasons which have partly been given. For whatever reason, there is minimal emphasis on intrinsic cultural *quality* as such. Of course, the notion of varying quality and of programming standards finds a place in the public debate, but the emphasis of the system is not strongly oriented in this direction. Illustrative of this is the clear choice to use limited financial resources to secure a wide range of representation, even at the expense of quality. The system is not geared to concentrating large sums of money for quality programme production, which, in any case, might be unrealistic as a goal. On questions of taste and decency, there is no formal nor, it seems, informal regulation or codification in matters of sex or violence (Jurgens, 1990). It is not a subject which has figured much in public debate. Almost the only relevant clause in the Media Law is one which rules on the time at which films certified as unsuitable for children may be shown on television, as well as requiring provision of adequate advance information when such films are shown on the subscription film channel.

Shocks to the Value System

The values embodied in the system, as described, overlap and are often mutually reinforcing. If there is an element of contradiction, it is probably to be found in the contrast between the stress on freedom and the very detailed and strictly enforced regulatory system, within which autonomy over content decisions is guaranteed. In general, it can also be expected that such a complex structure of regulation would inevitably be vulnerable to changes in the society or in the surrounding media environment. The first major legislation, the Broadcasting Law of 1967, was an ambitious attempt to establish firm foundations for an open public system, which would be responsive and adaptable to changing circumstances and social values. It was put to severe test during the 1970s, when the new system (which was also expanded from a one- to a two-channel network) did not quite work according to earlier value traditions.

The most fundamental change had been the opening for new entrants to broadcasting, which had led, according to critics, mainly to an increased popularization, cultural 'dilution' and secularization (less religion and politics). The exception to this was the new Evangelical Broadcasting foundation, which managed to get enough members to gain a minority share in television output. On the other hand, even more success was achieved by a new general interest broadcaster, of a politically liberal or neutral tendency, the TROS, which became the most popular programme provider in audience terms. It was followed by another success story, Veronica (a former pirate transmitter), which sought out and gained the attention of youth in particular, becoming equally popular on the basis of style as well as programming.

A degree of competition for the audience thereafter developed amongst the four large older-style 'confessional' broadcasters and between them and the newcomers. While a place in the system has never been secured on the basis of the size of audience reached, there is always a risk that a serious loss of audience share presages a loss of 'members' and eventual extinction. In any case, the effects of the newcomers and of increased competition during the 1970s on programme performance seemed clear enough, and many critics, of the traditional school at least, believed that the founding ideals had been betrayed.

The most threatened or lost values were, on the one hand, those of *diversity* (at least as defined in political and religious terms, as against a concept of consumer sovereignty and choice) and of conventional *public service values* – especially those of culture and general education. The emphasis on attracting audiences led to an increase in entertainment and fiction programming, although the law still required balanced programming overall. One can only assume that the lost values, as perceived by the critics, were compensated by new values of viewing pleasure, as perceived by much of the audience.

At the time to which this discussion refers (late 1970s, early 1980s), the impact of cable and cross-border reception was not regarded as a serious threat to the system or to its values. Despite foreign alternatives available to a fair proportion of the population, the great majority of viewers stayed loyal to the national broadcasters on their two channels. For this reason, there were few fears about damage to the national language and culture, and the more popular programming which was being enjoyed at home was in the Dutch language at least. Most of the alternatives were either from Belgium (thus also in Dutch) or Germany and in any case constituted programming provided under strict public service-type rules.

However, the electronic writing was beginning to appear on the wall of history, as the prospect of cross-border satellite transmission and extended cabling became a reality. A major enquiry was commissioned by the Government to provide advice on the likely impact of technology and other changes and to help in planning new legislation. This enquiry reported in 1982 under the significant title, *A Coherent Media Policy*, since the keynote was to attend to the communication system as a whole: broadcasting, press and new electronic media. This is also a reminder of one of the core value complexes of the society: coherence and community, balance of interests, keeping things under control and keeping an eye on the inter-media effects. The main value issues attended to by the committee of enquiry (WRR Report, 1982) were: how to maintain openness and diversity; continued autonomy; the trend to commercialization; the protection of Dutch culture, faced with an increased international flow of programmes; the consequences of policy liberalization; the protection of the public service system, especially in its cultural and informational role and its function of promoting national integration and national identity; and the protection of privacy in the wake of new technological developments.

It does not appear, either from research commissioned, or the content of the 1982 report, or the draft law which emerged in 1985, that the question of a threat to values relating to violence, sex, taste and decency was high on the agenda of concerns in the changing media environment. The WRR report paid some attention to three relevant concerns which had been voiced about ongoing changes affecting the media: the possible effects of violence; the threat to national identity; and cultural 'levelling down'. In each of these cases, the report reached reassuring conclusions, partly based on the lack of evidence to support an alarmist view of the power of the media to produce either violent behaviour or 'cultural fragmentation', partly based on a view of the inevitability of social change and of some increase in market orientation of the system.

Despite the fact that from 1983 onwards, during the period when the new Media Law was being drafted and debated, the extensive

Dutch cable system became a target for international communication satellite channels, especially Sky, Super and Music Box, there was little change in what might seem to be a complacent attitude to threats from across the border. The authorities did fight a rearguard action for a time against some of the commercial implications of change (the challenge to national advertising regulation and competition with the home advertising business), but the tendency of European regulation was recognized as encouraging the new trends and not easy to resist indefinitely. For present purposes, it is sufficient to note that it was the values of 'non-commercialism' and those relating to the national culture (especially in relation to the large youthful audience attracted by the satellite channels) which were seen to be under threat, rather than values relating to violence, sex, decency, etc.

Recent Developments

Since the Media Law was passed, there have been some developments which are relevant to the discussion (Brants and McQuail, 1992). One has been the introduction, as permitted by the law, of a subscription film channel, which is available to most households. This is not a remarkable change, although it does make available relatively 'adult' films, usually in the early hours of the morning. It is also not an option that has been widely taken advantage of. The rate of subscription was initially too low for profitability, and the channel has not made a really significant impact on the television scene.

Another policy-led change is the addition of a third television channel to the national public system. This has entailed not only an increase in viewing opportunity, but also a reorganization of channels. In practice this means a profiling which gives a clearer choice to viewers between a more neutral-popular, a more 'confessional' and a third channel, with more information, news and culture (but also a good deal of sports programming). Although the legal requirement of balanced programming (by category) applies equally to all channels, this change does represent a concession to the principle of 'consumer sovereignty' and to the demands of the audience-market system. In practice, it is also a tacit acknowledgement of the fact that television can no longer be used as a means of bringing 'culture' to an unwilling public, as in the days of the old confessional or public service cultural mission.

However, the major recent event relevant to the development of television in the Netherlands has been the arrival, since October

1989, of a commercial service, RTL-4, originating from Luxembourg as a daughter company of CLT. In reality this is a Dutch enterprise, aimed at the Dutch market, which it reaches by way of the Astra satellite and the cable system (80 per cent penetration). It is financed by advertising and competes both for the audience and a share of the Dutch advertising market. It was accepted under Dutch law, on the grounds of its being a foreign station, only after considerable doubts and difficulties and against the preference of the Government.

In a sense this development was the result of a policy failure, since the principle (really necessity) of allowing a private commercial channel to operate had been accepted by the Government as early as 1985. The general idea was to allow one or more of the popular existing associations to change their status from public to commercial organizations. However, no workable plan for this was ever accepted by the Government, and the initiative was seized by other interests.

RTL-4, within a year, became a more or less established part of the national system. It follows the rules laid down by the EC Directive on cross-frontier television and, to some extent, conforms to the main conventions of Dutch broadcasting, although not to the requirements for a balanced (by category) programme schedule. Only recently has it decided to provide advertising on Sundays. It is politically neutral and carries a large component of easy entertainment and American series. The main criticisms are the familiar ones of cultural 'trivialization', 'commercialism', low quality programming in general. It has not given rise to much complaint on grounds of violence, sex, indecency, etc. Its interests would not, in any case, be served by providing the kind of content that could be criticized in this way. Essentially, its success lies in being able to behave as a private commercial station in an otherwise highly regulated environment. It has, however, changed the whole media scene, largely by capturing a larger average audience share than any of the national channels (now over 25 per cent) and a significant part of advertising revenue.

The political response has been to move quickly to develop a legal framework for commercial television within the country, with the aim of reducing the advantage to this quasi 'pirate' and of reasserting policy control over the system (although at the time of writing the law had not yet been changed). There are also attempts to streamline the public sector and make it more competitive and attractive to audiences. It is not yet clear what the consequences of such moves will be, but it is certain that another irrevocable break with the past has been made. The Netherlands will soon belong to the ranks of countries, de jure as well as de facto, in which the public sector operates alongside a viable and growing private commercial sector, with the familiar consequences of competition for audience share, pressure on programming policy and on resources for 'quality' programme production. It looks as if the realities of European-style deregulation and of frontiers open to a large and steadily increasing supply of television may have brought the era of a distinctive type of public broadcasting to a close.

Conclusion: Towards a New Equilibrium?

It will appear from this account that the Netherlands has sought to protect a somewhat distinctive set of values and standards in its broadcasting system. In general, the values are those appropriate to a society which has a long history of political freedom and debate and which is both relatively small in terms of population and internally heterogeneous. The Netherlands has never nurtured any pretensions to being a primary producer of quality television culture, but it does place a high value on artistic culture in general and also on science and information of all kinds, not only because of its own traditions, but also because it has to make a living in the world by the application and handling of many forms of information.

This version of the situation offers some clue to the way in which threats and promises of the expanding communication system have been approached. At the same time, it should be said that the approaches followed have not always been compatible: there is a strong thread of inconsistency, especially between a commitment to freedom and the strength and detail of regulation of broadcasting. This is matched by a struggle between two deeply rooted tendencies in the society: one towards individualistic commercial entrepreneurship and another towards an egalitarian and communal social order. Ideally, some might hope, the former would have free rein internationally and the second prevail at home. This would seem to apply to the mass media at least. In today's world, the distinction is no longer easy to maintain, however, at least not for audiovisual media. The domestic system has thus gradually been slipping out of the traditionally firm control.

This has mainly been viewed as problematic for the cultural and political functions of the broadcasting system. Prized values of diversity and debate are at risk of being subverted by a bland and homogeneous international media culture. While in the past the protection of the Dutch language and national culture did not seem to have been given, overtly at least, a prominent place in media policy, there are probably more expressions of concern to be heard these days, when the real threats are greater. On the other hand, there would seem to be little that could be done to counter this danger. The political will remains, nevertheless, to maintain the system as long as possible and to work within the European framework to keep some control of the international environment. The question of standards of morals and decency has not been high on the list of problems, much less so, for instance, than the gradual encroachment of 'commercialism' in its softer forms and the draining of audiences away from the public system.

There have been some signs of concern about standards of the kind referred to. It would be surprising if this were not the case in a society which likes controversy and diversity and which also has a history of religious commitment and of conflict of ideas and values. One example of concern was the move made in 1988 by the then Minister responsible for broadcasting to suggest to the Chairman of the NOS the need to consider a voluntary code relating to morals and decency, especially given the legally guaranteed autonomy of broadcasting in respect of programme content. The instigation came mainly from smaller religious parties in Parliament (Jurgens, 1990). Another example was the more recent protest from feminist groups against the representation of women in the Veronica late night 'soft-porn' programme, *Pin-Up Club*. Neither example made a large impact or is likely to lead to any change in the system, which will continue to rely on the many extant forms of self-regulation, within the freedom guaranteed by the Constitution. However, the kind of social pressure which these examples show to exist will play some part in setting limits to what is possible, without there being written codes, whether formal or informal.

For the time being, there is a wait and see attitude about the likely fate of the values and principles which have been described. The system has not broken down, and the political will to support it remains largely intact. It is possible that internal and external changes have provided a needed safety valve and that a new equilibrium will follow the expected legalization of commercial participation in broadcasting. Nevertheless, there is more anxiety than there used to be about the viability of the traditional arrangements for securing social-cultural goals and less confidence in the effectiveness of any regulatory system to protect them.

References

Brants, Kees and McQuail, Denis (1992) 'The Netherlands', in EuroMedia Group (ed.), *The Media in Western Europe*. London: Sage. pp. 152–66.

Geersing, B. (1989) 'De betekenis van pluriforme publieke omroep in Nederland', *Mediaforum*, 1: 4–8.

Jurgens, E. (1990) 'Subtiele Britse censuur', *Mediaforum*, 5: 55–8.

Wieten, J. (1979) 'Media Pluralism: The Policy of the Dutch Government', *Media, Culture and Society*, 1 (2): 171–80.

Wigbold, H. (1979) 'The Shaky Pillars of Hilversum', in Anthony Smith (ed.), *Television and Political Life*. London: Macmillan. pp. 191–231.

WRR (Scientific Council for Government Policy) Report (1982) *A Coherent Media Policy*. The Hague: State Publishing House.

8

Vulnerable Values in a Changing Political and Media System: The Case of Sweden

Stig Hadenius

The original organizational structure of Sweden's broadcast media, dating from the 1920s, followed the British model. As in many countries, there was a struggle among representatives of different interest groups that wanted to influence the new medium. The radio industry, for example, wanted rapid expansion. Newspaper publishers were a restraining force, however. They were afraid of the new medium. Just as in the 1950s, when television was introduced in Sweden, the press was worried about this new source of competition. Could newspapers survive when newer, faster and – so they thought – more convenient media were available?

During the pioneering days of Swedish radio, the Government's Telecommunications Board (Telegrafstyrelsen) was another major force which influenced the pace of expansion and the structure of the new radio service company, AB Radiotjänst. This company was owned by the press and radio industry, but it was controlled by the Cabinet and Parliament through laws and agreements. It enjoyed a broadcasting monopoly and was financed by means of licence fees from owners of radio sets. Advertising was not allowed.

The structure of the broadcasting media in Sweden changed relatively little until the late 1950s. AB Radiotjänst evolved into the Swedish Broadcasting Corporation (Sveriges Radio). This company, with its national and regional channels and two terrestrial television channels, was owned by grassroots 'popular movements' (spanning a very wide range of voluntary organizations), the press and a number of private companies. Finance still came from licence fees, now mainly on television sets. The relationship between the Government and Swedish Broadcasting, which now delegated day-to-day operational decisions to its four programming subsidiaries, was regulated through laws and agreements.

But satellite technology would radically alter the situation of Swedish media, as it did with the media in many countries. In the spring of 1991, four additional satellite-relayed channels were broadcasting to a Scandinavian audience. All of these channels were advertiser-financed. This meant that Sweden's old commercial-free broadcasting monopoly was broken. Discussions were under way within and amongst the Swedish political parties on establishing a third terrestrial television channel and introducing advertiser-financed television. In March 1991, a parliamentary commission made a preliminary recommendation to proceed along these lines.

As for 'vulnerable values' in the broadcast media, there have been three main areas of discussion in Sweden. The first concerns 'objectivity' in the mass media; the second, whether television should be financed by licence fees or by advertising; and the third, various ethical issues related to programming. Behind the debates of recent years, of course, the issue of the influence of international and transnational media on Swedish news reporting and media structure has also occupied centre stage.

To understand how value concerns have been aired in Sweden, however, they must be placed in their political and structural context.

Political Changes

Stability and slow change have characterized the political system in Sweden. The same five political parties were represented continuously in Parliament between 1920 and 1988, although most of them changed their names. Since 1932, the Social Democratic Party has dominated the country's Cabinets, losing power only in 1976–82 and at the 1991 election.

Both this political stability and Sweden's long period of Social Democratic rule are unique in the Western world. In Denmark and Norway, the Social Democrats enjoyed a similar position of power, but it ended in the 1950s. The question of why Sweden displays a different political pattern than its neighbours can be debated, and there is no simple answer.

One probable reason, however, is that Sweden is one of the most highly organized countries in the world. More than 90 per cent of all employees are trade union members. Political parties have had close ties with various powerful organizations; most conspicuous has been the link between the country's leading employee organization (the Swedish Trade Union Confederation, LO) and the Social Democratic Party.

But on the non-socialist side, too, there are close connections between political parties and diverse interest groups. The Centre Party (formerly the Agrarians) has close ties with farmers' organizations. The Swedish Employers' Confederation and other business organizations have supported various non-socialist parties, especially the Moderates (formerly Conservatives) and the Liberals.

It nevertheless seems that during the late 1980s and early 1990s, Sweden's political climate changed dramatically – perhaps more than during any other period since World War II. The political system became less stable, and the level of voter support enjoyed by the Social Democrats fell considerably. At the same time, nationwide employer and employee organizations became weaker and other special interests stronger.

In public discourse, people increasingly say that there is no longer any 'Swedish model', a system characterized by strong centralized organizations in the labour market, an extensive and efficient public sector and a large measure of political stability. Also typical of the present time is that it is increasingly rare for people to talk about centralized public-sector solutions to social problems. Instead terms like 'alternatives' 'competition' and 'voluntarism' are far more acceptable. The issue of public sector efficiency has increasingly become the focus of debate.

What has happened in Swedish politics during the past few years is probably not temporary but represents a genuine shift in values. In the final report of a Government-appointed enquiry, entitled *Democracy and Power in Sweden*, political scientist Olof Petersson writes:

> The changes in Swedish society are partly explained by internal tensions among the various special features of the Swedish model. Many of yesterday's solutions, such as large-scale programmes, standardized systems and public sector expansion, no longer appear feasible. These changes thus compel us to seek new systems for organizing society. On point after point we can therefore observe how the features once associated with the Swedish model of society are today challenged and reassessed. (*Demokrati och makti i Sverige*, 1990: 390)

There are, of course, direct and indirect correlations between the political situation and the structure of the mass media. Strong political parties and great political stability have repercussions on the organizational structure and the contents of the broadcast media. With less stability and weaker interest organizations, the media are in a new situation.

Changes of Media Structure: National and International

Radio and, later, television were organized differently in different countries but with similar outcomes. The result was large nationwide companies that controlled their markets. Unlike newspapers, broadcast media were – almost without exception – strictly regulated. The mechanisms for financing radio and television admittedly varied – some companies ran advertising, others charged licence fees – but this was not important. The crucial thing was the result: large, strong nation-wide broadcasting units. The Swedish Broadcasting Corporation thus had its counterparts in most Western countries.

Radio and television eventually became important at the regional and local levels too, but most important was their national role. Television acquired great national significance even in countries like the United States, where competition prevailed. At the same hour, a majority of the people were watching the same news programmes (Hultén, 1984).

Today the situation has been partially transformed at least, and we can anticipate new and far-reaching changes. The old monopoly situation has vanished. In Sweden, satellite-beamed television began to reach people's homes, distributed mainly via local cable systems, early in the 1980s. Since then it has expanded rapidly. By the spring of 1991, nearly 40 per cent of households could receive satellite-beamed television channels. According to optimistic forecasts, by the mid-1990s the figure will be 70 per cent of households.

The London-based channel known as TV 3 began its broadcasts to the Scandinavian countries on New Year's Eve 1987. It is owned by Swedish-born financier, Jan Stenbeck, and is advertiser-financed. By the spring of 1991, TV 3 was broadcasting about 55 hours a week – mainly non-Swedish programmes, including movies, popular television series and sports. The channel has, however, gradually increased the percentage of its programming produced specifically for a Scandinavian audience. In 1990 it also began brief news broadcasts. TV 3 was expected to make a profit in 1991.

In the autumn of 1990, TV 4 was launched by Nordisk Television, with far greater ambitions and broader ownership than its competitors, TV 3 and the Nordic Channel. TV 4 is based entirely in Sweden, has public service ambitions and uses extensive Swedish material. Its public service ambitions are similar to those of Swedish Broadcasting. From the very start, one of TV 4's aims has been to be awarded the right to establish a third terrestrial television channel on which advertising would be permitted.

During its introductory period, TV 4 has had obvious difficulties reaching a large audience – except for a few programmes. For example, during its first six months, the channel was in no way able to compete with the two Sveriges Television (SVT) channels. It has also had a tough time making inroads against TV 3.

The various new Scandinavian television companies that are now broadcasting via satellite have changed the situation of Swedish Television. SVT no longer enjoys a monopoly, although it still dominates the field and has by far the largest number of viewers. The non-Scandinavian television channels, especially CNN, have also brought major changes.

CNN can be watched by a large percentage of American households and also by audiences of various sizes in about 100 other countries. Since the Gulf War began, CNN has assumed a prominent role among the American television networks in terms of new reporting. In Sweden, the number of people watching CNN increased sharply during the Gulf War, since most local cable networks include CNN in their menu of channels. A survey taken in Sweden during February 1991 revealed that nearly 10 per cent of respondents had obtained most of their information about the war from foreign TV stations, that is, mainly from CNN.

Also important is the fact that CNN influences the contents of other television channels and other media. Most Swedish news desks keep CNN running 24 hours a day. For many of them, CNN's material was the most important way of illustrating the events that unfolded during the war against Iraq early in 1991.

But CNN is not the only international television channel that has changed the situation of Swedish television and its viewers. Competing head-to-head with CNN are Britain's Sky News and the BBC. But during the period being discussed here, there was no doubt about CNN's leading role. This was true all over the world.

The interesting question is whether CNN will maintain its lead in the international television news field or whether it will run into competition. It seems possible that the unique position that CNN enjoyed during the Gulf conflict will be a one-time phenomenon. A number of European television companies have also joined forces to plan a prospective European news channel, Euronews. Of the Nordic countries, Finland is participating in this project, while the others are remaining outside. It is uncertain when this European news channel might be able to begin broadcasting.

All the talk about CNN has distracted attention from radio. International radio broadcasts play a crucial role for many. The importance of the BBC World Service can hardly be overemphasized. BBC radio broadcasts were the most important single news source for large numbers of people in the war against Iraq.

There are many other international radio broadcasts, the main ones being the Voice of America and Radio Free Europe. These stations have not enjoyed the same reputation for objectivity as the BBC. In spite of this they have undoubtedly played a major part in disseminating news and moulding opinion, especially in Eastern Europe.

Radio is certain to become even more international. Satellites can relay not only television pictures, but also radio signals. We will soon have a number of thematic international channels, specializing in music, news, and so on.

Despite all these rapid developments and the new television channels, the national public television company is still dominant in Sweden. The following section examines the rules governing it and the monitoring agencies that were created to safeguard those values that the Cabinet and Parliament regarded as important to protect.

Regulation of Public Broadcasting

In Sweden, a public service ideal along BBC lines has been the guiding principle ever since the first radio company was established in the 1920s. The situation has naturally changed as radio and especially television have become internationalized. The television channels now being relayed by satellite fall outside the strict regulations that have prevailed in the Swedish broadcast media.

The rule system approved by the Swedish Cabinet and Parliament thus applies only to the Swedish Broadcasting Corporation (Sveriges Radio, SR) and its four programming subsidiaries: Swedish Television (Sveriges Television, SVT), the Swedish Radio Company (Sveriges Riksradio, RR), the Swedish Educational Broadcasting Company (Utbildningsradion, UR), and the Swedish Local Radio Company (Lokalradion, LRAB). The ultimate purpose of the rule system is to protect the values that the Cabinet and Parliament believe are essential to maintain in broadcasting. Generally speaking, they have been approved under conditions of broad political consensus.

The operations of Swedish Broadcasting are regulated by a Radio Act approved by Parliament and by an Enabling Agreement between the Swedish Government and the Company. Among other specifications, the Radio Act stipulates that broadcasting operations must be carried out in an impartial and objective manner. But it emphasizes that this regulation must be interpreted in the light of the far-reaching freedom of speech and information that must prevail in the broadcast media. It also states that in their work, the programming companies must uphold the basic concepts of democratic government and the principles of the equal value of all people and the freedom and dignity of the individual.

There are also regulations in the Radio Act stating that no Government authority has the right to examine in advance or to prohibit a broadcast because of programme content. However, a special panel known as the Radio Council (Radionämnden) may examine programmes after they have been broadcast. The law also declares that the programming companies shall be obligated to make public the decisions of the Council in cases where their own company has been judged to have violated the law of the Enabling Agreement.

The Enabling Agreement contains regulations similar to those applied to the printed word: protection of sources, the designation of a 'responsible publisher' for every programme (meaning that this person and no one else can be subjected to legal action) and a special system of court procedures. Swedish free-press legislation is structured in such a way that, in principle, the law stands on the side of the media, and it is very difficult to win a verdict against a news medium.

The agreements between the Government and the broadcasting companies contain applications and refinements of the rules in the Radio Act. The responsibilities of the programming companies are defined, and their tasks are delineated. For example, the agreements state that programme operations should take into account the central position of the broadcasting media in society. They also say that the companies are responsible for broadcasting the news; stimulating debate; examining public agencies, interest organizations and companies; and covering cultural life. However, these sections of the agreements are phrased in very general terms.

The task of the Radio Council is to examine programmes after they have been broadcast and to decide whether they have lived up to the programming rules and guidelines stated in the Radio Act and the agreements between the Government and the programming companies. The Council is a public agency. It functions both as a monitor on behalf of the Cabinet and Parliament and as a body that the general public can turn to with their complaints about broadcasts. The Council has described itself as a 'court-like' body (Hadenius and Weibull, 1989).

Political Journalism in Sweden

Swedish newspapers have traditionally had close ties with political parties (Hadenius, 1983). The majority of newspapers have had a party identity, and many have had financial or organizational links with one party. The system of Government press subsidies that was established in 1971, totalling about SEK500 million (£45 million) during 1990, can be explained largely by the role of Swedish newspapers (Hultén, 1984).

For many years, radio in Sweden was completely unpolitical. It had no news desk of its own; the news was supplied by Tidningarnas Telegrambyrd (TT), a national wire service owned by the newspapers. Not until 1936 did Swedish Radio start a news magazine programme of its own, with the typical name of *Dagens Eko* (*Echo of the Day*). This programme had only a vague connection with the news. In its early stages, television also had a semi-official character. The trend toward greater openness and independence began cautiously only after World War II on radio and during the late 1960s on television.

One reason why there was no real political journalism for years in Swedish broadcast media was undoubtedly that the Cabinet and Parliament – which decided the structure and policies of these media – did not want radio and television programmes that might 'disturb' the established political system. Another was that leading politicians were closely allied with the press, which regarded broadcast media as competitors (Gustafsson and Hadenius, 1976).

Because of the close ties between the press and political parties, and the semi-official position of the broadcast media, not until relatively recently can we speak of a Fourth Estate in Sweden. During the 1970s and 1980s, however, there was a marked change in the role of the print and broadcast media in the political market. This was based on what – in Sweden – was a new ideology of journalistic independence, influenced by media practice in English-speaking countries.

Today it goes without saying that journalists must be independent of people with various kinds of power, especially political power. Their job is to be representatives of the public, examining and questioning authority. They should disclose matters of general interest, but which the people in power wish to conceal for one reason or another (Hadenius, 1990).

In recent decades, politics in Sweden – as in most countries – has become increasingly media-orientated. Press conferences and surprise announcements on television, radio and press are daily occurrences. Meanwhile, the position of Parliament has become weaker. This is most evident during election campaigns and Cabinet crises. What matters is setting the agenda of the media. A struggle is under way here, both between rival political parties on the one hand and between politicians and the media on the other.

We may now consider the main value-laden controversies that have arisen in Swedish media discussion.

Debates over Values in Swedish Broadcasting

The objectivity debate

During the 1960s and 1970s, when Swedish television and radio were gaining a freer position vis-à-vis political parties, Cabinet and Parliament, a marked change occurred in the contents of political programmes. Journalists assumed a questioning attitude they had never shown before. These programmes were often controversial, and they were perceived by many viewers as unfairly slanted.

Critical journalism was evident in feature stories, news items and discussion programmes. It is hardly surprising that this new brand of journalism, which had an even larger impact because of longer transmission hours and the expansion of Swedish television to two channels in the late 1960s, triggered irritation and strong criticism from various quarters. The critics also took a number of steps:

1   Complaints were lodged with the Radio Council.
2   Open criticism was voiced in articles and political speeches, and behind-the-scenes pressure tactics were employed.
3   Studies appeared aimed at determining the degree of objectivity on television and radio.

The Enabling Agreement between the Government and the Swedish Broadcasting Corporation states that SR shall provide objective and impartial news reporting. Political scientist, Jorgen Westerstähl, came to play a major role in these discussions, because he tried to define objectivity and conducted a series of studies of the extent to which Swedish radio and television were living up to the requirements of the Radio Act and their agreements.

According to Westerstähl (1971), the concept of objectivity contains four requirements: truth, relevance, balance and neutral presentation.

The truth requirement is the simplest to define but the most difficult to measure. It also lay outside the studies that Westersthäl and others conducted. The relevance requirement means that an event should be given the prominence and the amount of space that can be regarded as reasonable. But the major question, obviously is: What is reasonable, and what is not reasonable? Who should decide how much space a news item should be given in order for the relevance requirement to be regarded as fulfilled?

Impartiality can be measured, according to Westerstähl, by studying balance and presentation. Impartial news reporting must be balanced reporting. It should give the various parties that are involved the opportunity to present their respective versions. The neutral presentation requirement is also indisputable to someone who aims at impartial news reporting. One of Westerstähl's classic studies (1971) concerned media coverage of the Vietnam War during one period of 1968. In it, he examined how the different sides were presented by the media, for example, in terms of their successes or failures in the war and in terms of their good or bad relations with the civilian population.

Westerstähl classified various newspapers on a scale and then compared radio and television coverage with that of the news- papers. He found that the editorial policies of the broadcast media were roughly in the middle but were more negative than those of the wire services.

His studies were subjected to fierce criticism by journalists. One objection was that impartiality occupied too large a role at the expense of objectivity. Another was that comparisons among media implied that one which ended up in the middle of the scale was 'best' – even though a middle placement did not necessarily mean that the medium in question had been the most objective.

Werterstähl's studies were conducted mainly on behalf of the Swedish Broadcasting Corporation and the Radio Council. These organizations trusted his studies and – despite pronounced mistrust by journalists – they had a major impact on Swedish broadcast journalism. They represented a reaction against the new journal- ism, more independent of political parties, that was increasingly beginning to appear in various media during the 1960s.

Swedish journalism lacked a tradition of behaving as an indepen- dent Fourth Estate. Many journalists had undoubtedly overstepped their bounds. Criticisms levelled at some journalists for taking sides in news programmes and thereby violating the rules of the broadcast media were also largely justified.

At the time, some journalists thought that press freedom was synonymous with the right to crusade for their own or other people's ideas (Fjaestad and Holmlöv, 1975). Their intentions and their opinions were often evident in their stories. At worst, the audience could not find out what an interviewee had said, but only what the journalist felt about what he had said.

This was not good journalism, and it is understandable that the reaction against it was strong. Readers want to form their own opinions, not to be lectured to by self-appointed preachers. Journal- ists and newspapers also reacted against advocacy journalism.

The objectivity debate in Sweden is an example of how 'vulner- able values' in the broadcast media can come up for discussion. On the one hand, there was a new approach to their work by journalists, and on the other hand there were the expectations and demands of politicians.

What has been the outcome of this struggle during the 1980s and early 1990s? It is, of course, difficult to make a fair assessment. Put simply, the relationship between the mass media and politicians has increasingly come to resemble that prevailing in English-speaking countries. Politicians have taken a number of steps to protect themselves from journalists; for example they have hired information officers and speech writers. It is generally accepted that media representatives are an interest group – separate from the other power groupings.

The influence of politics on the media is still considerable. Many newspapers are owned by political parties, and their editors-in-chief are selected on political grounds. Representatives of the various parties sit on the boards of the broadcast media companies. The future of the broadcast media is being decided by a parliamentary panel consisting only of politicians.

News journalists have nevertheless clearly refused to let political parties lead them by the nose. In a study of how journalists perceived their profession, they gave the lowest rating to the task of 'presenting, even in news stories, those ideas with which my newspaper most closely identifies'. Only 1 per cent of journalists regarded this as 'extremely important' while 85 per cent considered it 'not important' (Petersson and Carlberg, 1990). Objectivity has become a norm, which naturally does not mean that it is always observed.

In discussions of journalism in the late 1980s, some argued that the objectivity debate had made journalists downright afraid of showing their opinions. They all followed the same pattern. Their programme segments and features were too bland.

It is the task of the Radio Council to decide whether the Swedish Broadcasting Corporation lives up to the requirements of objectivity and impartiality. Most of the Radio Council's rulings have dealt with shortcomings in these areas. During the ten years from 1978 and 1988, two-thirds of its negative verdicts against programmes concerned violations of these rules. When, for example, during a white-collar employees' strike in the engineering industry in 1988, Pehr Gyllenhammar, the head of Sweden's largest company, Volvo, appeared in an 'infotainment-type' programme to be interviewed about the strike, the Council found the programme in violation of the rules, because no arguments from the other side were presented in a clear fashion.

In such verdicts, the programming company, however, not the individual journalist or editorial staff, is declared in violation of the rules. The management of each programming company must then decide what action should be taken if the programme is or is not declared in violation. Verdicts against a programme must be publicized as soon as possible in the medium concerned.

Television without advertising – a controversial value
In many Western countries, it has been self-evident that one or more television and radio channels should be financed by advertising. The three Scandinavian countries, however, have been among the exceptions. In Norway, Denmark and Sweden, the broadcast media have been free of advertising.

For many people in Sweden, freedom from advertising has been the most important and the most vulnerable value in the broadcasting media. But especially since television broadcasting began, some people have campaigned for the introduction of advertising. They have nevertheless been in a minority among decision makers.

The opponents of television commercials won a clear victory when the organizational structure of Swedish television was decided in the 1950s. During the 1960s, advertisers and corporations conducted an intensive campaign on behalf of commercial television. They established a special organization – the Society for the Promotion of Television – which seemed to score successes. Various public opinion surveys over the years have demonstrated that there is indeed support for television advertising among the Swedish public; in Parliament, however, opinion has been against it.

During the 1950s, Sweden, like many countries, was the target of advertiser-supported 'pirate' radio stations broadcast from international waters. Their programming was dominated by light music, news and entertainment. The most successful Swedish transmitter of this kind, Radio Nord, was anchored outside Stockholm. With hindsight, it is clear that Radio Nord pioneered a new style of radio for Sweden, but its operations were vehemently opposed by both the Government and the Swedish Broadcasting Corporation.

A law was enacted which banned radio transmission from international waters. Radio Nord and the other broadcast stations were silenced. Interestingly, this episode led to important changes in the programming of Swedish Broadcasting. A new third radio channel was established, broadcasting mainly light music and news.

But the more heated debate on advertising concerned television. In 1969, a second television channel was introduced in Sweden. This was preceded by a lively debate on how the new channel should be financed. Supporters of commercial television attacked the broadcasting monopoly for failing to allow diversity, arguing that an advertiser-supported channel would earn more money and thus be able to show better programmes. They also maintained that the Swedish business sector would benefit from the introduction of commercial television.

The Social Democratic Cabinet settled for a system where there would be a 'stimulating rivalry' between the two channels but decided that this would take place within the same company and continue to be financed by licence fees. The result would be some degree of competition, but it would not occur on commercial terms (Hadenius and Weibull, 1989).

The issue of whether or not to allow advertising on television was debated throughout the 1980s. To a growing extent, of course, this debate took place in the shadow of expanding satellite channels and cable networks. It became increasingly apparent that the monopolistic Swedish Broadcasting Corporation was facing outside competition. Many of the commercials appearing on satellite-relayed television were Swedish-produced and could be received in Swedish homes.

Nevertheless, opposition to television advertising was particularly vehement in the three Scandinavian countries. Why have television and radio commercials been viewed as such major threats – and why should advertising be more dangerous to television than perhaps anything else? Why has advertising been the most intensely debated topic in discussions of the broadcast media in Norway, Denmark and Sweden? As a rule, this issue has been assigned an ethical dimension.

There is no simple answer. There is a form of anti-commercialism in the Scandinavian countries which maintains that commercialism is admittedly not completely harmful, but that it should be kept within certain limits. This kind of puritanism has been cultivated in the socialist parties and among their activists in particular. Around 1900, when the Social Democrats were establishing newspapers, they expressed the hope that these could survive without having to accept advertising. The newspapers would not be 'buyable', as they put it. But Social Democratic newspapers were forced to participate in a tough competitive market. They had to accept advertising, and they were unhappy that non-socialist newspapers were more successful as advertising media than socialist ones.

Among the opponents of television advertising, we can find the same energy and frenzy as among the opponents of Swedish nuclear power. They draw connections between television advertising and various shortcomings of commercialized society. They believe that although advertising is accepted in such places as newspapers and billboards, there must be an 'ad-free zone' and that television and radio should be such zones.

American television and radio have often been cited as frightening examples of what happens when commercial forces are let loose. Some have argued that it is not possible to combine commercial television with public service broadcasting of the Swedish type. Advertiser-supported television is compelled to aim continually for higher viewer statistics and is therefore uninterested in high-quality programmes that only attract small numbers of viewers. Another argument has been that advertisers would gain a direct influence on programming, making it more difficult to uphold the objectivity requirement.

There have also been strong commercial arguments against television advertising. They come from its competitors. Newspapers and magazines have been afraid of competition from broadcast media in the advertising field. Newspaper publishers have enjoyed a strong position, because they have close contacts with the people who wield political power. Only a few newspapers in Sweden have forcefully presented the opinions of those who favour television advertising.

An alliance between the opponents of advertising and groups with direct interests in the advertising field – especially representatives of newspapers – has worked to block commercial television. They were successful until the point when internationalization broke the broadcasting monopoly in Sweden.

In terms of viewer statistics, Swedish Broadcasting has in fact weathered the new competition very well. But the London-based TV 3 has also scored successes. Especially during 1990, it carved out a position for itself in the advertising market. A new argument has consequently emerged: Swedish advertising money is disappearing from the country.

Meanwhile, Swedish Television has been hit by rising expenses. The company has had to carry higher costs of in-house productions, while buying foreign television series and programmes at higher prices because of competition in the market. As a result, even the most rabid opponents of television advertising have had to give ground.

Around 1990, the dominant topic of discussion related to broadcasting no longer concerned whether or not advertising should be accepted on television, but what shape it should assume. There were disagreements both within and among the political parties as to how the new structure should look. Their discussions continued as TV 3's satellite broadcasts captured a growing audience and established itself more and more firmly in the advertising market.

In March 1991 the different sides reached an agreement in principle to establish a third terrestrial channel, which would not be part of Swedish Television. It would be financed by the sale of advertising. A number of conditions would be attached to its broadcasting licence:

1 Its ownership must be broadly based in Swedish society.
2 A certain percentage of the new channel's advertising revenues must be paid to Sveriges Radio.
3 The holders of the broadcast licence must pay for the construction and expenses of a third terrestrial distribution network.
4 Its programming would have to meet certain public service requirements.
5 Commercials must be limited to time blocks and not be allowed to interrupt programmes.
6 Certain types of advertising should be prohibited: for example, political advertising, commercials for wine and liquor, and advertising aimed at children.

The Cabinet and Parliament have thus tried in these ways to protect 'vulnerable values' that television advertising could threaten.

At the time of writing a discussion was under way over whether there is any constellation of potential owners who might be willing to apply for a broadcasting licence to operate this third channel. The cost will be substantial, and there is great uncertainty over the likely amount of advertising revenues. Another inhibiting factor is that the Cabinet and Parliament have reserved the right to reassess the situation after a number of years. A company may thus have its broadcasting licence taken away after a period of expensive investment.

The interesting point here is that by making this decision, Sweden has abandoned one of the values that it has protected for the longest period. However, the two television channels operated by the public service company, Swedish Broadcasting, will remain free of advertising. Critics of the March 1991 agreement maintain that these two public channels will have insufficient funds, since the politicians are unwilling to increase the licence fee level. They also believe that the battle for viewers will become just as 'commercial', even if the public company does not sell advertising.

Ethical concerns
Sweden's Freedom of the Press Act is part of its Constitution. The Cabinet and Parliament have few and limited opportunities to interfere with the press. On several occasions, legislation has been proposed to provide better protection to individuals and to restrict crime reporting, for example, but these have not won a political majority. In Sweden it has been regarded as in the public interest

not to surround the activities of the media with excessively restrictive laws. Other interests have been subordinated to this principle.

Instead, we have had an efficient self-policing system. The Swedish Broadcasting Corporation has accepted the ethical rules adopted by representatives of the print media. These rules are very specific in a number of areas, for example, respect for individual privacy (*Spelregler för press, radio och TV*, 1990).

Compared with other countries, for example, Swedish crime reporting is very restrained. Media organizations have established precise rules about when the name of an accused person may be disclosed. This may be done only after conviction for a serious offence. An ordinary citizen can thus count on anonymity in cases where he has not been convicted of a very serious crime.

The issue of disclosing names came to a head in 1986, when a man was detained on suspicion of having assassinated Prime Minister Olaf Palme. In almost every country outside Sweden, his name was revealed. It was also published in a few Swedish newspapers, but not revealed on radio or television. In the broadcast media and in most Swedish print media, he was referred to as the 33-year-old. After he ceased to be a suspect, those newspapers that had nevertheless published his name were found guilty of libel and were ordered by the courts to pay heavy fines.

The situation is different when people in the public eye are involved. A remarkable change has occurred in this area in recent years, especially in the broadcast media. A senior civil servant, business owner or politician can expect to have his name revealed even if he is only a suspect in a crime. The same applies to such television celebrities as actors and personalities. The reason why the media make exceptions from the otherwise strict rules in these cases is that they regard it as in the public interest that the activities of these people be made known.

In recent years, there have been a number of cases where the need to disclose names has been challenged, and where it has been apparent that such disclosure has done far more damage to the person in question than any legal punishment. A leading banker suspected of a minor tax violation can expect heavy publicity in the print media, radio and television. The same is true of a Member of Parliament suspected of driving under the influence of alcohol, or a prominent lawyer accused of a conflict of interest. These people would probably not have had their names disclosed in years past, but it happens today. In several cases, their names have been disclosed first on television (Hadenius and Weibull, 1990).

In Sweden, as in other countries, there has been debate about violence and pornography in the visual media. But this has been more closely associated with the videocassette business than with radio or television. One reason is that television has been relatively restrained about showing programmes or movies containing violence or pornography. Among members of the public, there is a high level of tolerance for erotic films, but the limits are far stricter when it comes to violence. Typically, the groups that have criticized television and video have focused almost exclusively on violence, especially in videocassettes.

The contents of satellite channels beamed toward Sweden are regulated by the Cable Act. This law is very liberal and contains restrictions only on brutal violence and violent pornography. But satellite channels have not chosen to compete with public service television by emphasizing violence or pornographic movies. Instead, TV 3 in particular presents more entertainment and simple game shows.

Another problem area is treatment of crime and accident victims. Since 1923, when the Swedish press established its ethical code, this type of material has been handled with caution. Such caution used to be even more pronounced on Swedish radio and television, where crime and accident reporting was very limited until the late 1970s. During the 1980s, crime reporting became more common in the broadcast media, but the treatment of victims was still characterized by great reticence. Over the past few years, however, there has been a change. This is particularly evident in the news programmes of the new Swedish satellite channel TV 4. Even so, this does not approach the level of exploitation of the kind that often occurs in the evening newspapers. It should be added, however, that in an international comparison, Swedish evening tabloids are very moderate.

Conclusion: Looking Ahead

Ethical concerns usually predominate when vulnerable values are debated. This is true around the world. The fact that Sweden, as well as other Nordic countries, deviate from this pattern can be explained primarily by their cultivation of a public service tradition in radio and television. Because of their general norms and specific guidelines, ethical problems have been peripheral. Only in exceptional cases have the broadcast media deviated from what could be accepted by the vast majority of viewers and listeners.

Instead, the debate in Sweden has centred on rule systems and their application, especially in relation to political issues. Objectivity issues occupied centre stage for a long time. They arose when television and radio gained a freer, less official position. Because radio and television became more important to political debate and political decision making, they received even closer scrutiny.

Today the issue of objectivity in the broadcast media is less prominent. The various programming companies enjoy a high degree of independence, and politicians have no direct influence on programme content. On the other hand, it can be noted that today more politicians sit on the boards of the programming companies than ever before. Politicians will also have an absolutely crucial influence on the restructuring process now under way at Swedish Broadcasting.

In Sweden, as in other countries, the broadcast media are undergoing a deregulation process. The rules under which they will operate have not yet been formulated. But it is clear that the situation in the broadcast media will become more commercial and that Swedish radio and television will experience problems similar to those found in numerous other European countries.

The deregulation of the broadcast media, along with intensified competition in the media sector, can be expected to result in a completely new situation – new, that is, to the Scandinavian countries though more prevalent elsewhere in Europe. An indication of this is the new type of crime reporting that TV 4 has introduced.

Furthermore, quality-related issues have already become a focus of debate: will all the new channels be filled with simple home-made game and entertainment shows and with American soap operas?

Political discussion of media-related issues will only partly change in character; however, the issue of political advertising in the broadcast media is new and controversial. But, as previously, most essential will be how the various broadcasting companies present the political debate in news and current affairs programmes. Election campaign coverage will be followed especially closely by representatives of the political parties, and this is hardly anything new. But the picture is more complicated than before, with more channels and different owners.

Let me conclude by making a connection between this and the change of political climate that has occurred so rapidly in Sweden. The previous stability and Social Democratic dominance in the political system seem to have vanished. It is impossible to specify what role the media have played in this development. It is reasonable to assume, however, that they have helped to accelerate and amplify it.

The media in Sweden once had a stabilizing effect on the political system. The press was closely tied to the political parties, and the broadcast media had a semi-official role. Today the situation is virtually the opposite. The media have had a destabilizing effect, which impending changes in broadcasting are likely to intensify.

References

Demokrati och makti i Sverige (1990). Uppsala: SOU.

Fjaestad, Björn and Holmlöv, P.G. (1975) *Swedish Newsmen's Views on the Role of the Press*. Stockholm: Ekonomiska forskningsinstiutet vid Handelshögskolan.

Gustafsson, Karl Erik and Hadenius, Stig (1976) *Swedish Press Policy*. Stockholm: Swedish Institute.

Hadenius, Stig (1983) 'The Rise and Possible Fall of the Swedish Party Press', *Communication Research*, 10 (3): 287–309.

Hadenius, Stig (1990) 'Regeringen och massmedierna 1840–1990', in Stig Hadenius (ed.), *Journalistik och politik*. Stockholm: JMK, Stockholm University. pp. 8–48.

Hadenius, Stig and Weibull, Lennart (1989) *Massmedier*. Stockholm: Bonniers.

Hadenius, Stig and Weibull, Lennart (1990) *Sensations journalistik eller nödvändig granskning*. Stockholm: SIM.

Hultén, Olof (1984) *Mass Media and State Support in Sweden*. Stockholm: Swedish Institute.

Petersson, Olof and Carlberg, Ingrid (1990) *Makten över tanken*. Stockholm: Carlssons.

Spelregler för press, radio och TV (1990). Stockholm: Pressens samarbetsnamnd.

Westersthäl, Jurgen (1971) *Objektiv nyhetsfürmedling*. Gothenburg: Scandinavian University Books.

9

Television in a Small Multicultural Society: The Case of Switzerland

Ulrich Saxer

Issues about vulnerable values in multichannel television can be properly considered only when the problem-solving capacities of media systems are realistically taken into account. Too much discussion and too many media policy measures are motivated by wishful thinking – in Switzerland as elsewhere. To conceive the mass media in a functional–structural perspective, and in the light of empirical research, as problem-solving systems offers a chance to evaluate, judiciously and realistically, proposed or actual measures of television regulation, their likely efficacy and impact.

The functional capacity of a media system depends on its host society's resources and communication needs. Bearing in mind such societal prerequisites as integration, adaptation, goal-achievement and pattern maintenance, it is clear that national television stands a better chance of meeting these in well-integrated societies than in less integrated ones. It is normally not possible to compensate for large-scale societal defects, as some policy makers seem to imagine. It is also clear that small countries, such as Switzerland, need systems that are more flexibly adaptive to their international surroundings than do much larger states with more ample resources. The so-called 'next-door-giant' effect (Liu, 1972), which engenders uneven communication flows between large and small neighbours, cannot be judged only negatively, as nationalistic policy makers tend to do. The suitability and feasibility of media policy cannot be assessed unless the broader social context is considered.

Switzerland and its Media System

Five characteristics of Switzerland are particularly formative for the structures and functioning of its mass media.

First, with an area of 41,293 km, Switzerland is a small country, which has less than 7 million inhabitants (1989: 6,723,000) among whom over a million are foreigners (1,040,325), more than a third (38 per cent) coming from Italy. This population is unevenly distributed, due to the largely alpine nature of the country. Densely populated metropolitan areas contrast with thinly populated peripheries. In addition to the large percentage of foreigners, the population structure is characterized by a rapidly growing share of senior citizens and single-person households.

Second, Swiss society is plurilinguistic (73.5 per cent German speakers, 20.1 per cent French, 4.5 per cent Italian and 0.9 per cent Romansch in 1980). Due to topography, there are more cultural segmentations than in most countries.

Third, the Swiss economy has functioned successfully on the whole, enjoying high levels of productivity, personal income and employment, compared with other states in Western Europe. Work incentives are also high, as are standards of education. There are marked standard of living disparities, however, between the more privileged and less well-off members of the society.

Fourth, the Swiss political system is highly differentiated and exceptionally demanding, since, in addition to its electorally representative institutions, it is constituted as a direct democracy on three levels: the confederation, the regional states and the local communities.

Finally, in the last decade, structural change has accelerated, though less dramatically than in other societies. Switzerland has become an information society with a highly developed communications infrastructure. It has also moved further in the direction of a multiculturally divided society with many signs that political consensus is eroding.

These characteristics have given rise to the following main problem areas:

First, because of the high degree of cultural segmentation, Switzerland needs integrative institutions, among them mass media. At the same time this system of institutions must be differentiated enough to cater for the very different needs of a multicultural society.

Second, the Swiss political system requires highly efficient and (again) differentiated political and media institutions, which can disseminate adequate political information to citizens on the local, regional and national levels.

Third, the resources that the Swiss media system possesses to satisfy these functional imperatives are sparse – particularly in television. Creative potential is limited; and in this calm small state national and international attention is rarely captured by significant or dramatic events. Moreover, because of linguistic pluralism, the main media markets are small.

Finally, developments in European politics may necessitate adaptations of outlook toward the outside world that are, to a degree, still unclear. Some segments of the population, however, are being drawn in on themselves by more private and hedonistic values. At the same time, there has been an increasing alienation from central political institutions and allegiances. All these tendencies suggest that certain previously established patterns are now endangered, which, in the eyes of some, deserve protection as vulnerable values.

Among the structures of the Swiss media that must respond to the numerous and partially discordant expectations resulting from this constellation of problems and needs the following may be mentioned: a press system with an exceptionally large number of newspaper titles (275 in 1989, including 114 dailies: SZV, 1990); an electronic media system, in which television is still provided as a public service only by the Swiss Broadcasting Corporation (SBC), though private radio stations are permitted; a television system that transmits three full programmes in German, French and Italian, as well as regular broadcasts in Romansch; a thriving magazine industry; a vigorous book publishing sector; but an almost starving film industry. There is of course much functional complementarity among these different media.

Whose Vulnerable Values?

The task of identifying vulnerable values in television systems and protecting them by regulation or other steering devices is always difficult in a democracy. The liberal tradition, still quite strong in Switzerland, denies legitimacy to many media policy measures that might otherwise be entertained. Moreover, the global advance of deregulation has weakened the techniques of national media regulation as well as faith in its likely efficacy. Shifting values and a decline in value consensus in multicultural societies (Inglehart, 1990) have made efforts to uphold certain norms and standards of television programming against market forces yet more problematic.

What the problem boils down to is (a) which group or groups are legitimated to define such values and (b) which group or groups are influential enough to implant their definitions of those values in the media order and output? So far as the question of legitimacy is concerned, in a direct democracy like Switzerland the answer is every citizen, at least to the degree that legal proposals may be submitted for decision to the popular sovereign. In practice, however, the political process seldom culminates in such an open, final, collective decision. Far more often vulnerable values are defined effectively only by certain actors, more powerful, efficient or competent than the rest, to the benefit of their interests, and such definitions, backed up by group pressures, are de facto implemented in television programming. It has also to be borne in mind that media regulation and programming standards must be interpreted and applied by media regulators as well as by media executives and practitioners (who can sometimes operate in the media policy arena with a special though often disguised vigour).

This may serve as a preface to a rudimentary typology of actors in Swiss media policy. These pursue quite different strategies in defining and seeking protection for vulnerable values, that is, societal concerns of high importance. In the 1980s, all recognized that limited resources made the establishment of a second full-scale television system alongside the existing public one highly impractical. The possibilities of realizing certain values and standards in programming will therefore still be confined to one system. Meanwhile, programmes are entering the country from the outside that are not always compatible with officially defined Swiss values, with which Swiss media policy can deal only negatively (if it wishes) – that is, by excluding them.

Seven actor-groups can be roughly distinguished, each of which can aspire to play some part in defining and enforcing certain values for Swiss television.

Transnational actors. Among these the Council of Europe is particularly important for Switzerland, as the Swiss Government gave its provisional agreement to the European Convention on Transfrontier Television in May 1989. This actor's strategy is mainly guided by the traditional liberal ideal of a free flow of information. Transnational television industry players pursue more or less identical aims, in order to smooth the passage of programme exports.

National authorities. Such authorities, principally the Government, Parliament, the relevant ministries and regulatory bodies (among the last particularly the Independent Authority for Programme Complaints), contribute to the definition and protection of values in television programmes according to their positions in the decision process. In a direct democracy, the Government's strategy will usually be to seek consensus at almost any cost, so as to avoid the need for a plebiscite, the results of which are always difficult to predict. The customary fruit of such a strategy is compromise.

Political parties. Swiss political parties tend to react to issues in the media sector along traditional party lines, with the Right being more favourably disposed to private entrepreneurial activity, the Left favouring public service broadcasting; the former being also closer to the press, where it enjoys much support, the latter to television and the electronic media.

Representation of economic interests. Since the Swiss economic system penetrates the country's political system at many points, much support is given to policies thought likely to strengthen the competitiveness and prosperity of the national economy. Media policies opposed by leading representatives of the economic system stand little chance of being introduced.

Representatives of cultural interests. Churches, educational institutions, artists' associations, sports organizations, etc. – all advance their own preferred values. The churches, for example, call for programming in line with Christian standards.

Media organizations. As powerful audience multipliers, on which politicians depend heavily for access to the electorate, media organizations can often manage to obstruct regulations they deem unfavourable to their interests. Their influence on policy may be limited, however, when such media actors cannot reconcile their sometimes conflicting interests. Generally they tend to pursue two aims: to secure utmost freedom to act according to their organizational and professional cultures; and to ensure rewarding markets for themselves. The tendency of even public broadcasting to imitate the successful programming of private providers cannot be overlooked (Meier et al., 1989).

Ordinary citizens. So far as media policy is concerned, these are at the reactive end of the decision chain. Audience associations and pressure groups of different political colours speak in their name but with little authorization. The role of the general audience in Swiss media policy – except in the very rare case of the plebiscite – is limited to that of a consumer of media offerings. Its rate of consumption is presumed to indicate how far its preferred values in television coincide with those embedded in the various television products that the market makes available.

Which Vulnerable Values?

In Switzerland, as in many other countries, the result of this constellation of actors is a rather disparate mixture of social, political, economic and cultural concerns that different groups want to be respected in programming according to their opinions and beliefs. This is only to be expected in a multicultural democracy. The most powerful actors succeed in defining vulnerable values in the most compelling way: by legal authority and regulation. In the media sector the need to interpret legal prescriptions in terms of professional culture leads (and has led in SBC) to a framework of

internal organizational regulation. Thus there is always an inter-
action between two different sets of values: societal ones, such as
human dignity or the protection of juveniles; and those artistic and
journalistic norms of media organizations, which must always
transform the officially postulated values into pictures, words and
sounds, applying the routines of their crafts. It is not surprising,
therefore, that legal measures aim not merely to protect general
societal values in television output but to institutionalize certain
professional norms that may lend them support. For example, the
law requires adherence to certain professional norms of accurate
reporting and a balanced presentation of opinions in order to secure
– and this is the political value to be realized – a comprehensive and
reliable basis of information from which citizens may form their
political judgements. In other words, vulnerable values endorsed by
legal regulation and controlling institutions pertain on the one side
to the functioning of Swiss television, where they are formulated as
norms of performance, and on the other side to certain societal
concerns.

On the *performance level*, a draft federal bill on the future of
Swiss television and radio (published 28 September 1987 but still not
passed at the time of writing) aims first and foremost to secure
SBC's position as the main television and radio service operating in
and for Switzerland. The prime concern is to maintain a full range of
national television, though not at the expense of press interests or
those of the Swiss film industry. This qualification reflects a widely
shared belief that the country's scarce media resources should not
be squandered in destructive competition but should contribute to a
functional complementarity, particularly since an advanced information society needs a highly differentiated media system. For its
part, SBC's Concession (issued by the Swiss Federal Council, 5
October 1987), mainly mentions certain norms of professional
culture, which the organization is expected to respect. These are
spelled out in internal manuals and codes and chiefly refer to
informational and cultural standards.

On the *societal level*, those values that are accepted more or less
universally by the most influential actors are of a very general
character, and a multicultural society's interpretation of them tends
to be polyphonous. Such widely endorsed value concerns include:
human dignity; cultural identity; the integration of Switzerland and
maintenance of an optimal position for it in the world; fair trading
conditions; a suitable information level for democracy; and the
physical and mental well-being of the population.

Although these values and norms are more or less esteemed
throughout Swiss society, since different sectors attach different

weights to them, there is *no fixed rank-order of vulnerable values.* Moreover, they differ in the degree to which they are observed in practice. They differ in stability as well – that is, their standing and interpretation vary over time. Finally, it is obvious that the system of regulation and control, designed to ensure the conformity of television output to these values, cannot be more stable, consistent and effective than the real adherence of the Swiss population to them in practice will allow.

Protection Systems

The legal framework

Rules and mechanisms for the protection of such vulnerable values are incorporated into a broader framework of law that regulates television in Switzerland. Its chief sources are: the European Convention on Transfrontier Television of 5 May 1989; Article 55 bis of the Federal Constitution; the SBC Concession (1987), including its elaboration in various internal regulations; an Order concerning experiments in local broadcasting, 2 June 1982; a Federal Decree concerning satellite broadcasting, 18 December 1987; and regulations governing advertising on television, issued 15 February 1984. There is also the above-mentioned draft bill for the future governance of radio and television. Otherwise, provisions for controlling violent and pornographic materials in media output may be found in the general penal code.

The coherence of this system of broadcasting law is relatively loose. This is because difficulties of consensus-building among divergent influential actors have encouraged Swiss legislators to react to developments in the media sphere instead of striving to steer them in advance.[1] They usually intervene only when problems in or related to the media sector are so severe that they can no longer be ignored.

In addition to espousing the principles of a free flow of information and ideas, the independence of broadcasters and the audience's right to unimpeded access to international television, the *European Convention on Transfrontier Television* favours European audiovisual production and lays down certain minimum standards of advertising control. In the main, Swiss law complies with these obligations, which are particularly binding for smaller states with limited international influence. The more closely Swiss interests are interwoven with broader European developments, the less can the country try to realize its own particularistic values, for example, by denying certain foreign programmes access to Swiss screens. To enhance its international presence Switzerland can only aim to place some of its domestically made programming in satellite channels. For Switzerland, adjusting its regulations on television advertising to European norms has also proved to be (and still is) a laborious task. In this field, the value of fair trade is in some conflict with that of cultural identity (realized by sticking to national or regional cultural norms).

Interestingly, Article 55 bis of the *Swiss Constitution* defines the tasks of Swiss television in functional terms by specifying certain effects that the broadcasters are supposed to attain with regard to the audience: notably cultural development, a free formation of opinions and the feeling of being entertained. This is difficult to gauge of course, since being entertained, for example, is a highly individual and variable matter. It might appear that audience research could play a decisive part in evaluating whether the broadcasters have met their legal obligations, really kept viewers amused and made their audiences more educated and ready to form opinions. It seems, however, that Swiss lawyers have not appreciated this consequence of the constitutional text! What has happened, so to speak, is a personalization of values. On the other hand, by insisting that broadcasters cater for the different needs of the regions, and that their news reports should be accurate and balanced, Article 55 bis of the Constitution upholds the values of an integrated and informed society on the macro level.

Under the influence of the various actors in Swiss media policy, the *draft bill on the future of television and radio* mainly points in two directions: a cautious holding open of the eventual possibility of authorizing a private Swiss television service; and a securing of the structural foundations of SBC, so as to ensure the continuing presence of a strong national public broadcasting organization. This draft reaffirms the previously mentioned general societal values and organizational norms of performance in terms similar to those that appear in the SBC Concession. Being the product of much compromise, however, the draft has more the character of a late reaction to ongoing international and national developments than that of a determined effort to steer a positive course amidst them.

According to the *SBC Concession*, the Swiss public broadcaster's programmes must 'uphold and develop the cultural values of the country and contribute to the spiritual, moral, religious, civic and artistic development' of the audience. They should transmit information that will allow viewers and listeners freely to form their own opinions and should also satisfy their needs for entertainment. An accurate and balanced service of news and public affairs commentary must be provided. The programmes must also 'serve the interests of the country, reinforce national unity and solidarity and promote international understanding'. These norms and standards (derived from Article 55 bis of the Constitution) uphold an élitist (or bourgeois) cultural ideal, and the civic ideal they reflect is that of the politically interested and active citizen. Participation in elections and plebiscites has steadily declined in recent decades, however, while the spread of cultural pluralism has long legitimized sturdy strands of popular culture (demonstrated, for example, by the rapid acceptance of private radio stations: cf. Saxer, 1989). This helps explain corresponding changes in SBC's programming profile, justified by changing interpretations of the Concession. Swiss German television especially turned politically to the Left in the 1970s, violating, according to critics, norms of objective and balanced reporting (Saxer 1979). In the late 1980s, under the pressures of increased competition, SBC's programming also became culturally less demanding (ignoring the terms of the Concession, according to some commentators) in order not to lose too large a share of the Swiss audience to foreign channels. Nevertheless, by the end of the decade SBC was a minority broadcaster in Switzerland. Its evolution in the period was a striking illustration of the difficulty of protecting societal values in broadcast programming against the grain of sociocultural change, changes in journalistic culture and the heat of competition from rivals not bound by the same standards.

Swiss penal law still includes quite strict proscriptions against pornographic materials in the mass media (Article 204). In response to changing social attitudes towards sex and erotic display, however, these are being revised so that in effect only hard pornography will hereafter be banned. But gratuitous portrayals of violence, unless justified on artistic grounds, have been prohibited since 1 January 1990 (Article 135). This shows that Swiss legislators are still willing to defend norms of official culture – at least when offence against them is made visible by and in the media. Of course these provisions are partly explained by the aim of protecting young people from the harmful influence of certain kinds of media output, but they may also be interpreted as an attempt to tame deviant consumer habits by imposing traditional cultural norms on media production.

Similar taming efforts are responsible for the elaborate *regulations of advertising in television* (18 articles in all), which were revised several times in the 1980s. An outcome of conflicting international and national pressures, business interests and cultural considerations, these amount to little more than a precarious, to some degree accidental, and weakly sanctioned compromise. The aim is to curb the ever more aggressive system of broadcast advertising by means of definitions. Through the following legal distinctions (which accord with requirements of the Council of Europe Convention on Transfrontier Television), an attempt has been made to satisfy as many interests as possible, protect the vulnerable values involved and identify the permitted forms of advertising as clearly as possible:

1 Programme vs advertisement: The distinction seeks to ensure transparency by clearly indicating the source of the message.
2 Integrity of programmes vs interruption: The distinction is designed especially to protect programmes of presumed cultural worth.
3 Suitable vs unsuitable times for advertising: The distinction creates a hierarchy of days in line with the ecclesiastical calendar. It also aims to protect young people by relegating the advertising of certain products to late hours.
4 Transparent vs surreptitious advertising: The distinction endeavours to curb advertisers' ingenuity in masking their messages.
5 Advertising vs sponsorship: The distinction paves the way for special conditions intended to prevent undue influence of sponsors over programme content.
6 Acceptable vs unacceptable advertising: The distinction turns on ethical standards, including norms of honesty, fairness and avoidance of misleading claims, to ensure advertisers' conformity to them.

Regulatory institutions

The Swiss Federal Transportation, Communications and Energy Department is in charge of supervising the performance of Swiss television, as is the Federal Court as a last resort. In addition, an Independent Authority for Programme Complaints was created in 1984, as required by Article 55 bis of the Constitution, to adjudicate complaints of alleged Concession violations in the output of Swiss broadcasters, succeeding a similar though not constitutionally mandated body. This addition to the regulatory apparatus came into existence largely as a reaction to the alleged leftward drift of SBC programming in the 1970s, which had provoked much criticism. It is worth reviewing the work of the Authority and its predecessor in some detail, because, since their inception, they have evolved a set of criteria for evaluating the conformity of Swiss television to valued societal and professional norms.

The number of complaints these bodies have had to consider have varied greatly over time. They reached a peak in 1980/1, with 30 complaints criticizing SBC's coverage of youth riots in Zurich;

dropped from 39 in 1984 to 18 in 1987; but subsequently rose to 32 in 1989. The main target of complaint throughout has been Swiss German television, which never fully succeeded in regaining a reputation for abiding by the standards it was supposed to observe. This suggests that once public trust in a medium's respect for widely accepted norms is shaken, it will take much time and journalistic effort before it can be restored.

The content of the complaints received by the authorities also differed during the 1980s. At the start of the decade the main points of complaint concerned how broadcasting had dealt with political and ideological controversy, and a supposed lack of objectivity and balance in news and current affairs programming. Of course there will have been an unknown share of organized protest in these complaints. In later years, the spectrum of offending themes and modes of presentation widened to include economic, religious and moral issues, and criticism increasingly focused on entertainment (and 'infotainment') programmes alongside the usual objections to more politically oriented programming per se. This may be interpreted as a faint reflection of the previously mentioned value shifts in the Swiss public at large, mirrored in the more hedonistic style of 'infotainment' programming.

The reasoning of the Authority also changed over time, especially after 1988. Its focus shifted from a predominant attempt to secure high standards of specifically journalistic performance to a more broadly based attempt to protect social, cultural and moral values. At the same time the verdicts became more legalistic and less professionally oriented. There has been much dispute over this shift in the Authority's approach, with particularly harsh criticism coming from journalists and the political Left.

Last but not least the Authority's procedures changed as well. There are many signs that the originally populist basis of the institution – with easy access for any plaintiff – is being reduced and that more and more it is lawyers who are doing the complaining. This is not difficult to understand when one notes the overall score of complaints rejected and accepted by the Authority. In only 4 of 111 complaints made against Swiss television in 1984–9 did the Authority decide that the Concession had been violated. Thus, the unorganized citizens, the last group in the previously outlined typology of seven media policy actors, really remained last, despite the Authority's availability as a port of call for viewers' complaints. The relatively flattering result for public television suggested by these figures was achieved, however, only by dint of SBC's laborious, costly and time-consuming defensive strategies. Thus, the Authority's attempts to influence journalistic culture and to protect societal values more generally has actually operated in two directions: on the one hand, it has mediated between broadcasters and complainants, helping them to conclude their disputes in amicable settlements; on the other hand, it has served as a strong threat system – at least that is how many broadcasters perceive it – even though its legal sanctions are quite limited. If the Authority finds that a broadcaster has violated the Concession, it can ask management to take steps to prevent a repetition of the offence in the future, and, failing that, it can apply to the Government to enforce the measure concerned. Yet SBC's reactions to the Authority's infrequent requests of this kind have so far been modest and grudging.

Attempts to influence (if not regulate) Swiss television may be made by all the other actor groups not dealt with here, but only those of the churches are institutionalized, and indeed they have managed to secure privileges in religious programming in both radio and television. Naturally, much lobbying is done behind the scenes by all actors, including audience associations chiefly advancing populist appeals, each striving to win greater respect for their values in the output of Swiss television.

The Efficacy and Functional Impact of Regulation

It is of course difficult to assess the efficacy and functional impact of Swiss control systems for the protection of vulnerable values. After all, there is no control group – Switzerland *without* protection systems – which would allow their effectiveness to be pinpointed. This concluding section can therefore offer little more than estimates and educated guesses.

Efficacy
There are four sets of conditions and limitations on the effectiveness of protection systems in small, democratic, multicultural societies:

1　The international environment: the adherence of Switzerland to the European Convention on Transfrontier Television leaves little opportunity for it to resist an invasion of programming alien to its values – for example, by denying them access or censoring them.

2　In any case foreign television programmes are readily accepted by large parts of the Swiss audience, even when they do not comply with those values that are ostensibly protected by Swiss regulations.

3   To defy such consumer verdicts by protective measures would be difficult for a democracy, lacking sufficient legitimacy.
4   Cultural pluralism in democratic information societies dilutes the force of general values and consequently the incentive to protect them against the competing principle of a free flow of information.

In these conditions, protective systems against television imports that do not entirely conform to national values cannot work very effectively. This may be one of the reasons why 'fallout' from external television is not (yet?) a prime concern of Swiss media policy makers. The efforts of legislators and regulators are mainly concentrated on national television. Public pressure for its compliance is also greater than on programmes from abroad, because if one of the latter does not satisfy – or even offends – the viewer can just switch to another foreign channel. (The increasing practice of 'zapping' and 'grazing' strengthens this tendency.) National television is different, however, because it comprises only one service in one's own language, provided by a single broadcaster, and is therefore usually eyed with more value-involvement. Furthermore, although national and local parochialism are still alive in many parts of Europe, the gradual unification of Western Europe may induce more transnational sharing of values and more tolerance of programmes from other countries. Nevertheless, the Swiss film industry will continue to be supported by protective measures, and SBC will be expected to include a sufficiency of Swiss-made programmes in its schedules (though precise quotas will not be set). Efforts to place Swiss material on international satellite television channels will also persist. Yet an ever increasing acceptance of foreign programmes by Swiss viewers can be expected in the 1990s.

The effectiveness of legal regulations largely depends on the possibility of really sanctioning what they prescribe. In addition to the above-mentioned international factors, there is the consumers' verdict to be taken into account, against which no democratic media policy can prevail in the long run. Moreover, journalists, other media practitioners and business interests can often find ways of getting round the intentions of legal restrictions (as in surreptitious advertising techniques). It is true that SBC's compliance with the Concession has been relatively high, at least so far as the structure of provision is concerned. For example, the Concession's demand for a national system of television, delivering a full schedule of programming to each of the main linguistic regions, has been amply met. This is only possible thanks to a system of finance which, in a spirit of solidarity, seeks from the largest region support for the smaller ones. If the present financial difficulties of SBC persist, however, that spirit of solidarity could be strained. The Concession has also ensured the adherence of Swiss television to certain cultural values and standards, though this could prove more difficult as foreign competition intensifies. The attempts to regulate television advertising have probably been least effective. Limits on amounts of commercial time and the list of banned products have been changed again and again under economic pressure, and punishment of advertisers for infringing the rules has been extremely rare.

Regulatory effectiveness is also hampered by the fact that it must cope with the double task of protecting societal values and amending journalistic professional culture. A difficult course has to be steered between maintaining an essential freedom and flexibility for the journalistic enterprise while at the same time ensuring its adherence to societal expectations.

Functional impact

Finally, there is the matter of the functional impact of the Swiss control systems that have been established to preserve vulnerable values in television. The answer cannot be straightforward, since from a functional–structural standpoint the question must take the following form: do Swiss protection systems, by endeavouring to protect vulnerable values, increase, stabilize or reduce the problem-solving capacity of Swiss television? The chief dimensions to be considered here are: the scope of Swiss media policy; possible functions and dysfunctions of television for Swiss society; influential currents of social change; and the structuring and steering capabilities of democratic media policy for television.

So far as scope is concerned, the Swiss Government, as the principal actor of Swiss media policy, has certain limited possibilities of negotiating on behalf of Swiss values when issues of international communication arise in trans-European forums. It can also ban certain kinds of foreign programmes from Swiss screens, though at the risk of international disapproval and of opposition from parts of the Swiss viewing public. Hence, its main theatre of operation is Swiss television. In the absence of a consensus over the role of television in Swiss society, however, the Government tries above all to achieve compromise among the most important policy actors when deciding what values to uphold; and since the legitimacy of its initiatives in this area is precarious, it tends to fall back on a policy of protecting official cultural values in programming.

The functions and dysfunctions of Swiss television are similar to those found in other information societies. As elsewhere, many institutions, organizations and pressure groups try especially hard to put forward their definitions of reality and their agendas of social concerns over television as the most popular and influential medium of mass communication. Viewers, however, primarily use it as a means of entertainment. The older and less educated parts of the population watch television most often and patronize its entertainment offerings most heavily, thereby deepening the knowledge gap between themselves and other members of society, particularly regular newspaper readers. Generally, however, the Swiss are less fascinated by the television medium nowadays than they used to be; quite often it is reduced to the status of a secondary activity, accompanying other pursuits. In time, shrinking attention to it may parallel a shrinking value-involvement in issues of programming standards.

Three features of social change in Switzerland are relevant to the role of television. The increasing proportion of elderly people, still television's most faithful clientele, may strengthen pressures on it to respect traditional social values. The increasing alienation of many Swiss citizens from political institutions may diminish the future significance of television in politics. The diffusion of hedonistic and individualistic values may limit the ability of television to disseminate values of integration and solidarity as well as the norms and patterns of official culture.

In conclusion, if the structuring potential of Swiss media policy is relatively high, its steering capacity is on the whole low. It has secured the transmission of linguistically differentiated Swiss television programming, compatible with basic political and cultural values, in equal proportions to the different language regions, and it has also protected Swiss cultural industry. Viewers' consumption patterns, however, manifest preferences for supposedly culturally worthy programmes to only a limited degree. Public-virtue television contrasts, so to speak, with private-vice consuming habits. Moreover, as the professional culture of television journalism is increasingly shaped by international standards and routines, it may become less responsive to purely national concerns.

In short, the functional balance is ambivalent. At any rate, the case of Switzerland demonstrates how difficult it is for a small, culturally pluralistic society to establish systems of regulation and control that can really protect vulnerable values in multichannel television.

Note

1. On the one occasion when an attempt was made to frame a coherent overall media policy (in 1982) only fragments of it were introduced.

References

Inglehart, Ronald (1990) *Culture Shift in Advanced Industrial Society*. Princeton, NJ: Princeton University Press.

Liu, Han C. (1972) 'Foreign News in Two Asian Dailies', *Gazette*, 18 (1); 37–41.

Meier, Werner A., Schanne, Michael and Bonfadelli, Heinz (1989) *Auswirkungen internationaler Kommunikationsstructuren auf die schweizerische Medienkultur*, Final Report of National Research Programme 21: *Cultural Diversity and National Identity*, Zurich.

Saxer, Ulrich (1979) *Fernsehen unter Anklage: Ein Beitrag zur Theorie publizistischer Institutionen unter Mitarbeit von Marie-Therese Guggisberg*. Diskussionspunkt 5 des Publizistischen Seminars der Universität Zürich, Zurich.

Saxer, Ulrich (1989) *Lokalradios in der Schweiz*, Final Report, *Experiments with Local Broadcasting, 1983–8*, Zurich.

SZV (1990) 'Schweizerischer Verband der Zeitungs- und Zeitschriftenverleger', *Bulletin*, No. 2: 40.

10

Values and Normative Choices in French Television

Dominique Wolton

Vulnerable values, protected to some degree by legislation, exist in all areas of society: education, health, morals, politics. What makes television, and more generally broadcast communication, a special case is that it is a recent and prodigious activity in the history of societies.

The consensus on the media that has prevailed in Europe since the 1950s is now crumbling. Since the 1970s, new communication technologies, deregulation and the increasing domination of economic forces have gradually undermined a consensus based on the primacy of public television: a conception of television that implied a certain willingness to elevate the public, even if it also entailed a certain amount of politicization and bureaucracy.

In twenty years, the balance of values in broadcasting has swung completely around. The principle of maximum freedom has progressively taken hold, substituting today's preferred tyrannies, money and profitability, for those of the past, which were linked to politics.

While there are still regulations to uphold a certain conception of what television should be, it is less their content than their context of meaning that has changed. The regulations are much the same as they were (protection of minors, morals, violence, etc.), but the perspective in which they are applied is not. In the past, the perspective that prevailed was a particular model of television, consisting of a policy of supply and a conception of the role of television in society. Today, the dominant perspective is that of the audience, which is identified with demand; and, in the name of viewer freedom, the supply policy consists of offering those programmes assured of the greatest audience.

In a word, any voluntarist definition of television now appears outmoded, conservative, bound up with statism and with hindrance to freedom. Freedom of commerce, on the other hand, is perceived to be the best means of offering the public what it wants.

We have moved from a policy of supply to a policy of demand. Value and quality are strictly equated with the choices of the public. There is no point in posing questions of determinate finality; by its choices, the public will decide. Value and quality flow from the audience, or, to put it another way, the yardstick of quality is the size of the audience. This has the obvious advantage of simplifying the problem considerably. It is no use wondering about programme quality or about what values should be upheld – answers to all our questions will be furnished by the market, that is, the audience for the programmes . . . .

While it could be considered progress that, after thirty years, the problems of values and quality are posed not only in terms of supply, but also taking account of demand, we have now reached the opposite extreme, in which the entire meaning to be given to these issues comes down to a consideration of demand.

This simplification of the problem is all the more harmful in that cable and satellite, by multiplying capacity in the means of transmission, are only *accentuating* the importance of the question. The more channels there are and the more numerous the images they broadcast, the more important is the question of the values that need to be defended and the level of programme quality that ought to be maintained.

This question is ultimately more important today than it was twenty years ago; yet we act as if it were less so simply because in the meantime the rule of consumption has supervened. But the increase in programme supply, like the expansion of transmission capacity, only heightens the importance of the question of values.

The internationalization of production and transmission in no way eliminates the problem of common values that need to be upheld and protected within each cultural space. On the contrary, it makes it more acute.

In other words, and contrary to current modernist thinking on the subject, the problem of values is not at all diminished by the explosion of communication, the internationalization of production and transmission, or the gradual entry of television into the era of economics and profits. Far from making the issue obsolete, these developments only emphasize its importance. The explosion of communication will accentuate the critieria of norms and values, making these a problem for the future rather than the past.

What this clearly means is that there is much less chance of consensus on the vulnerable values in need of protection, since these go against the grain of the current liberal ideology. There is instead a likelihood of violent conflict.

The Recent Evolution of the Public–Private Balance in French Television

France, and more broadly Europe, although France has perhaps been the archetype, has for a long time been characterized by a consensus concerning television as a public service.[1] The expansion of television occurred principally after 1960 (there were fewer than a million receivers in 1958), with the first major stage of development being between 1964 and 1974. From the creation of the Office de Radio Diffusion–Télévision Français in 1964 (ORTF) until its break-up in 1974, there was a strong Left–Right consensus for public television, with no advertising until 1968. A second channel was created in 1964, giving rise to the beginning of a form of competition, and a third channel in 1971. At the time, the consensus against commercial (that is, privately owned) television was total. From 1974 to 1981, competition was installed within the framework of the public service, and television was established as a public enterprise obeying economic constraints.

The year 1981 saw the return to power of the Socialists, who were completely hostile to commercial television and who wanted above all to strengthen public television. But the atmosphere of liberalism at the time, as well as the struggle the Socialists had waged since 1978 for 'Free Radio', led them to pass the law of 29 July 1982. This statute formally adopted the principle of freedom of communication and created an accompanying regulatory authority which, while its name would be changed twice by the two laws which would follow (Haute Autorité in 1982 and la Commission nationale de la communication et des libertés in 1986), would never succeed in establishing its autonomy or even less its independence.

In the area of television policy – as in other areas, for that matter – the reign of the Socialists would lead to a complete turnabout. Having come to power declaring their intention to strengthen 'definitively' the public television service, they would go on, principally following the wishes of the President, to create a private pay-television channel (Canal Plus) in 1984, then the first privately owned general-interest channel (La Cinq) with the Italian Media magnate, Silvio Berlusconi, and finally to launch a private music channel, which became M6 in 1986.

The Right, returned to power in the 1986 legislative elections, had to go one better than the left and decided to 'liberate' television even more by privatizing TF1. This was the law of 1986.

The result in 1988, seven years after the arrival of the Socialists in power, was that France had gone from three public channels to seven channels in total, of which only two (A2 and FR3) remained public!

This slow and inexorable dismantling of the public television service, leading to what is called a 'PAF' (*paysage audiovisuel français*, 'French audiovisual landscape') dominated by commercial television, illustrates the slow crumbling of the consensus in favour of public television. In 1988, following the re-election of François Mitterand and with a very slim majority in Parliament, the Socialists were not about to revise fundamentally the liberal law of 1986. They would content themselves with amending it slightly. This is the current situation. The crumbling of the consensus has been stronger and more systematic among the political, economic and cultural élites than among the public, which for its part has become more and more favourable to commercial television, but less out of support for its values and programmes than out of disappointment over the lack of renewed vitality in public television. But since the public has seen commercial television as all the more attractive for being freed of pointless constraints, while public television was otherwise bogging down, everyone has concluded that the public, too, has definitely 'had enough' of public television.

We have moved from a strong consensus for public television to a consensus that is a little weak and somewhat craven in favour of commercial television. The crux of the misinterpretation is certainly that the public's support for competition, and thus for the virtues of commercial television, is not being accompanied by a systematic indifference toward public television. Once again, the interest in commercial television and in competition between the two sectors is being misunderstood as the end of interest in public television. The latter, however, being deeply caught up in a process of self-destruction, has done much to give credence to this idea!

The Present Regime for Protection of Vulnerable Values in the French Broadcasting System

The current system comprises what was enacted in the law passed by the Right and then modified by the Left upon its return to power in 1988 following the presidential elections. It is a contradictory mixture of the old values of public television and the new practice. This practice is tending increasingly toward a system emptied of any normative constraints, which are associated with outmoded statism, in favour of the single accepted and hypostasized constraint, that of the market; and all this in the name of freedom of the citizen.

This contradiction, particularly visible in France, where, especially after 1975, a theory of public television was so strongly expounded – even if the practice frequently fell short of the model –

allows one to wonder whether, after the current liberal phase, there will be a return to the idea of public television; or whether, on the contrary, the problem of a television upholding certain norms will finally disappear. In a word, will the principles of quality, public service, programme diversity and programming orientation outlive the model of public television that gave birth to them, or will they die with it? The strength and the weakness of Europe is to have identified public television with respect for certain public norms. What is at stake in the future is to know whether these values will be maintained under competition.

On paper, in terms of the texts of the authorizing legislation, the French system is almost perfect. Unfortunately, the regulatory authority, the Conseil supérieur de l'Audiovisuel (CSA), remains too politically partisan, as evidenced by the fact that its composition, like its name, has changed three times in five years since its creation in 1982.[2]

The CSA looks after equality of treatment, respect for pluralism, protection of juveniles (including a 'watershed' of 10.30 p.m. for the showing of films classified as unsuitable for children under the age of 13), defence of the French language, free competition, control of advertising, assignment of frequencies, etc. It can issue directives elaborating the public and private networks' legal duties on behalf of these values. It can enjoin any network it deems to be in breach of its *cahiers des charges* (or licence obligations) to take the necessary steps to get back into line. It can levy fines for non-compliance or even suspend a delinquent channel. For the private sector, it grants cable and satellite concessions. For the public sector, it names the directors of the channels and ensures the sovereignty of state control. It also plays an important part in the matter of new communication technologies. As a regulatory authority, it straddles an 'old-fashioned' administrative and political role, a 'modern' role that is more economic, regulatory and pro-competitive, and an 'ethical' role that it has difficulty assuming, given the excessive politicization of its members.

The traces of the old-style regulation which mixed politicization, administration and cultural ambition are found most readily in the list of the responsibilities of public television.

Public television must, for example, cover the entire territory of the country, bringing 'news, entertainment, and cultural enrichment' with a 'cultural, educational, and social' mission and highlighting the 'national heritage' (Article 3). It must favour pluralism in the expression of different currents of thought and ensure 'respect for the individual, equality of men and women, and protection of children and adolescents' (Article 5). It must air

religious broadcasts (Article 19), original works for television of EC
origin (60 per cent of the time) and works in the French language
(50 per cent of the time) (Articles 26 and 44). It can show no more
than 192 films per year, with no more than one commercial break
per film. There may be no more than six minutes of advertising per
hour on average (nine minutes for commercial television).

Thus, quickly catalogued, are the rules of law intended to protect
vulnerable values in French broadcasting.

The Ambivalence of the Rule of Law

The explosion of communication over the last twenty years, with the
multiplication of channels and the increase in capacity for producing
and, above all, broadcasting programmes, has only accentuated the
challenge to the values that had been accepted at the beginning of
television. Those values have increasingly become associated with
the 'past', on the simple reasoning that they were 'imposed' values
which no longer had any legitimacy once the public, the only true
arbiter, could freely express its choice among several channels. In
this era of satellites, when the magnitude of costs seems to preclude
any other logic but that of the market, how can those values,
considered so vulnerable and fragile, be preserved?

The change that has in fact occurred in the broadcasting landscape, reinforced by the movement of ideas in favour of freedom of
communication, shows the ambivalence of the rule of law. Everywhere, and especially in France, the law is presented as the means
of defending democracy and fragile values. But what do we
observe? In almost every country, the law, which is supposed to
protect certain values, in no way forbids the adoption of the strict
logic of the market, a logic which considers explicit protection of
certain values to be archaic.

And yet, the results after fifteen years of the 'modernist revolution' in television are rather disappointing. There is the problem of
violence; the ever more numerous 'infantile' programmes; the
relegation of all cultural or documentary broadcasts to the 'ghetto'
after 10 p.m.; the invasion of variety shows; the standardization of
line-ups around three or four types of programmes that are virtually
identical on all of the channels; the proliferation of channels, but
the crushing similarity of programmes; and so on. What is most
interesting is that everyone admits that television has gone to the
dogs but accepts this as the ransom of the law of the market! The
situation is enough to make a good number of people choke, such as
those television professionals who, between 1950 and 1970, under

production conditions much more difficult than those of today and with less sophisticated instruments for measuring their audience – which they never had the feeling they were forgetting – nevertheless offered programmes that were more diversified and often of much better quality – even if these days one no longer speaks of the 'quality' of a programme but only of its 'audience', as if the two were synonymous!

The paradox today is that never have the values in need of protection been so fully defined in the texts of legislation; never have the conditions for producing and broadcasting programmes been so favourable; never have the tools of audience analysis been so sophisticated; and yet never has television been so bad! The triumph of the rule of law, considered an improvement over the prior 'nothing but politics' regime of television in France, signifies in reality two simultaneous and contradictory phenomena: the end of consensus for a particular model of public television and acceptance of, if not outright support for, all the consequences of the revolution in communication.

As such, the rule of law does not always represent the transcription of a consensus nor even the means of generating a new norm. The law can also be a figleaf covering an unadmitted contradiction. Why, after all, should the law, any more than cultural policy or values, be able to transcend the merciless conflict between norms and interests?

The call to the rule of law, as a means of establishing a widespread consensus on communication, can be seen as much as a means of extending the logic of democracy and increasing the principle of institutionalization as it is a means of momentarily neutralizing a collection of contradictory logics.

Ultimately, the law as an organizing principle for reality itself suffers from the contradiction of being at once the symbol both of triumphant liberalism, which knows no law but that of the market, and of a certain normative process which is meant to promote a certain ethic in television and communication.

In reality, the current situation is characterized by a juxtaposition of more or less contradictory value systems which have momentarily found, in the triumph of the rule of law, the means to hold together their contradictory logics. The law is thus a symbol of a relation of forces, rather than of a transcendence of them; but then, that is what it always has been!

By facilitating the evolution from a logic of administration to one of politics and then to one of economics, the law has merely expressed the relation of forces, rather than opposed it.

This critique of the dominant legal ideology has but one aim: to show that the law, which the recent, and very questionable, consensus favours as a means of transcending contradictions, is perhaps only a means of allowing them to coexist temporarily.

Vulnerable Values in France

In France, the gradual abandonment of the values of public television results less from economic and technological causes than from a political and ideological movement, linked in notable part to the internal collapse of the public television service. The discovery of the market came only afterward.

In a society where the logic of politics tends to dichotomize all problems, including those of broadcasting, what factors of cultural unity nevertheless exist and can serve as a base of common values?

Going beyond opposing political ideologies are four areas of broad social consensus.

First, there is centralization. The regional movement, which is strong in Great Britain, Germany and the USA, has never been powerful in France; and, notwithstanding various measures to decentralize, Paris remains the centre of all aspects of the country's cultural life. The French language is likewise the subject of a broad consensus, although one which has the disadvantage of greatly undervaluing the principal source of vitality in the language, namely, the fact that it is spoken in other countries around the world. The consequence of this two-fold phenomenon is that France is fairly well protected against an invasion of foreign programmes – much unlike the situation in Switzerland, Belgium, the Netherlands or Northern Italy.

Second, there are few problems of national or linguistic identity.

Third, there is the overdetermination caused by a political approach to television, which explains, for instance, why all projects for educational television in France have so far failed to get off the ground.

The fourth and most recent consensus, which appeared during the reign of the Socialists, amounts to an emotional attraction to the market economy, large communication companies and commercial television, combined with a sort of nostalgia for the virtues of public television.

In these four base areas there is a certain amount of agreement concerning the values in need of protection: a reticence against too much sex and violence; defence of the French language and French cultural production; and, finally, a feeling of national identity and, more broadly, political sovereignty that needs to be preserved.

Here the difference is apparent between France and our neighbouring countries, for example, Germany and Great Britain.

What remain as subjects for discussion, and what can in a sense be considered the vulnerable values of today, can be summarized under five points: the relationship between public and private sectors, as well as the degree of concentration that should not be exceeded; economic regulation of the industry, especially the degree of protection for authors; the balance between print journalism and radio and television; the degree of voluntarism needed in order to maintain a national production capacity, particularly the quota proportions for the broadcasting of French and European works; and, finally, the relationship between general-interest and special-interest or 'theme-oriented' television channels.

These five dossiers are today beset by conflict and opposition. If one is willing to admit that throughout history, values in need of protection are the subject more often of conflict than consensus, one can hypothesize that indeed these are the vulnerable values of the present.

Vulnerable Values for the Future in a European Context

These are three in number.

First, the defence of a certain *European identity* which is different from that embodied in North American productions. This must start with the *defence of cultural diversity* and not with the affirmation of an artificial unity which does not yet exist. As I have explained at some length in the fifth part ('*Les sirènes de la télévision européenne*', 'The Siren Songs of European Television') of Wolton (1990), it is by favouring the inherent cultural diversity within Europe that a European cultural unity can best be preserved for the future. Protecting European identity has to begin with protecting the cultural identities of different countries. This is well demonstrated by the cases of Italy, Belgium and Switzerland, multilingual countries which can survive only on condition that their multilingualism and multiculturalism is maintained. These three countries foreshadow today the questions of identity that Europe will be facing tomorrow. And, as can be observed in Hungary, Czechoslovakia, Romania and Yugoslavia, the return of Eastern Europe to the democratic fold in no way invalidates the importance of questions of nationality and cultural identity within these countries.

As stressed in Wolton (1990), there is no communication without identification; the greater the development of processes for communicating, the stronger are the processes of identifying. The two go together and the worst mistake would be to believe that new communication forms lead eventually to the disappearance of old identities. The contrary is in fact the case. Thus, the only way to develop communication within Europe is to develop simultaneously the identifying processes. These are a condition of communication and not an obstacle to it, as one theory of communication would too naïvely have us believe. The explosion of communication in all its forms, especially through the medium of television, is going to require new theoretical work on the definition of identity and the relations between identity and communication. From this point of view, Europe constitutes a fantastic laboratory, provided that we can get beyond the most classic common premises and ideological notions concerning 'identity' and 'communication'.

Second, there is a need to clarify the relationship between general-interest and theme-oriented television. This is a crucial matter (as I also pointed out in Wolton, 1990), because the power of television is first and foremost that of an egalitarian medium addressed to all. In our apparently egalitarian society – in reality very hierarchical and segmented – television is one of the truly egalitarian factors. Television programmes for the masses, because they are directed at everybody, never really satisfy anybody, but the medium's essential function as a social link resides in this apparent contradiction. In our complex societies, general-interest television is one of the only existing dimensions of this social link; and it is one which cannot be fulfilled by theme-oriented channels, which enclose each category of viewers in its own programming ghetto.

By presenting different kinds of programmes on the same channel, general-interest television obliges each viewer to admit that the programmes he or she does not watch have as much legitimacy as those he or she does. It is a school for tolerance at the same time that it is, for the largest part of the population, their window on to the world. The more numerous and diversified the programmes offered by television, the more this window is opened wide. General-interest television is for culture what universal suffrage is for politics – the democratizing factor. Nothing would be worse for One Europe than the disappearance of general-interest television in favour of a collection of theme-oriented channels, which might be 'profitable' but at the cost of making a decent level of general-interest programming impossible to sustain. There is an idea of social equality in mass-audience programming that simply disappears with theme-oriented television.

The risk is one of creating a two-level broadcasting system with mass-audience programming of poor quality for the greater part of the general public and theme-oriented programming of better quality for various smaller publics. Theme-oriented television thus appears as a means, not of reducing social and cultural inequalities, but of maintaining and even, in a sense, legitimizing them.

Third, there is a need to strike a balance between public and commercial television. While the main problem remains that of the balance between general-interest and special-interest channels, everyone understands that this balance is attained more readily if there is also a balance in each country between public and commercial television. The reason is that public television recalls more readily – even if it cannot always achieve them – the ideals of general-interest television. When commercial television is too dominant, the risk is that general-interest programming is maintained at an inferior level and that programmes of quality take refuge in a collection of privately owned theme-oriented channels.

If we want general-interest television to be of better quality, then we must have a public sector strong enough to oblige the general-interest commercial channels to raise the quality of their programmes. There is a false idea that only with theme-oriented television can we have quality programmes. As history has shown, television for the masses and television of quality are not mutually exclusive, and there is no doubt that high-quality general-interest public television could prove the point once again. So, for that matter, could commercial television, which could be just as good as public television.

In France today, commercial television is dominant and constitutes the norm of general-interest programming; public television is merely following the same model, which has been gradually imposed by the commercial channels. If we do not want this model to become eventually too impoverished, it is vital to strengthen public television so that it can in turn strengthen the model of general-interest programming.

There is thus a direct link between balanced competition between the public and private sectors and maintaining general-interest television. In general, the more the laws of economics are imposed on television and, more broadly, on communication – particularly through the introduction of new communication technologies – the more television will appear as an essential factor of cultural and national identity. While there is still no such thing as world-wide television in terms of *programmes* (even if there is now a world-wide market for programming), world-wide television news has long been believed to be possible. One of the consequences of the Gulf War (August 1990–February 1991), however, which for the first time permitted truly international coverage of the news, was to show that, despite what had been thought, there was also no such thing as 'world-wide news'. Public opinion in Arab countries in fact gave Western news a rather bad reception. The indispensable awareness of the 'historical relativism of information' is what I examined in a book written after the Gulf War (Wolton, 1991), in an attempt to understand the role and the status of news in a universe overly dominated by the media.

Not only is there no 'international communication', there is also no 'international information'. This two-fold conclusion, radically opposed to the most classic theses about the revolution in communication and information, leads to a re-emphasis of the importance of the contexts of national and cultural identities and, for television, the necessity of strengthening its role as a social link *inside* a national community – independently of its necessary or desirable submission to the logic of economics. The more television becomes international in terms of its technology and economics, the more it appears that its survival in the role of a social link inside the national economy depends on its ability to remain a high-quality general-interest service in terms of its programmes. Today this is probably the main issue at stake, the vulnerable value to be given priority in each country. But one also observes, as I have already said, that this vulnerable value is a subject not of consensus, but rather of dissensus. One can say that the dominant vulnerable values of today are to be sought not in subjects where there is agreement, but in subjects where there is confrontation.

Conclusions

These are six in number.

First, the vulnerable values at any one moment are usually something to be extracted, like a sort of accounting balance between opposing protagonists. What one calls consensus on essential values usually turns out to be consensus on problems of the *past*, not the present. Vulnerable values of the past can be subjects of consensus, those of the present are usually subjects of antagonism!

Second, different countries do not, in any case, go about protecting vulnerable values in the same way. This is because the values that are more or less common to Western societies have become media subjects in themselves, through history, culture, legislation, religious behaviour – national factors which differ from one country to another. What is thus of most interest is not observing the common desire to protect the same values, but understanding how these have been diffracted in the media by different national prisms.

Third, it is important not to overestimate the power of the law, especially in the area of communication, because that power is bounded by two impassable limits, influence and non-communication, neither of which lends itself to legal treatment. The law sanctions developments and consensus, but it does not create reality; it comes *after*, not *before*, so it cannot be expected to do much for the protection of certain values. If there is no cultural consensus, particularly in an area so blurred and elusive as television and communication, there is no point in expecting too much from the law. The example of the supervisory authority in France attests to this: notwithstanding the 'fierce' determination to 'protect' public television, in fact over the last ten years everything has been done to the benefit of commercial television.

Fourth, if one wants to maintain the 'respect for differences in Europe' of which one hears so much, one has to start by admitting that the values which are the foundations of Western individualism (liberty, equality, respect for the individual, religious pluralism, the importance of the family and the child, necessity for rules of morality, etc.) are not experienced in the same way in different countries. This admission, moreover, raises the question of the limits to what some have too quickly called 'European law'. The absence of consensus is not something that should be hidden, since the antagonism between approaches is sometimes more fertile.

Fifth, this in turn raises the always interesting question of the relationship between law and culture. Will mutual economic and political penetration – in terms of the market in communication and the construction of Europe, respectively – lead to a nationalism of the rule of law? Up to what point is this possible or desirable? The question is all the more interesting for the fact that *all* the European countries want to protect much the same values, which belong to their common cultural heritage. The limitations of the law as a means of protecting vulnerable values in the area of communication stem from the fact that in communication there is always a discrepancy between the emitter and the receiver, between the message and what is done with it. The fluidity and fundamental ambivalence in every situation of communication is what undermines the effectiveness of the law, since the law always has to be able to reduce the ambivalence of a situation in order to deal with it.

In this area, it is the *principles* of law rather than the regulations to implement them that need to be emphasized, without failing to point out, even if it is not fashionable today to do so, the importance of the role of the Government in the area of communication.

Finally, the essential problem, if one dares affirm it, is to know whether mass media must follow only the logic of the market. This, undoubtedly, is the main vulnerable value in need of protection and promotion. Once this value is admitted, all the rest follow!

At the moment of writing unfortunately, it seems that the various countries are less mobilized by this vulnerable value than they are seduced by the scents and charms of commercial logic.

Notes

1. For more detail on the history of television in France, the reader may consult Chapter 1 (pp. 10–80) of Missika and Wolton (1983).

2. Three of the nine members of the CSA are appointed by the President of the Republic (including its Chairman), three by the President of the National Assembly and three by the President of the Senate.

References

Missika, Jean-Louis and Wolton, Dominique (1983) *Folle du Logis: La télévision dans les sociétés democratiques*. Paris: Gallimard.

Wolton, Dominique (1990) *Eloge du Grand Public: Une théorie critique de la télévision*. Paris: Flammarion.

Wolton, Dominique (1991) *War game: l'information et la guerre*. Paris: Flammarion.

11

Vulnerable Values in Spanish Multichannel Television

Esteban Lopez-Escobar

In the 1980s, Spanish television evolved from a public monopoly, with only two state channels, into a competitive multichannel system. At present, there are 11 terrestrial channels (with yet more expected); a cable television sector, operating outside the law though not illegally (Lopez-Escobar and de la Viuda, 1990–1), that reaches over one and a half million homes; and increasing reception of foreign television stations via SMATV (Satellite Master Antenna Television).

Distinctive features of the organization of television in Spain include the following:

1 A public sector comprising not only two national channels (TVE1 predominantly for majority interests and TVE2 catering more for minority tastes) but also a considerable number of public regional channels, operating under the authority of Governments of the autonomous communities.
2 No exaction of a householder licence fee to finance this public sector.
3 The heavy reliance, consequently, of most services on advertising revenue (there are two advertising-financed channels and a subscription-funded Canal Plus), supplemented by state subsidies to the public channels.
4 A marked disparity between fairly widespread recognition of certain values that television may uphold or undermine and the lack of an elaborated enforcement machinery for protecting them.

In these conditions, the new multichannel situation has created a new audience map, and all the networks and stations are increasingly guided by the ratings. The two national public channels, which once commanded the attention of all available viewers, have experienced a progressive decline in their audience shares and hence also in their advertising income. With an audience of over 50 per cent in peak time for the two channels combined, they still hold the lead, but their financial situation is weakening. As a result, the national public broadcaster faces a double uncertainty: first, over strategy, whether to fight hard to hold the mass audience or to concentrate on a distinctly public service programming profile; and, second, over the likely policies of its state patron, including how much subsidy support it can expect, should advertising revenue continue to fall in the future (Holder, 1991).

Structure

National public television

The governance of Spanish public television is highly politicized, though much less so than under the Franco regime and somewhat less so than in the period before 1980 when the state directly controlled the two television channels. In 1980 Radiotelevisión Española (RTVE) was formed as a public corporation to provide television and radio services through separate subsidiary companies, Television Española (TVE) and Radio Nacional de España (RNE).

The television and radio companies are governed by an overall Administrative Council, separate Advisory Councils for television and radio and a Director-General. The Administrative Council consists of 12 individuals elected by the Spanish Parliament, most of whom are party representatives. The Director-General is appointed by the Government; ceases to hold office whenever Parliament is dissolved; has been changed with each main change of post-Franco Government; and in turn appoints the chief executives of the television and radio companies.

According to the law that established RTVE, the Administrative Council approves its 'plan of activities, establishing the basic principles and general lines to which broadcasting should adhere', responding to proposals from the Director-General. The Advisory Council is empowered to present opinions or reports to the Administrative Council about any of its programming policies.

In addition, in each autonomous community a regional advisory council of RTVE has been formed, which advises the regional RTVE executive on broadcasting matters. It is generally considered, however, that neither the national nor the regional Advisory Councils have exercised any real influence so far and that their effectiveness has been negligible. Nevertheless, they are able to express feelings about broadcasting problems in their areas. Although it is the only known case of its kind, it is worth mentioning a document issued in October 1990 by the RTVE Advisory Council in Navarra, which expressed concern about what they considered to be a progressive deterioration in the quality of programming on public television, 'which, in the name of supposed market orientation, is trying to achieve increases in viewing ratings without giving proper consideration to the means it uses'. The Council complained about programmes which were obscene, vulgar and in poor taste, 'if not decidedly coarse', and declared that 'the last straw was the broadcasting of films, some openly pornographic, at 10.15 p.m., a time at which many children and teenagers are watching television'.

Television channels of the autonomous regions
The same 1980 law that established RTVE also envisaged the possibility of eventually setting aside a third channel for regional services in the autonomous provincial communities.[1] In December 1983, a law activating this possibility was passed, though only after the Basque and Catalan communities had preemptively created their own television and radio corporations. Thus, regional television in Spain was initially spurred by concerns to express and promote the cultural identities of peoples with their own languages, including the Basques (Euskal Telebista now provides two services for its area, one in Basque and the other in Spanish), Catalans and Galicians. Thereafter the Parliaments of a number of other autonomous communities – Madrid (now a major broadcaster), Valencia, the Balearic Islands, Aragon, Andalusia and Murcia – followed suit (though not all these regions were broadcasting at the time of writing). The public regional television corporations have recently formed a consortium called FORTA to look after their joint interests – facilitating programme exchanges and co-production, networking the sale of advertising time and pooling resources for programme production.

The television and radio corporations of the regional communities have the same governing structure (Administrative Council, Advisory Council and Director-General) as RTVE nationally.

Private television
In 1988 the Spanish Parliament passed a law authorizing the Government to license three private television channels – nationwide in scope but with an obligation to provide some regional programming. The licences were awarded in 1990, initially for ten-year periods, to Tele 5 (a Berlusconi-backed station with access to Fininvest resources for programming, production facilities and advertising sales), Antena 3 and Canal Plus (a slow-starting subscription service). Tele 5 and Antena 3 had reached over half the country's households by the time of writing.

The terms of the law governing private television are not onerous and could be characterized as mainly technical. Ownership must be predominantly in Spanish hands. In addition to the demand for a certain amount of regional programming, there is an emphasis on domestic production: 15 per cent of total transmission time must be produced in-house, and at least 40 per cent should be devoted to Spanish or EC production, including feature films (but these targets are to be attained gradually over three years). Otherwise, a decree of the responsible Ministry, which approved the basis for licensing these operators, states in a clause on the 'rights and obligations of the licensees' that they should observe the same fundamental principles that were enunciated for national public television in Article 4 of the 1980 Law (dealt with below).

Vulnerable Values

An impression of the values that Spanish legislators and broad-casters might consider to be affected by how television is provided can be drawn from several sources: the founding law of 1980 that established RTVE as the national public broadcaster; a set of basic policy principles formulated by the RTVE Administrative Council in 1981; equivalent principles adopted by the autonomous regional broadcasting bodies; advertising laws and norms specifically; and concerns expressed in policies and debates over media depictions of sex and violence.

The 1980 Law

According to the preamble to the 1980 Law, television and radio are considered to be socially significant media from two standpoints. First, they are essential vehicles for (1) information provision, (2) participation of citizens in politics, (3) formation of public opinion, (4) enhancement of the educational system and (5) advancement of the culture of Spain, its regions and peoples. Second, they are indispensable means for upholding liberty and equality with particular regard to (1) the interests of minorities and (2) prevention of discrimination against women.

Although it may be a matter for debate to what extent these ideas have been followed up in practice, or indeed whether the legislators who endorsed them had clear notions in mind, the wording of the preamble particularly emphasizes civic values, national and regional identity concerns and assurances for minority interests in a frame-work of national integration.

Article 4 of the law deals somewhat more specifically with programme content and scheduling. This declares that 'the activity of mass communication media should take its inspiration from the following principles':

1 Information should be objective, true and impartial.
2 A distinction should be drawn between information and opinion; in the case of opinion, the identity of the holder should be indicated, and the opinion may be expressed freely within the limits of section 4 of Article 20 of the Constitution (see below).
3 Respect for political, religious, social, cultural and linguistic pluralism.
4 Respect for the good name, reputation and privacy of the individual and for all the rights and freedoms recognized in the Constitution.
5 Protection of young people and children.
6 Respect for the principles of equality set out in Article 14 of the Constitution.

The principles of 1981
In 1981 the RTVE Administrative Council unanimously approved a set of 'Basic Principles and Guidelines to Which Broadcasting Should Adhere'. The objective of this statement was said to be to establish 'the values of civic culture which should pervade the broadcasting activity of the public media', first of all by helping to consolidate the democratic process established by the 1978 Constitution. The Council was seeking to identify, it went on, 'a group of normative values which should be dynamic rather than merely restrictive'. The principles concerned were presented in two categories: those described as 'basic', which applied to all media and every type of programme; and those which were specific to particular areas of broadcasting.

The Council's basic principles may be summarized as follows:

First, to encourage viewers and listeners to identify with the values enshrined in the Constitution, which provide the foundations of national life; these are freedom, justice, equality and political pluralism. It is not enough merely to accept these principles passively; the media should actively contribute to their promotion and defence. Moreover, such a defence of democracy should not be thought of as limited to programmes that provide information and opinion but as extending to entertainment programmes as well. It is also relevant to programming for children and young people, which should be inspired by 'the values of freedom, solidarity, equality, non-violence, tolerance and respect for the law'.

Second, to foster and support feelings of national unity and solidarity among all Spanish citizens, in a society 'based on recognition of and respect for the plurality and linguistic, cultural and regional diversity of the human communities that go to form the Spanish nation'.

Third, to promote habits of dialogue, tolerance and openness; to favour debate as a means of settling disagreements and conflicts; to awaken the civic spirit as the fundamental basis for all social coexistence; and categorically to repudiate violent solutions.

Fourth, to encourage respect for the legitimate authority of public institutions (Crown, Parliament, Government, etc.) and of the Catholic Church and the other recognized religious confessions.

Fifth, to explain the problems of the national economy and to present them in their appropriate contexts. (The reason for this clause was that the restoration of democracy coincided with a difficult period for the economy, and the Government wished to avoid a possible identification of democracy with an unstable economic situation in the minds of members of the public.)

Finally, to strive to ensure that television and radio are living and faithful mirrors of reality, encourage participation on the part of citizens and promote their moral and aesthetic enrichment.

Norms for the television channels of the autonomous communities

The foundation documents of the autonomous television corporations mainly reiterate the above principles with only slight modifications. Most add another emphasis, however, which refers to the protection and promotion of regional culture and, where applicable, of the regional language. It should not be forgotten that the third channel was authorized with the goal of enhancing regional identity in all its manifestations. Thus, the last principle of broadcasting mentioned in the statutes of Euskal Telebista is 'the promotion of Basque culture and language'; one of the principles of broadcasting laid down for Catalan television is 'the promotion of Catalan language and culture'; and one of the principles of Galician public autonomous television is the 'promotion and dissemination of Galician language and culture, and the defence of the identity of the Galician people'.

Advertising rules

In matters related to advertising, particularly detailed standards have been developed. Advertising is subject both to the general law (*Ley General de Publicidad*) and to norms approved by the Administrative Council of TVE.

A 1988 version of general advertising law replaced one that had been promulgated in 1964 under the authoritarian regime of General Franco. Under the 1964 version advertising was deemed unlawful if its aim, object or form was offensive to the institutions that formed the basis of the nation, ran counter to the rights of the individual, constituted a breach of good taste or social decorum, or stood in contradiction to the law, to morals or to standards of good conduct. The more recent law declares advertising illegal if it (1) offends against the dignity of the individual or attacks the values and rights recognized in the Constitution, especially those referring to children, young people and women; and it bans advertising that is (2) deliberately misleading, (3) disloyal, (4) subliminal or (5) in contravention of the norms that regulate the advertising of certain products, goods or services. This law also specifically prohibits the advertising on television of tobacco products and of alcoholic beverages over 20 per cent proof.

The most recent version of the TVE Administrative Council norms on advertising was issued in 1990. This provides some pointers to the values that this key agency in the structure of state television considers to be its duty to protect. Three main value-sensitive matters are covered in it.

One concerns incitement to disorder or violence. Article 5, for example, states that advertising is not permitted 'which incites to violence or anti-social behaviour, which plays on fear or superstition or may indirectly encourage abuses, imprudent or negligent behaviour or aggressive conduct'. Advertising is also rejected which is 'liable to incite to cruelty towards and maltreatment of people or animals or to the destruction of cultural or natural riches'. Other references to violence appear in the norms concerning the protection of juveniles, in which it is stated that advertising 'must not be harmful to minors' and that it should 'not show minors in dangerous situations or in situations which might be likely to arouse violent or unjust attitudes or feelings which run counter to solidarity and undermine respect for education'.

A second area of concern is to uphold standards of good taste, particularly in the use of language. Article 7 states, for example, that advertising texts: 'must make correct use of language. Colloquial language may be used, but in no case should expressions be used which are obscene or coarse or which in any way offend against good taste and the feelings of the public.'

A third set of provisions focuses on the advertising of alcoholic beverages, supplementing the *Ley General de Publicidad* with the following restrictions:

1 Such advertisements must not be directed specifically at minors, nor, in particular, should they use minors as the main characters or present them drinking alcohol.

2   They should not associate consumption of alcohol with an improvement in physical performance, or with driving, nor should they include any theme or surroundings that refer to sport or sportsmen.

3   They should not give the impression that consumption of alcohol contributes to social or sexual success.

4   They must not suggest that alcoholic drinks have therapeutic properties, or act as stimulants or sedatives which can be used to resolve conflicts.

5   They should not encourage immoderate consumption of alcoholic beverages or offer a negative image of abstinence or sobriety.

6   They must not emphasize the high alcohol content of the drink, even where this is within authorized limits, as a positive quality.

In addition, the 1988 law authorizing private television provided for controls over the amount of broadcasting time that could be devoted to advertising. This was fixed at no more than 10 per cent of total transmission time, with a maximum of ten minutes of advertising permitted in any single hour.

Filmed sex and violence
The various laws on television say little about portrayals of violence and sexual conduct in programmes (other than what has been covered above). Some indication of possible expectations for television can nevertheless be found in rules that apply to film, notably in a decree of 1977 and a law of 1982.

The 1977 decree specifies that 'films whose main subject is sex or violence may only be shown in special rooms. In any case they are allowed to be shown only to persons of over 18 years of age.' The 1982 law requires that films which are pornographic in character, or which rely heavily on violence, should be classified with an X rating. Such films may be shown only in special auditoriums, which must have more than 100 and fewer than 200 seats. Advertising of X films may not include more than 'the technical and artistic information pertaining to the film, excluding any pictorial representation or reference to content, and must fulfil the requirement that this film is only to be shown in a special auditorium'. Moreover, publicity for these films 'may only be exhibited inside the premises where the film is to be shown and in the special informative or advertising sections of newspapers and other mass media'.

Otherwise, a 1982 decree, which was framed to regulate activities that could be harmful to young people and children, also refers to pornography. This reflects Article 20.4 of the Constitution, which regards the 'protection of youth and children' as one of the limits on the right of freedom of expression that it otherwise proclaims and guarantees. A preamble to the decree refers to the need to defend public morals and to support the rights to protection of the family, young people and children. It identifies pornography as a problem which is profoundly affecting society. In accordance with previous court rulings, pornography is defined as 'those photographs, drawings or any other graphic or visual means of expression or reproduction, including texts, which undermine the basic principles of collective sexual morality that are fundamental in every civilized society'. This decree bans 'any kind of publicity for activities that are contrary to morality and good behaviour'.

Debate over standards on Spanish television was recently stimulated by awareness that the increased competition for audiences was encouraging both the commercial and the public channels to offer programmes, which, even by an indulgent estimate, bordered on the pornographic. TVE itself announced the scheduling of films like *Emmanuelle* and *Histoire d'O* (to take a couple of the more provocative examples) at times when, according to its own organizational guidelines, a large number of children and adolescents might well be watching television. The most controversial development, however, was a decision by Canal Plus to broadcast a series of pornographic films commencing in October 1990. Since the films concerned had been X-rated, their showing in theatres would have been confined to X auditoriums as described above. It may be significant that this decision of Canal Plus seems to have created difficulty for its owners and shareholders, who are fearful of the impact of their involvement in such a strategy on their public image. The Spanish press has dealt exhaustively with these matters, which have also led to calls from several quarters for more effective controls over such tendencies.

Lack of Regulatory Machinery

Spain has not yet developed an effective framework of broadcasting regulation for enforcing the values outlined in the previous section of this chapter. Many of the values concerned have been expressed in the form of general principles without elaboration into more definite obligations. The regulatory machinery is either non-existent or politicized.

Although so far as public television is concerned, the Administrative Council has wide-ranging authority over RTVE policy, because of its partisan composition, it shows more interest in the politics of broadcasting than in programming standards. In both state and regional television, the Advisory Councils have not been able to step into this enforcement gap.

Neither has the law on private television created an independent regulatory authority that could supervise programming with the aim of protecting the social values discussed in this chapter. Control over commercial television is vested entirely in the Government, principally in its Ministry of Transportation, Tourism and Communications. It is true that the private channels are supposed to abide by the programming principles enumerated in the 1980 law, and that the 1988 Law, which authorized their introduction, states that 'repeated violation of the obligations of programming and of the limits and rules on the transmission of advertising' is a grave offence, against which the Government may apply severe sanctions. This puts opportunities in the Government's hands to apply quantitative controls over the private sector (in programme scheduling, amount of advertising, etc.) with the aim of enhancing the quality of its provision; but so far no will to act in such a manner has been apparent.

In the public at large, however, a growing unease over this situation is engendering a movement for improvements in television programming – in state, regional and private television channels alike. In October 1990, for example, a Spanish Congress of Television Viewers' Associations held its second convention in Barcelona and decided to set up a National Federation of such organizations. The main proposals adopted at this Congress were reminiscent of initiatives taken in other countries to counter dangers of a cultural decline in television. These included: (1) a demand addressed to both the Government and the television authorities to keep so-called 'junk programmes' (those containing large amounts of sex and violence) out of prime time schedules; (2) insistence on more care over the use of language in programmes, avoiding expressions that are coarse, obscene or in bad taste; (3) concern about the promotion of false models of individual and social behaviour on television; and (4) a demand to cease the exploitation of women as advertising stereotypes and sex objects.

Another Spanish body that is pressing for more sensitivity to standards in programming is the National Consortium of 'Clean Broadcasting' Associations. Its aims are to encourage the communications media to devise and adopt ethical codes for the guidance of its practitioners, and to inform consumers about ethically dubious programmes, so that they can withhold their support from companies that have helped to finance them. This movement is advancing the cause of what it calls an 'ethical ecology' in television and radio, and it has been prepared to initiate legal actions against programmes and advertising that could be deemed harmful to children and young people. It has asked banks and other financial institutions not to sponsor or support such programmes and advertising, and it is launching a campaign for the adoption of more stringent legal controls over programming injurious to the moral and physical welfare of young people.

It is also significant that the Catholic Church has thrown its weight behind such endeavours. Many bishops, for example, have denounced programmes that exploit sexuality as a way of attracting a larger number of viewers.

Conclusion

Thus, in a situation where few regulatory influences on broadcast content are operative, both public and private television companies have increasingly relied on appeals of violence and sex – in informational as well as entertainment programmes. This has apparently happened because, in the opinion of the managers of these organizations, this is necessary if television is to make 'good business sense'. This criterion applies as much to the public as to the private television networks, since so much of the former's revenue comes from advertising. Except for legal bans on the most blatant specimens of pornography, there are no effective mechanisms to curb these tendencies or to resist the resulting pressures on programme quality and diversity. Many Spaniards feel that until now the Administrative Councils of RTVE and the autonomous television corporations have mainly exercised a political role. The Advisory Councils have had little influence. The law that instituted private television did not foresee the need for an independent regulatory authority.

On the whole, Spanish policy makers have shown a great interest in questions of broadcasting technology and administration but very little in programming matters. On the other hand, the relative inertia of voluntary associations toward broadcasting policy in the past seems to be changing, as certain sectors of Spanish society sense that important social values are under attack. Such public impulses may eventually influence politicians and the television authorities to modify their policies. As matters stand at present, however, the Spanish political and broadcasting systems have given little priority in practice to the task of preserving those values to which so much lip-service has been rendered.

Note

1. According to Article 2.2: 'The Government will be allowed to concede to the Autonomous Communities, when authorized by a law of the Cortes Generales, direct charge over a television channel which falls under state control and which is created specifically for the ambit of each Autonomous Community.'

References

Holder, Stuart (1991) 'No Certainties', in *A Broadcasters' Guide to Spain*. London: International Thomson Business Publishing. p. 36.

Lopez-Escobar, Esteban and de la Viuda, L.A. (1990–1), 'La televisión no pública', *Situación* (special issue on Informe sobre la información: España 1990): 175–86.

PART III

POLICIES AND DIRECTIONS

12

Defending Vulnerable Values: Regulatory Measures and Enforcement Dilemmas

Wolfgang Hoffmann-Riem

The broadcasting orders of Western Europe, once organized root-and-branch along public service lines, are all now (or fast becoming) mixed television economies. In such systems the battle for the public interest must be waged on three fronts, developments on any one of which may affect how important values fare on the others. These are (1) the regulation of private television, (2) the definition and pursuit of new missions for public television and (3) the invigoration of processes of public accountability. In this chapter, I review the strategies and measures available on the regulatory front and assess their prospects for effectiveness. In the following two chapters, Jay G. Blumler and I explore role options for public television, when it is one major force in a multichannel framework, and what may be required to hold all the principal broadcasting authorities to public acount in these now highly complex systems.

The foregoing chapters revealed a broad spectrum of values designated for protection and a variety of ways in which their protection is being sought. Certain patterns, however, emerge. In what follows, those patterns will be typified, although many specific details must necessarily be omitted.

Typology of Precautionary Measures to Protect Vulnerable Values

Sets of conflicting concerns and interests
Government regulation may be better understood if the values which it seeks to protect can by systematized. Two important groups can be identified initially.

The first includes values protected by the legal and social systems: for example, protection against defamation, breaches of confidentiality and of privacy, and safeguarding the moral development of juveniles. Much of the protection considered necessary can be supplied by the courts under the general legal system, but where broadcasting poses special problems, then special regulations may be needed. The latter may not be designed solely to inhibit broadcasting but may be intended to ensure its freedom of expression. For example, absolute protection of private data or the moral development of children might harmfully limit free discussion of matters of real public interest. Government regulation may, therefore, strive to strike a balance between such conflicting values, with freedom of communication on the one hand and the value at issue on the other. The nature of the society can be defined by reference to the point at which the balance is struck, closer to freedom of communication or to such other values.

A second group of regulations deals with values that are to be protected by the communications order itself, with freedom of communication as the most important of all. Associated with it is diversity in the range of media and in their contents. So too are the protection of national and European production resources, with corresponding outlets, and of multilingualism in countries where there is more than one language in widespread use. Protection is usually secured by positive precautionary measures: for example, structures intended to achieve a variety of competing broadcasters, to combat concentration of ownership and to ensure adequate access to air time by various groups. Most important of all, is the protection from the state or powerful interest groups of the independence of the broadcasting order.

There are, however, conflicting interests within the broadcasting order: media companies, journalists, advertisers and the audience itself have interests which overlap but do not coincide completely. The balance to be struck between them may be achieved by, for example, restrictions on advertising, statutory protection of the rights of journalists or guarantees of access for certain groups, such as minorities. In addition, a public access channel can be provided, affording anyone an opportunity to make their views known through broadcasting.

Various approaches to governmental regulation
The regulation of broadcasting does not differ in principle from the regulation of other social fields, in particular, so-called economic regulation. States, therefore, adopt similar regulatory techniques, although tailoring them, in the case of broadcasting, to specific features of that medium.

Two forms of control can be distinguished. The first may be termed imperative and imposes directions on broadcasters' conduct by means of specific requirements, orders and prohibitions, with sanctions in the case of failures to comply. The second may be termed structural, depending upon a general framework to control indirectly the conduct of broadcasting organizations and others active in the same field. In this way, the basic economic structure, including the mode of finance, may be stipulated or special procedural or organizational rules created. Such structural requirements are intended to ensure that those subject to them are steered towards achievement of the desired goals and that development does not proceed in a rampant, uncharted way. Both imperative and structural forms of control can be employed at the same time.

These two kinds of control are now described in greater detail.

Imperative control for safeguarding generally protected values threatened by broadcasting activities.   Imperative control is used, primarily through prohibitions, when broadcasting might otherwise threaten values afforded protection under the general legal system: for example, to defend the rights of the individual or the interests of the state. Thus measures may be taken to preserve human dignity or protect religious feelings; to curb advertising of drugs or alcohol; or protect the symbols of the state from being debased. Imperative control may make use of the general law, but it may also rely on norms formulated specifically for broadcasting. Examples of the latter include the regulations on advertising contained in Articles 11 and following of the European Community Television Directive (and the media laws of many individual countries), the juvenile protection rules established by the German state media authorities or the Code of Practice published by the Broadcasting Standards Council in Britain.

Imperative control for safeguarding the communications order or other values related to communication.   Alongside such negative requirements, prohibitions and orders, there are others intended positively to protect freedom of communication or the communications order itself. These include measures designed to ensure the ability of the broadcasting order to function. The regulatory purpose may be technically-directed; for example, to prohibit, by the granting of licences, unauthorized use of the spectrum. It may also be programme-directed, of which the US Fairness Doctrine, the Swedish emphasis on objectivity in news reporting and the British stress on 'due impartiality' may serve as examples. Other forms of imperative control include directions on the broadcasting of advertising in blocks or requirements on the transmission of specific kinds of material, such as educational material for schools.

Quotas offer further examples, whether relating to information or cultural programmes (as in the licensing procedures of the British Independent Television Commission) or designed to ensure that national or regional productions comprise a certain proportion of overall programming (as in French Belgian policy). The last of these may be influenced not only by broadcasting policy considerations, but by economic and social ones.

Structural control of externally pluralistic competition.   Regulations aimed at setting basic structural conditions for the operation of broadcasting are also of special importance. 'External pluralism' is the term often given to reliance on economic competition to ensure diversity in systems where private enterprise is present. Efforts are made to ensure access to programming by various interest groups so that the widest range of programming may be provided. The analogy is with the private press (Fowler and Brenner, 1982). In principle, everyone has the right to become a broadcaster, just as he or she has the right to become a publisher of the written word, making whatever profit can be realized, whether through advertising, Pay-TV, or sponsorship. The state remains largely uninvolved, leaving the broadcaster, once a licence has been granted, to self-control. Supporting legislation is intended to do little more than to ensure fair competition and secure the smooth working of self-regulation.

An alternative model of external pluralism to that based upon the market can be seen in the group broadcasting practised in Holland (see Chapter 7). The guarantee of diversity comes from the competition of various social groups, each, with access to a proportion of total air time, competing for the public's attention. The state provides a constitutional framework, with appropriate safeguards for the broadcasters and the public, and allocates the frequencies.

Structural control of internally pluralistic programming.   In contrast to the externally pluralistic system, where the individual member of the audience chooses between a variety of programmes produced from a variety of diverse sources, each differently orientated, the internally pluralistic system offers diversity from the same source. This is the model most commonly followed in public service broadcasting, whose practitioners have been expected to offer a diversity of subject matter and treatments within their overall scheduling responsibilities. To ensure an adequate range of programmes, the state may need to provide a framework. German public broadcasting has taken the construction of such a framework with particular seriousness, creating pluralistically composed decision-making bodies, the Broadcasting Councils (*Rundfunkräte*). Similarly, numerous 'grass roots' organizations participate in the ownership of Sveriges Radio in Sweden. But reliance may also be placed on other factors, such as the professional inclinations of those responsible for programmes. These can be seen at work in the conduct of the BBC, where, despite much sensitivity to informal interest group pressures, there is no provision for pluralistic representation on its Board of Governors.

The market plays little part in the funding of this form of broadcasting, since it has scant interest in, for example, minority programmes. The usual source of funding is the user-licence or state subsidies (as used in Spain, for example) although some broadcasting organizations supplement their main income from advertising sources; for example, in France, Germany, Italy and Spain (typically with safeguards to prevent advertisers from influencing programmes).

Structural diversifications. Broadcasting orders, though different in character, all have their defects. Public service broadcasting can be too close to Government (as in France) or to political parties (as in Italy and Germany), which poses threats to its independence. Privately-run broadcasting, reliant on the market, can be dominated by powerful economic interests. Moreover, it can fail to provide a range of output, being absorbed with the production of mass-entertainment programmes. The recent evolution of 'dual broadcasting systems' in many countries may enable the two types to complement one another. I have called this principle of reciprocal compensation 'structural diversification' (Hoffman-Riem, 1990, 38ff.). The twin pillars of such systems, one private and the other public, are differently structured in order to take advantage of their respective strengths and to compensate for the weaknesses. This principle was clearly formulated by the German Federal Constitutional Court (*Bundesverfassungsgericht*), which held that a 'basic provision' of programmes by public broadcasting was indispensable and that the imposition of less onerous 'public service' obligations on private broadcasters could only be justified by the survival of the public sector (*Bundesverfassungsgericht*, 1986: 157–60; 1987: 325–6).

In reality, not only are differently structured broadcasting systems set up alongside one another; mixed forms may also be instituted. Thus market-based broadcasting is not always allowed to operate as it pleases. Even in the US, which has the longest tradition of commercial broadcasting, the Communications Act recognizes certain programme commitments. The British commercial system, with the ITV companies regulated by the IBA, was protected from financial competition by a statutory monopoly. The group broadcasting system in the Netherlands depends in part on quasi-market financing, that is, on the dues paid by their members identified by their subscriptions to programme guides. Many internally pluralistic public television channels in Europe have also been based upon partial financing via the market, through advertising.

Combination of structural control with imperative control. Broadcasting orders typically display a mixture of structural requirements and imperative directions and prohibitions. The latter are usually meant to compensate for weaknesses in structural control; for example by directing the inclusion of certain kinds of programmes. They are, however, less likely to be observed when they conflict with the interests of the broadcasters, either economic or editorial. Where economic competition is the main agent of regulation, then the requirements on the private broadcaster are likely to be lightest. It was no coincidence that the British Government, when proposing greater competition between British commercial broadcasters, also indicated a lighter regulatory regime to be imposed on private operators by the new control authority, the Independent Television Commission (Home Office, 1988). German legislatures, by comparison, have proceeded cautiously, insisting, for example, that, where competition was limited, private broadcasters must provide programme services in line with the internally pluralistic model. The same requirement may be imposed when an acceptable number of competitors fail to provide the necessary degree of diversity.

Bodies Charged with the Regulation of Broadcasting

The type and intensity of the special measures taken to protect vulnerable values in broadcasting depend on the model of control favoured by the Government. Special broadcasting supervision is less rigorous, for instance, where the model is found in the marketplace and there are already adequate supervisory measures, such as anti-trust laws, in place, even if these must sometimes be adapted to the particular circumstances of broadcasting. The further the model departs from that of the marketplace, then the more is special treatment necessary. However, that does not mean that marketplace broadcasting can be entirely free from other forms of regulation. In fact, one cannot find anywhere the conviction that the market alone suffices as regulator for achieving desired effects and avoiding dysfunctional ones.

The Broadcasting Act passed by the British Parliament at the end of 1990 provides a useful example of a compromise between the pure doctrine of reliance upon the market as regulator and provisions to avoid its potentially deleterious consequences. The Act is full of constraints on the future licencees which are economic and editorial in their impact. The French *Loi relative à la liberté de Communication* and Germany's state media laws show a similar penchant for control, although there are weaker requirements in the Italian Act on the Regulation of the Public and Private Broadcasting System (*disciplina del sistema radiotelevisione pubblico e privato*, 1990).

The protection of vulnerable values enshrined in statutes needs the support of organizations to oversee the fulfilment of normative requirements. Special supervisory bodies are therefore created. Exceptionally in France, the Conseil Supérieur de l'Audiovisuel (CSA) has duties extending over both private and public broadcasters, but in Britain, as in most countries, responsibilities are confined to the private sector. Germany has separate organizations in each of its sixteen states, but in other countries one finds centralized broadcasting supervision, although most such agencies are decentralized to a degree (for example, with regional sub-offices). Legal autonomy from Government, however, does not necessarily ensure independence in day-to-day work. Governmental or parliamentary involvement may include regular monitoring of activities, influence on senior appointments, or a crucial role in income and expenditure decisions. Informally, too, a Government may make its influence felt, but the extent to which this happens depends on the local political culture. For years the British Government refrained from exercising the very considerable powers of intervention which it had over both the BBC and the Independent Broadcasting Authority. In contrast, both the French and German Governments were de facto in close touch with the broadcasters, although the CSA now enjoys a greater measure of practical independence than did its predecessors.

Most of these supervisory bodies that license and monitor broadcasting are led by a Board, usually small in membership (between, say, 7 and 13 members). They have a staff entrusted with the day-to-day running of the organization and preparation of the Board's business. In Germany, the practice is to have larger boards, often operating quite lethargically and leaving true authority to the Director, a monocratic position (Wagner, 1990: 131).

Beside the supervisory bodies, there are occasional examples of agencies with a limited range of concerns. In Britain, for example, there is a Broadcasting Complaints Commission to deal with matters of fairness in programmes and the invasion of privacy. There is also a Broadcasting Standards Council whose remit is confined to the portrayal in television and radio programmes and advertisements of violence, sexual conduct and matters of taste and decency.

These two British organizations, dating from 1981 and 1988 respectively, may deal with both public and private broadcasters. Of course, in Sweden and Switzerland, where private television has not yet been introduced, only public broadcasters are answerable to the Radio Council and the Independent Authority for Programme Complaints, respectively. In many other countries, the public broadcaster does not have to account to an outside agency. The BBC, through its Board of Governors, is required to regulate itself within the terms of its Royal Charter and subject to the provisions of its operating licence granted by the Home Secretary. In Germany, the public broadcasters similarly regulate themselves, with the Government becoming involved only in the case of a default.

In spite of the increasing Europeanization and internationalization of broadcasting, its supervision remains a national affair. Neither the EC Television Directive nor the Television Convention of the Council of Europe provides for any mechanism of pan-European supervision. However, although the supervision of even transfrontier broadcasting remains an internal matter, nations within the European Community have obligations to one another and to the EC itself, which has powers to penalize defaulters. Lacking such powers, the Council of Europe intends to sustain its Television Convention by the creation of mechanisms for reconciling differences, including the establishment of a Standing Committee and conciliation and arbitration procedures.

Such expedients, for punishment or conciliation, will only be invoked when member states cannot secure observance of legal requirements within their own territories. To achieve the latter, it is necessary not only to enact suitable norms of broadcasting law, but also to provide for the continuous monitoring of them. The two European instruments, the Directive and the Convention, assume that this monitoring will be performed as a duty by the individual states. When a violation is suspected, the monitoring power cannot prevent the transmission of a programme from outside its borders, and it can stop a retransmission only in the event of particularly serious and repeated violations.

Such weaknesses of enforcement at the European level make it desirable to examine the means adopted to prevent offence at source and to protect vulnerable values at the national level.

Fields of Supervision

This section describes the main fields of attempted regulatory supervision found in West European broadcasting systems, principally in the television sector.

Awarding of licences as the point of departure for supervision
Licensing procedures have, as one of their primary objectives, the avoidance of chaos in use of the ether. The granting of a licence is the start of a procedure for laying down conditions for transmission. Formerly, no charge had been levied by Governments for use of the spectrum, but this position has been changed in Britain by the terms of the Broadcasting Act, 1990. Nevertheless, special obligations will be established, requiring observance of legal requirements and codes of practice, for instance. That may only be the beginning of the demands made on licensees in return for granting a licence. In France, conditions are additionally set down in the individually-negotiated *des charges cahiers*, following award of the licence. Licences in Germany can be tied to additional terms and conditions. These must, of course, remain within the framework of broadcasting laws, which nevertheless permit detailed commitments. Since several applicants normally compete for the same licence and licences are generally awarded in so-called comparative allocation procedures, the licensing authority is basically able to select the applicant with the most attractive offer and to bind him or her legally to his or her promise. Although in Britain, the best offer in programme terms will not necessarily guarantee success, the undertakings submitted by the winning applicant, in order to pass the prior quality threshold, will also become binding conditions of his licence (see Chapter 5).

Licences, once granted, are normally held for lengthy periods. Even following the expiration of the licence, the holder has a good chance of renewal, particularly since it is by no means certain that a different applicant would offer better programming. The legal or de facto protection of the licensee's status may make it difficult for the supervisory body to enforce obligations or to set new ones. However, under changed circumstances, it is normally possible, although only under impeded conditions, to supplement the conditions of the licence, and, in the event of failure to observe the duty, the licence can be suspended or revoked (with fines possible as a lesser penalty).

Maintenance of pluralism and diversity

In all broadcasting orders, television is seen in its relations to the workings of democracy. The German Federal Constitutional Court has recognized the fundamental importance of mass communication for the free formation of opinion. It has called for positive assurances that all citizens shall have access to those forms of communication considered important for their political, social and cultural orientation. Other courts, such as the French Conseil Constitutionel, have stressed the relationship between broadcasting and democracy – as do the founding documents of Spanish and Swedish television. Demand for pluralism in broadcast programming mirrors the anchoring of Western social orders in the concept of pluralism. In the process one finds a growing awareness that it is not only information programmes which are important for the formation of citizen's opinions, but also, and perhaps most importantly, entertainment programmes. This is especially true of television as the entertainment medium par excellence. Accordingly, the calls for pluralism are by no means confined to a diversity of information in special news and current affairs programmes, but also relate to the operation of broadcasting as a whole. These break down into a number of normative requirements.

Impartiality, fairness and balance.

Despite the changing perception of the importance of entertainment programmes, special measures exist to protect news and current affairs programmes. The US Fairness Doctrine provided the precedent for this, even though the Federal Communications Commission (FCC) has recently sought to rescind it. The doctrine imposed two main duties: to provide a reasonable amount of time for the discussion of controversial issues; and, secondly, to allow opposing viewpoints to have reasonable opportunities for exposure. Broadcasters in Germany are expected to observe a minimum level of balance, objectivity and mutual respect. Individual programmes must not exert a one-sided influence on the audience. The Broadcasting Act, 1990, binds the British broadcaster more tightly still, requiring the person providing the service to ensure that 'due impartiality [be] preserved . . . as respects matters of political or industrial controversy or relating to current public policy'. The Swedish Radio Council has assessed broadcast programmes for objectivity and impartiality after their transmission.

These obligations are particularly difficult to administer, as the fate of the Fairness Doctrine shows. Controversial topics or opinions may be treated by broadcasters only to a limited extent, partly because they go to great lengths to avoid affronting certain segments of their audience or straining excessively its tolerance of minority views. As a result, attempts to require the comprehensive treatment of political or other public controversies present a nearly unsurmountable task. Similar difficulties are met in enforcement of the duty to give relevant parties opportunities to present their contrary positions. This takes time and, according to current opinion, it is often less attractive for the majority of the audience than the simplified expression of a single position. The advertising industry, moreover, is hardly interested in supporting a controversy-laden programming environment. It therefore comes as no surprise that, even during the full validity of the Fairness Doctrine, the large US networks made an effort to limit the spectrum of controversy. They also specifically decided not to accept commercials on controversial social issues, since they could then be obliged to carry commercials with an opposing message. While taking pains to enforce the Fairness Doctrine, the FCC therefore practised a considerable degree of moderation. In only 0.15 per cent of complaints did the FCC intervene against broadcasters (see LeDuc, 1987: 179). Broadcasters were able to avoid stiffer sanctions, sometimes by offering to rectify an omission. In more than sixty years of broadcasting regulation in the United States, there are only two examples of licence-renewal refused on grounds relating to the Fairness Doctrine. The decision in 1988 to abolish the Doctrine is still a major subject for debate in the United States.

In other countries, there are in certain respects better prospects for enforcing such programming requirements. As a broadcaster as well as the regulator, the IBA in Britain was able to impose lasting influence on the structure of the Independent Television network's schedules and, in particular, to enforce the duty of impartiality. The financial stability provided by the advertising monopoly enabled the ITV companies regularly to serve relatively small audiences. Future plans for increased competition in Britain will alter this position, however. With fewer powers, the supervisory bodies in France and Germany have taken fewer steps to enforce programming obligations. Intervention to prevent one-sided programming was, however, unnecessary since commercial broadcasters tend to avoid alienating sections of their audience. None the less, when, in response to advertisers' needs, programming in its entirety is structured to increase viewers' dispositions to purchase, a more subtle one-sidedness may ensue. No steps for correcting this tendency have yet been devised by the supervisory bodies.

Provision of a forum for the responsible airing of civic affairs and political debate.   Closely related to the programme commitments just outlined are the requirements to ensure the appearance in programmes of socially relevant forces and groups. German broadcasting law specifically provides for this to happen. However, it is hard to enforce, not least because there are no criteria for determining social relevance. Moreover, the demands for balance can lead to broadcasting-by-stopwatch, already to be observed in more than one European country. Public broadcasting in Germany was often paralysed in the 1960s and 1970s by considerations of this kind. However, the more pluralistic the broadcasting order becomes, the less urgent becomes the need for each broadcaster to take all interests into account. Consequently, such an obligation was not placed on Dutch confessional broadcasting. Even there, however, NOS, the public broadcaster, serves as a source of balance in reserve.

Presentation of news with due accuracy.   News programmes are usually subject to additional obligations connected to professional ethics traditionally observed by journalists. For instance, incoming news reports must be scrutinized before transmission to establish their origins and their truthfulness. In their transmitted forms, they must be objective and independent. There is often a requirement for a clear distinction between broadcast news reports and commentaries on the news. It is not easy to enforce requirements of this kind, however, since their strict imposition can dampen free communication and robust public debate, as well as curbing, through limits on investigative journalism, the role of the media as a watch-dog. In the interests of a lively democracy, therefore, but also to avoid controversy, supervisory bodies commonly exercise restraint in their approach to this facet of their role.

Maintenance of cultural and linguistic pluralism.   Efforts to conserve the cultural identity of the nation or of particular groups within it are an important element within the overall object of maintaining pluralism. Neither programme directives nor prohibitions can play decisive parts in this process, however. It is more important to devise a broadcasting structure in which local or regional voices, or the voices of important social sub-groups, can be regularly heard alongside the national voice. Special problems arise when there are active cultural minorities, as in Spain, especially when they use their own languages to reinforce their distinctiveness. The pressure of such minorities for access to broadcasting has been taken into account in a number of European countries by the creation of special language services: in Catalan and Basque, for example, in Spain (see Chapter 11), or in Welsh in the case of the United Kingdom. The linguistic division is similarly recognized in Belgium by the existence of separate French and Flemish services. Belgium has gone a step further in attempting to limit the cultural threats resulting from programming by foreign broadcasters, long accessible in the country through extensive cabling. Its efforts to tie the dissemination of foreign programming by cable networks to the payment of levies to fund national audiovisual productions have met with opposition, however, from the EC Commission (de Coster and Stephane, 1990).

The protection of multilingualism often presupposes financial support for minority broadcasters. Thus, in Switzerland, the public broadcasting system involves a form of internal compensation to ensure that minorities, like the Italian-Swiss in the Ticino, have their own programming.

Guarantees of this kind apply primarily to public broadcasting. Commercial broadcasters are inevitably circumscribed by their need to address commercially-viable audiences, though linguistic minorities in one country can sometimes be reached over satellite or cable with programming in their own tongue from other countries. Such foreign provision, however, is likely to satisfy their identity needs to only a limited degree.

Even where there is no linguistic difference, the need for commercial broadcasters to attract audiences of a sufficient size also limits their preparedness to serve regional audiences or sub-groups. Rules that seek to promote local or regional television therefore meet with opposition and are largely of no effect. Networks are in most cases created to supply programmes from other regions, so that any local or regional emphasis may tend to be marginal. The opposition raised in Germany to proposals to regionalize private television is a good example of this. The state media authorities wished to enforce 'regional window programming' on the operators. However, despite the fact that their nationally distributed services were licensed region-by-region, RTL-Plus and SAT-1 voiced massive protests against the proposal, yielding only to the argument that continued resistance would cost them their licences for the terrestrial distribution of their services. Although they sought to reduce their costs by offering to broadcast joint regional programming, the state media authorities stood firm.

Ensuring a variety of mutually independent broadcasters. Broadcasting under the market model presupposes a variety of broadcasters to ensure competition and provide choice. But a prime incentive within a commercial model is to maximize profitability through concentration of ownership, presenting private broadcasting with one of its greatest problems. Italy illustrates the problem clearly. In the absence of Government regulation, the successful Fininvest group (led by Berlusconi) was able, within a short time, to gain influence over all of the country's national commercial television networks. The group also has considerable press interests, leading to cross-ownership within the two media. The new Italian broadcasting law, passed in 1990, has largely accepted the situation and requires only minor adjustments to be made.

Despite the argument that concentration could lead to greater efficiency, all broadcasting laws and supervisory authorities go to great lengths to stem its advance. Typical instruments include measures to restrict both cross-ownership and, within the same medium, multiple ownership. But their success has been only limited. In the first place, the rules are often full of loopholes and ignore relevant devices, such as the creation of networks to supply programmes. Then the rules often fail to deal successfully with the ability of the true owners to conceal their identities behind figureheads or within the maze of elaborate corporate structures. The supervisory bodies may be under-equipped in resources and skills to gain the necessary insights into what is actually taking place (cf. for example, Thaenert, 1990).

Such failures are often compounded by the tendency of states to respond to growing concentration of ownership by making statutory amendments, relaxing requirements or granting exceptions. It is economic reality which dictates to the legislators and the administrators, not the other way round. However, the will to regulate remains vigorous, and defensive action has at least put the brake on spiralling concentration.

Supervisory bodies appear to be caught in a dilemma, operating on the presumption that only the economically powerful can be successful in the long run (this is at least true of cost-intensive television) and believing that an interlocked multimedia system may be able to achieve efficiencies of programme supply and distribution. Accordingly, their criterion for licensing too often becomes one of economic and distributive efficiency.

Their own standing will often depend upon their success in promoting an economically successful system. It was no coincidence that, at the outset of commercial television in Britain in the 1950s, the Independent Television Authority encouraged publishers to participate. The FCC in the United States gave encouragement to economically successful companies, such as Rupert Murdoch's Fox Broadcasting, to launch a fourth television network. In the interests of global economic expansion, the Commission has encouraged a degree of cooperation among companies which would not have been tolerated in the domestic market. The German media authorities, in expanding television, have favoured companies with strong press interests. The requirements placed upon licensees have often been drafted to favour those already in the media field over those coming from other branches of industry or commerce. A similar pattern has been followed in France in granting the fifth and sixth television licences, where the authority concerned (the CNCL) intentionally supported multimedia concentration, giving preference also to media companies with international operations.

Strengthening of national and regional production resources. Maintenance of diversity can also be applied to the goal of protecting cultural identities at European, national, regional and local levels in the face of increasing transnational (especially US) communication. Rules on quotas of programming have consequently been devised, covering, among other matters, proportions of production from European or national producers, with some share of those figures reserved for independent production houses. They may also cover proportions of news programmes or programmes reflecting regional cultures.

A central objective of many quota rules is to ensure domestic production, thus safeguarding it against an infiltration of foreign culture through foreign programmes, particularly of American origin. On the assumption that externally based programmes are unable to pay regard to those cultural aspects unique to the country receiving them and that, in particular, internationally orientated commercial programmes tend to be omnipresent, the aim of the precautionary measures in this area is to maintain the special cultural characteristics of a nation or a region. At the same time, however, they aim to maintain jobs in domestic production – and, presumably, also the tax-paying power of national firms. This is important not simply from an economic perspective, but also from a cultural one, since otherwise the know-how and other aspects of the production infrastructure necessary for indigenous identity-forming programmes would be lacking.

Experience with quota rules elsewhere is extremely ambivalent. Canada, which has made extensive use of them in an attempt to fend off the influence of its powerful neighbour and so prevent the

Americanization of its programming, has been unable to record any notable success. It has, however, reinforced domestic production, even raising standards to the point where US producers cross the border to employ Canadian facilities and skills.

The enforcement of quotas by supervisory bodies is not easy, precise definitions being hard to establish and ways of circumvention being numerous. It is no coincidence that the EC Television Directive deals extensively with definitions, and this despite the fact that the quota obligations which it contains are formulated rather weakly.

Protection of juveniles and educational programming for children

Children and young people are also television consumers and, especially among problem groups, may tend to watch addictively. Broad agreement exists that the likely socializing effects of television require special precautions, particularly in the case of children and young people. The measures can be divided into two groups, one negative, the other positive.

The negative measures take two forms. The first is of the absolute prohibition of certain kinds of programming, a ban on such things as incitement to racial hatred (a constraint applying also to adult audiences). The second reflects an attempt to make the viewing of certain kinds of programmes difficult for children, such as those portraying violence. One approach is through the so-called family viewing (or 'watershed') policy which restricts such programmes to times of day when children are less likely to be watching. Codes of practice often exist, sometimes enshrined in statute (Germany), sometimes issued by supervisory bodies (United Kingdom), sometimes in the self-regulatory documents of the broadcasting industry itself (the former NAB Codes in the United States). Difficulties of definition occur again and, in countries where freedom of communication is virtually absolute (the United States), the proscriptions are milder than in countries (Germany and the United Kingdom) where it is more natural to restrict freedom of communication in the interest of other values.

The enforcement of these rules is difficult since, in this case too, the language used is not easily translated into practice, and, moreover, there is a well-founded risk that they might be used to suppress contents which are, for other reasons, undesired. There has been vigorous opposition, particularly in commercial broadcasting circles, to the imposition of specific programming obligations. It seems that programmes permeated with violence are more appealing to viewers than other kinds of programme; advertising-financed schedules, dependent upon high viewer ratings, make particularly intensive use of violence as a dramatic tool.

The more heated the battle for ratings, the smaller the chance for the observance of the corresponding duties (cf. Barnett, 1988: 117; Hoffmann-Riem, 1981: 168ff.). Whereas the mass-orientated pro-grammes of the larger commercial operators directed at all seg-ments of the population observe a certain degree of restraint, some cable operators have virtually specialized in filling a self-created gap in the market with violent and pornographic materials. Operating on the questionable assumption that children do not have access to such channels or will be restrained from watching by their parents, the supervisory authorities tend to apply little pressure. However, there are differences in attitudes to be observed; the most consistent supervision appears to be exercised in Britain and Germany.

Children are large-scale consumers of television, with their use of it declining as they become a little older. Positive measures for their protection include the provision of programmes designed for them, age-group by age-group, and intended to produce pro-social effects. While the public broadcasters have produced some remarkable programmes for children, it has been less easy to encourage private broadcasters to follow their lead. The relative lack of success by the FCC may serve as a model of the difficulties of creating obligations to provide programmes for children and then enforcing them. The duty to televise such programmes, which was weakly structured from a legal standpoint, was only at the outset obeyed by the networks: in the course of time, the programmes were shifted to less desirable time-slots and then dropped altogether. Advertisers have little interest in educative programmes for children, preferring child audiences as the addressees of toy-related (and other) advertising messages in entertainment programmes for children, as well as in programmes appealing to both adults and children.

In the early days of cable television in the United States, however, some notable children's programmes appeared, not through the actions of supervisory bodies, but as a result of economic pressures, since they served a useful purpose in attracting additional subscribers to the cable stations. Even such children's programming does not, however, appear capable of resisting its displacement by more entertainment-orientated fare when the time is needed for other purposes (see LeDuc, 1987: 65).

An apparently contrary trend to American experience can be noted in Germany. With the exception of SAT-1, the private terrestrial television broadcasters have included a remarkable variety of children's broadcasts (Schmidt, 1990). They not only appeared interested in making a good impression on the public, but also wished to guide the viewing habits of children and young people towards the private sector as future members of its viewing audience. Moreover, children and young people command enough money to constitute, for certain goods, a sufficient market to appeal to advertisers. It is, however, too soon to establish whether these programmes have 'pro-social effects' or simply meet the needs of their audiences for attractive material.

Maintenance of standards in matters of violence, sex,
taste and decency
Reference was made above to the protection of children from material which was also thought to be harmful to adults. Such material includes the portrayal of violence, sexual conduct and matters of taste and decency. Some countries, however, do not accept that their adult audiences should be protected by any additional measures (for example, the US and Germany). However, the creation of the Broadcasting Standards Council in Britain extended the protection of these values further than before. The Code issued by the Council in 1988 shows how difficult it is to translate standards into practice. In addition, it is necessary for supervision to be exercised with great sensitivity, if it hopes to avoid risking the suppression of opinion. Particularly in matters of taste and decency, there can be rapid swings of opinion within a society, but it cannot be the task of a supervisory authority to thwart social change or otherwise seek to guide it from a moral standpoint. In addition, political minorities often tend to go to the limits of that which is tolerated, not least with the object of attracting attention otherwise denied them in the media. There are difficult questions here of the distinction between providing a legitimate forum for controversy and the no less legitimate goal of upholding minimum standards for all.

Control of advertising
Advertising forms the most important basis of finance for private broadcasters; a number of public broadcasters also fund themselves in part from the same source. The possibly harmful consequences of advertising for programming have led to the establishment of restrictions on the nature and quantity of advertising allowed. Advertisements may only be transmitted at certain times and in limited amounts and certain forms, spliced together in blocks, for example. They must be clearly distinguishable from programmes and the advertiser kept from exercising an influence on the accompanying programmes. Somewhat different rules exist for programmes supported by sponsorship.

The limited rules which governed advertising in the United States have almost all disappeared, but both the EC Television Directive and all the principal guidelines for Western European broadcasting organizations contain some clear instructions. Since the interests of advertisers and of commercial broadcasters conflict with them, the instructions are frequently violated in many countries. Supervisory bodies often have difficulty in interpreting their rules in practice, and advertisers are more inventive in devising new forms of advertising than either the supervisory bodies or legislatures are in thwarting them (see especially Saxer's discussion of how such problems have arisen in Switzerland: Chapter 9 above).

Product placement, concealed advertising, and sponsorship have all recently presented challenges to the supervisory bodies, with which they have dealt at best uneasily. The advertisers, testing the regulators' tolerance, are always shifting their ground, devising new forms of advertising as soon as the regulators have come to terms with the old. The internationalization of media has also helped to shift the limits of tolerated advertising. Often it does so unobtrusively, since, even when commercials are edited out of an imported programme, their influence on the dramatic structure and content of the programme itself may survive undetected by the audience. Teleshopping has carried the integration of programmes and advertising a stage further and, in the face of the EC Television Directive's verdict that it was a form of advertising, has led to a relaxation of restrictions on advertising time in order to accommodate it. In the mixture of entertainment and salesmanship which the form provides, the needs of the consumer for protection are overlooked.

Although rules on the placement of advertisements may be the easiest to enforce, broadcasters may circumvent them by fragmenting programmes into a series of natural breaks or scheduling a single programme as if it were several, separate, programmes (cf. Annan Committee, 1977: 165). Restrictions on advertising in conjunction with children's programmes may be inhibited by fears that they will lead to the disappearance of specially made programmes for children.

Protection of the integrity of works of art
In Italy, the question of the interruption of creative works for advertisements achieved a particular importance. Distinguished directors and other film-makers, supported by the public, have long objected to the practice. The absence for many years of regulations governing private broadcasting meant that commercial interests, which wanted the interruptions to continue, easily prevailed. However, the Broadcasting Act, 1990, has made some modest

concessions to the concern, following expressions of political support for the film-makers' protests.

Review of Methods of Supervision

The foregoing sections, which are intended to be illustrative only, have, I hope, shown clearly that the supervision of broadcasting is faced with enormous difficulties. It must often be exercised against the interests of those being supervised, making the task of imposing all manner of regulations difficult.

With the transition to the market model of broadcasting, the duties of supervisory bodies change. This may be shown by the succession in the United Kingdom of the IBA by the ITC. As was stated earlier, the former Authority, in its role as a broadcaster, could actively influence programme content in the directions it wished; more than a watch-dog, it hunted with the hounds. The new Commission is a classic, detached supervisory body. Apart from granting licences and, within the limits afforded by the Broadcasting Act, 1990, attempting to influence the quality of programming by its choice of licensees, the Commission is confined to monitoring the licensees' observance of the Act. The Act provides room for the exercise of some judgement by the Commission on subjective issues. But its freedom to choose between a range of decisions is not on the scale enjoyed by its predecessor.

In all broadcasting orders, regulatory norms are characterized by relatively vague and usually broad delegations of power (cf. Hoffmann-Riem 1981: 278ff.; Ziethen, 1989). The latitude with regard to franchising is particularly wide: in selecting certain applicants and specifying obligations, there is room for exercising (political) influence. The transfer of certain aspects of decision-taking in the selection of franchisees to the market – of which the cash-bid in Britain is one example – is an indication of efforts made to limit the discretion of the licensing body; but, as is shown by the exceptions available in the United Kingdom, the licensing body's decision-making and structuring power also remains, in part at least, intact.

The most important supervisory instruments on a general and abstract level are the influence of the structure of the broadcasting order and the setting forth, in legal forms and in guidelines, codes etc. of additional obligations. The specification of corresponding requirements in the licence conditions given to individual broadcasters, or possibly later additions to them, represents an attempt to detail the amount of latitude each broadcaster enjoys and defines more precisely the mutual rights and duties in its relationship with the supervisory body.

The actual exercise of supervision, ensuring compliance with the provisions of statutes, licences and codes, is conducted in a number of ways. Broadcasters are, for instance, required to notify changes of ownership or substantial alterations in the pattern of shareholdings. They may be required, as in Germany and in the United Kingdom, to retain recordings of programmes for certain periods of time or may be able to invite advance comments from the supervisory body on a programme likely to be controversial. However, systematic ongoing control of, for instance, the conduct of programming, which the former IBA in Britain was empowered to perform, is nowhere to be found. In some cases, the supervisors may be free, or may be required, to investigate matters only on receipt of a complaint.

A not wholly unexpected ally for the supervisory body in its role as monitor of performance is the competitor who loses no opportunity to draw attention to alleged breaches of a rival's obligations which might enable the rival to increase his market share. Many supervisory agencies are familiar with the friendly telephone call which brings to notice some supposed lapse on the rival's part.

When a breach is discovered, the supervisory body is usually able to adopt one of a graduated series of responses, moving from warning notices through fines and the withholding of advertising time, to suspension and, ultimately, the loss of the licence. The possibility of refusing to renew a licence when it expires is an especially important instrument with great practical use, although it is not expressly mentioned in the law as a sanctioning tool. Procedural requirements may also have the force of a sanction. For instance, the American broadcasting industry generally regards the costly procedure of a formal FCC hearing as a severe sanction, to be avoided in the interest of saving time and other expense, but also of avoiding public discussion. Experience suggests that the availability of a range of sanctions, to be used appropriately in each case, is a better means of enforcing conformity than a few, perhaps drastic remedies which the supervisory body might be unwilling to invoke. The French have recently moved in this direction in order that their supervisory structure may exercise control with more subtlety.

Guidelines for Practical Supervisory Action

Not only in the area of broadcasting supervision, but also generally in the area of economic supervision, regulatory practice has shown that supervisory bodies by no means confine themselves to the formal instruments provided in the Constitution, but seek to supplement these by resorting to a number of further measures and special strategies.

Informal cooperation

Supervisory bodies usually prefer to resolve conflicts by informal means rather than have recourse to their formal powers. The tools they employ may extend from 'raising eyebrows' to informing the public and threatening to use the official sanctions. They try to avoid friction and to prevent the differences from ending up in court. Networks of a formal and informal kind are developed to deal with most problems. Supervisory reality is not marked so much by orders and licence revocations, as by telephoned requests and pregnant phrases uttered during cocktail parties.

Not only does the informal route cost less, but it can be advantageous to both sides. The supervisory body may be given information, which it might not readily obtain from a formal request. It can agree to overlook a failing for a short time in return for a promise to rectify the matter voluntarily. The broadcasters, for their part, can use the informal route to influence the supervisory body's perception of a problem and so divert sanctions otherwise almost certain to fall upon them.

Methods of this kind have surfaced in other fields where the same relationships between supervisors and supervised exist. Their value in broadcasting comes from the often sensitive nature of the material under discussion and the concern of the broadcasters for their independence. Few cases are precisely the same, so, in this way, specific directions can be avoided in an area where precedents have special dangers. The danger in dealings of this kind can be summarized in the words, 'agency capture', to indicate that the interests of supervisor and supervised have merged, with serious consequences for the interests of the consumer (see generally Bernstein, 1955; Peltzmann, 1976).

Cooperative relationships may also be cemented on a personal level. There is a continuous exchange of employees between the FCC in the United States and the broadcasting industry. No such exchange yet exists on the same scale in Europe, but the 'revolving doors', which allow the uninhibited transfer of the respective approaches to problems, are starting to turn. The utility of the existence of informal links is quite obvious in the media sector where concerns for freedom of expression and ample information flows have a special significance on two counts: the rights due in a free society and the often quite remarkably vaguely formulated description of the regulators' task. The legal authority to supervise thereby turns into 'chartering powers' in working out the substance of – or refraining from the use of – conceivable supervisory action.

In Germany there is a second set of doors permitting movement between the supervisory authorities, ministerial bureaucracies and the political machine in general. For example, the directors of many state media authorities are recruited from the chancellery offices of the state minister-presidents, where they had previously been engaged in drafting the broadcasting laws which they must then operate.

Identity of interests in the success and protected status of broadcasting
Reference has already been made to the tendency, as time passes, for supervisory bodies to find their interests in the success of the enterprise coinciding with those whom they are supervising. This contributes to maintenance of the *status quo* or permits deviations from it only gradually. As a result licensees can usually depend on the renewal of their licences. While such a situation prevents many surprises – challengers have difficulty in proving an ability to offer better programmes – it has the effect of reducing the tactical options available to the supervisory body in doing its work. A similar constraint arises from the long-term nature of many licences. A failure on the part of the supervisory body to exercise its ultimate sanction by revoking a licence encourages the belief that it will never do so, thus weakening its authority.

The broadcaster's popularity with the audience also provides a useful tool in generating political pressure against any threat to its protected status. The French Haute Autorité was forced by public opposition to pull back from attempts to limit increases in signal strength from the transmitters of certain radio stations. Broadcasters, as employers and holders of economic power, may also be able to cultivate support from lobby groups that benefit from their programming policies.

The broadcasting industry as proponent of regulation
Although burdensome regulation often provokes criticism from the broadcasting industry, which complains of pettifogging controls, it can nevertheless also appear to welcome supervision. In 1969 and 1970, a large section of the broadcasting industry in the US appeared to regard the continued existence of a regulatory framework as important to the protection of its status. In other fields of economic regulation, there is often a cyclical phenomenon where, in

times of expansion, companies push for the breakdown of regulatory barriers, but, once times become harder, regard regulation as a useful buffer against competition from newcomers. Thus, in US television, the FCC for years protected the networks against the expansionist drives of cable operators, but relaxed its guard when, in better times, the networks themselves appeared more profitable.

Incrementalism

Reference was made above to the reluctance of supervisory bodies to make drastic changes, preferring to change gradually. The process is often characterized by a failure to enforce old rules with their former rigour, paving the way for new rules or no rules, as in the case of the gradual retreat by the FCC from the Fairness Doctrine.

When major changes are introduced, such as a move from regulation to widespread deregulation, they tend to come about incrementally and after lengthy preparation.

When the initiative for change rests with them and is not imposed by the Government, regulators usually wait until the political climate is favourable, whether the change is in the direction of greater or lesser control. Where the move is a deregulatory one, then the regulators will wait until the broadcasting industry itself is in sympathy. This helps to ensure unanimity of interests and the likelihood of favourable publicity from the industry itself.

Transitional problems are, if possible, kept to a minimum, perhaps by phasing action over a long period to lessen their impact, as in the case of the United Kingdom's Broadcasting Act, 1990. Steps are often taken to minimize the effect of changes on accumulated holdings ('grandfathering', as it has been termed). An illegal situation can be dealt with by making it legal, recognizing the reality that the removal of the illegality is, for one reason or another, impractical. This course has been pursued in France and Germany. In the area of advertising control, breaches of regulations may be disposed of by modifying the regulations to meet the breach at least half-way. The relaxation in Germany of the advertising rules in the Interstate Treaty provides an example of this, as do the statutory amendments made in France following the failure of the Haute Autorité to enforce limitations on advertising.

Priority for limited self-regulation

The difficulties confronted by supervisory bodies and the respect shown to entrepreneurial autonomy have encouraged the tendency to leave matters to the broadcasters' own sense of responsibility. The German state media authorities, for instance, initially tried to entrust the allocation of scarce frequencies to a share-out agreement among the competing licence applicants themselves, with the supervisory body acting only as a moderator. In the United States, the FCC left to the National Association of Broadcasters the devising of a code on the depiction of violence, using it as a guide in laying down requirements for its licensees, until anti-trust objections necessitated the rescinding of the code.

Safeguarding the supervisory authorities' organizational interests
Public authorities develop an interest in their own survival, even when their mandate has disappeared, and they are generally successful in surviving. The FCC succeeded in living through the deregulation of the broadcasting order in the United States, while, in Britain, although the IBA did not itself survive all the changes of the Broadcasting Act, 1990, its successor, the ITC, recruited the great majority of its staff from former employees of the IBA.

Incorporation of broadcasting supervision in the political arena
Supervisory authorities must always be aware that they are locked into their respective political arenas. The French Haute Autorité and the CNCL had a taste of this when they were dismantled. The IBA experienced it too when it was obliged to observe Government restrictions on reporting in Northern Ireland. Political influence may be exercised in a number of ways: in the selection of personnel or in the use of special directives and the pressure of adverse criticism made directly by Ministers or through their parliamentary supporters. More fundamentally, politicians can act through Parliaments to amend constitutional arrangements under which supervisory bodies and the broadcasters are required to act. Pressure groups can exert influence and, as in Belgium and Germany, may be represented in the governing structures of the supervisory bodies.

The latter, however, are not wholly at the mercy of pressures on their independence, for they may often play one group off against another. While a political party in power occupies an advantageous position, the wishes of an Opposition party, which may one day form the Government cannot be completely disregarded. Experience in different countries shows differing degrees of success among the supervisory bodies in resisting these challenges.

The degree of pressure is related to the importance attached to the activities of supervisory bodies and the broadcasters. In Britain, the BBC is more vulnerable to political pressure, because of its status, than was the Independent Broadcasting Authority and its franchisees. In Germany, the political parties have tried harder to secure their positions in the public sector of broadcasting than in the private. In the broadcasting councils of the former, there is a legally shared responsibility for programming policies with the broadcasters. In the state media authorities for private broadcasting, there is none.

Ritualistic Elements in Broadcasting Supervision

The difficulties confronting the supervisory bodies which have occupied much of this chapter raise the question of whether the main task of supervision lies more in the area of political legitimation and less in influencing the conduct of broadcasters. As early as 1950, M. Edelman, author of the well-known book, *The Symbolic Uses of Politics*, developed theories of this kind in relation to the FCC in the United States (Edelman, 1950). More recent literature has emphasized the symbolic-ritualistic character inherent in certain aspects of broadcasting supervision (Hoffman-Riem 1981; Streeter, 1983). A look at the new Broadcasting Act in Italy shows, for example, that it was not set up in such a way as to have fundamental influence on the broadcasting order. Nevertheless, its enactment satisfies the demands of the Italian Constitutional Court and, presumably, the expectations of the general public as well. When many sets of European regulations are examined, it is evident that, in the light of foreign experiences, especially in the United States, some could never be expected to be effective. However, for instance, in view of the heated controversies in Germany over media policy, it was both politically and legally impossible to introduce private broadcasting without wrapping it in a network of regulations. It cannot be ruled out that the German state legislatures were primarily interested in the effect of supervisory instruments in conferring political legitimacy, thereby seeking to satisfy the public with the requirements prescribed in them. It is not unusual for such prescriptions to be incorporated in legislation even when their effectiveness is limited. Their political value may lie in their proof of political activity or in the deflation of public opposition.

That is not to say that broadcasting rules and the tools of regulation are necessarily ineffective and justified only by their role in legitimating the broadcasters' activities. At the same time, it must be doubted whether supervision of those activities can ever achieve the goals set in circumstances of keen economic and journalistic competition among the broadcasters. Even when this is not the case, the rules may still have their worth in, for instance, the area of ensuring legitimacy and in providing justifications and levers for civic groups, concerned with the public interest in television, to press regulators for more forthright action. If the objective of regulation, that is, the protection of the vulnerable values as defined in this volume, is taken as the standard, then the legitimating role of the regulatory arrangements should not be seen as an end in itself. A system should, instead, be constructed to protect those vulnerable values as effectively as possible. The undeniable difficulties associated with designing and imposing standards should only be a spur to devise the regulations and supervisory structures, together with an effective scheme for their administration, that can operate in a broadcasting system which is being increasingly run on economic lines.

Prospects

No overall appraisal can be made without the exercise of extreme caution. The experience of most Western European countries in dealing with private broadcasting and its supervision is too recent to allow definitive assessments. However, it would already seem that structural arrangements for assimilating private broadcasting into the traditions and practices of public service broadcasting are lacking.

Such assessment can also be impaired by the fact that supervisory bodies are often quite reluctant to report on their regulatory successes and failures. Research on this topic, particularly empirical research, is virtually non-existent. It is therefore widely left out of consideration in policy discussions.

Although the United States and the United Kingdom have had longer regulatory experience, recent changes in the broadcasting environment in both countries make it less relevant to prognoses about the future. In the case of the United States, there has been a conspicuous failure to sustain a strong public sector alongside the private sector, which much reduces the value of any evidence drawn from it for regulating the European dual broadcasting system.

In making such assessments of past performances as are set down in this chapter, use has been made of documents published by the supervisory bodies in different countries, scattered observations in the literature, our colleagues' national case studies and the writer's own research (Hoffmann-Reim, 1989). Overall, the assessment must be sceptical rather than optimistic.

It would be wrong, however, to give the impression that broadcasting supervision is of no consequence whatsoever. It contributes in every country to a relative ordering of the broadcasting systems and aids by avoiding clear abuses and preventing blatant violations of the rules. But it always approaches its limits when it fails to comport with the interests of the broadcasting industry. Particularly in the case of programme content, supervision has been relatively helpless and unsuccessful. It has often reacted to this, as we have seen, by weakening the supervisory standards or abandoning them altogether.

The supervisory bodies have perceived private broadcasting as subject to a distinct regulatory model and have consistently regarded their task as one of ensuring its ability to function. By the forms of contact outlined above, they have seen to it that supervision has become sufficiently aware of the interests of those regulated, realizing that the supervisory structure can only survive when it pays a certain amount of consideration to the broadcasting industry's own interest structure. As a result, its protection of vulnerable values tends to be weak; its effectiveness depends on the extent to which those values are also accepted by the broadcasting industry itself.

References

Annan Committee (1977) *Report of the Committee on the Future of Broadcasting.* Cmnd 6753. London: HMSO.

Barnett, Stephen R. (1988) 'Regulation of Mass Media', in Stephen R. Barnett, Michael Botien and Eli M. Noam (eds), *Law of International Telecommunications in the United States.* Baden-Baden: Nomos. pp. 81–246.

Bernstein, Marver H. (1955) *Regulating Business by Independent Commissions.* Princeton, NJ: Princeton University Press.

Bundesverfassungsgericht (1986) 'Judgment of 4 November 1986', in *Entscheidungen des Bundesverfassungsgerichts*, vol. LXXIII (1986). Tübingen: Mohr. pp. 157–60.

Bundesverfassungsgericht (1987) 'Order of 24 March 1987', in *Entscheidungen des Bundesverfassungsgerichts*, vol. LXXIV (1987). Tübingen: Mohr. pp. 325–6.

de Coster, Simon-Pierre and Stephane, Robert (1990) 'Measures Taken to Maintain the Quantity and Quality of Audiovisual Production in the French-Speaking Community of Belgium', paper presented at a conference on Vulnerable Values in Multichannel Television Systems: What European Policy Makers seek to Protect, Liege, Belgium.

Edelman, Murray (1950) *The Licensing of Radio Services in the United States, 1927 to 1947.* Urbana, Il: University of Illinois Press.

Fowler, Mark S. and, Brenner, David L. (1982) 'A Marketplace Approach to Broadcast Regulation', *Texas Law Review*, 60 (2): 207–57.

Hoffmann-Riem, Wolfgang (1981) *Kommerzielles Fernsehen: Rundfunkfreiheit zwischen ökonomischer Nutzung und staatlicher Regelungsverantwortung: das Beispiel USA.* Baden-Baden: Nomos.

Hoffmann-Riem, Wolfgang (1989) *Rundfunkaufsicht in Grossbritannien, USA und Frankreich.* Düsseldorf: Presse- und Informationsamt der Landesregierung Nordrhein-Westfalen.

Hoffmann-Riem, Wolfgang (1990) *Erosionen des Rundfunkrechts: Tendenzen der Rundfunkrechtsentwicklung in Westeuropa.* Munich: C.H. Beck.

Home Office (1988) *Broadcasting in the '90s: Competition, Choice and Quality*. Cmnd 517, London: HMSO.

LeDuc, Don R. (1987) *Beyond Broadcasting*. New York: Longman.

Peltzmann, Sam (1976) 'Toward a More General Theory of Regulation', *Journal of Law and Economics*, 19 (2): 211–40.

Schmidt, Hendrik (1990) 'Mit dem Li-La-Launebär zum Erfolg', *Media Spectrum*, 28 (11): 64–7.

Streeter, Thomas (1983) 'Policy Discourse and Broadcast Practice: The FCC, the US Broadcast Networks and the Discourse of the Marketplace', *Media, Culture and Society*, 5 (3/4): 247–62.

Thaenert, Wolfgang (1990) 'Programm- und Konzentrationskontrolle privater Rundfunkveranstalter', in DLM Jahrbuch 89/90, *Privater Rundfunk in Deutschland*. Munich: R. Fischer. pp. 31–51.

Wagner, Christoph (1990) *Die Landesmedienanstalten: Organisation und Verfahren der Kontrolle privater Rundfunkveranstalter in der Bundesrepublik Deutschland*. Baden-Baden: Nomos.

Ziethen, Michael P. (1989) 'Rechtliche Spielräume der Lizenzierung und Kontrolle: ausgewählte Regelungsfelder', in Gerd-Michael Hellstern, Wolfgang Hoffmann-Riem, Jürgen Reese and Michael P. Ziethen (eds), *Rundfunkaufsicht, Bd. III: Rundfunkausicht in vergleichender Analyse*. Düsseldorf: Presse- und Informationsamt der Landesregierung Nordrhein-Westfalen. pp. 59–161.

13

New Roles for Public Service Television

Jay G. Blumler and Wolfgang Hoffmann-Riem

As the foregoing analysis makes plain, it is no easy task to redirect the energies and efforts of profit-pursuing communication providers 'from the outside'. Regulatory measures can lay down certain framework conditions within which broadcasters must operate – for example, setting terms of fair competition to establish a 'level playing field' of entrepreneurial combat. They can aim to block undue concentrations of media power and inhibit gross abuses of such power. They can hold the line on matters susceptible to specific and unambiguous rulings (like the number of permitted minutes of advertising time per hour).

External regulators' abilities to influence programming, however, are normally indirect, limited and modest. Partly this is because democratic societies are wary of the risks to free expression and citizen choice of far-reaching content controls. Partly it reflects the inherent elusiveness of human communication and creativity. In great part it is because no amount or form of regulation can transform the economic driving forces that will predominantly spur the behaviour of audience- and revenue-seeking competitors in a multichannel television system. This does not mean that private providers should be relieved of obligations and expectations to serve the public interest. But since there can be no guarantee that the offerings of commercial programmes will be primarily shaped by such considerations, there must be well-organized alternatives to a broadcasting market.

One such alternative must be a principled, amply resourced and purposefully directed public television sector. Only strong public television organizations can be expected to serve the public interest 'from the inside': giving priority to the vulnerable values at stake in how broadcasting performs; and treating them, not just as imposed requirements for obligatory or token conformity, nor just instrumentally as means to audience maximization, but as ends in themselves.

Does This Really Matter?

The answer to such an ultimate question depends of course on one's values and how a medium like television stands in relation to them. In European eyes, public service broadcasting has always appeared to be a central value of a civilized society, not dissimilar to the notion and position of a university (Blumler and Nossiter, 1991: 422). In the United States, too, public interest advocates are struggling at present to upgrade PBS from its stepchild status, arguing that 'public television should be just as much a public commitment as our public libraries, hospitals, parks and universities' (Minow, 1991: 14). This is not to claim perfection for such institutions in practice. Public broadcasting has not been exempt from the sociological imperatives that oblige all large organizations to adjust to external power forces and internal factional rivalries. Nevertheless, throughout its history its executives and producers have appreciated, in ways not significantly open to profit-seeking businesses, the rich social and cultural potential of radio and television.

Thus, the balance of public and private forces that is eventually struck in the mixed television systems of the 1990s could be crucial in many areas. In *politics and public affairs*, it could determine how much priority is given to keeping the torch burning for the role of reasoned argument in civic and electoral choice. In *catering for children*, it could determine how much priority is given to broadening their horizons, stimulating their curiosity and serving their educative needs. In *global perspective*, it could determine how much indigenous material is available for viewer consumption and reflection amidst the incoming flood of external influences that inexorable processes of communication internationalization are increasingly unleashing. At *production level*, it could determine whether the imagination and ingenuity of creative programme makers are released or diverted and suppressed; imbued more or less with attributes of literate engagement and exploratory courage. At *audience level*, it could determine whether viewers are talked to predominantly as escapists, avoiding any deeper involvement, or as 'mature people who wish to be informed and entertained' (Smith, 1990: 16). In the realm of *standards*, it could determine how often the insidious equation of watchable television with trivialization, standardization, homogenization and inauthenticity is confirmed or countered.

The Challenge of Role Redefinition

The ability of public broadcasters to make a significant difference along these lines cannot be taken for granted, however, in current conditions of diminished authority, tighter funding and competition with private (national and international) rivals. They may be tempted to give top priority instead to the seemingly greater pragmatic urgency of beating back immediate or imminent competitive threats to their audience shares.

The most tangible and increasingly common way to measure competitive success or failure in any endeavour is numerical. In television, ratings measure the number of viewers programmes reach relative to those who have watched the available alternatives. The injection of market forces into European television systems virtually ensures that such ratings will become an ever more salient currency of evaluation in the general and trade press, among producers and in board-level deliberations. Public television bodies may set national viewing share targets as levels below which it would be fatal to fall. In such an atmosphere, ratings could even become crude indicators of how much 'public service', and in what forms, society is prepared to accept from its licence-funded providers. Those 'public service' elements could then be gradually reduced to only a few differences from what is commercially scheduled, just sufficient for public broadcasters to counter critics' charges of having completely abandoned their remit. At that point, however, such claims to distinctiveness of service could be difficult to sustain, since even commercial channels will occasionally put on outstanding programmes that transcend their usual levels of provision.

Thus, a future scenario of convergence, in which higher-quality programmes appear in a few 'bits and pieces' on all channels, however funded, is not implausible. Strong trends in that direction have indeed been independently reported by our colleagues in France, Italy, Spain, Switzerland and Belgium. Continuation of such a drift could undercut the rationale for the maintenance of independently financed public broadcasting corporations and strengthen the appeal of a video publishing model for realizing the public interest in television – by subsidizing worthwhile programming whatever its intended destination.

Public broadcasters must therefore work out a mission and role for themselves that can give principled guidance to their policies internally and justify their continuing claim on societal resources externally. Tackling this task is urgent, since public broadcasters will increasingly be on the defensive until it has been convincingly completed: reacting to competitive inroads in ways that reduce and blur their distinctiveness; conceding to private entrepreneurs the cachet of riding the waves of novelty and difference; and, ultimately, losing control of their organizational destinies.

This task of role definition will be formidable for three reasons. First, it poses new and unfamiliar challenges. When only public broadcasters provided programmes, they could be all things to all men (and women) – the Marks and Spencer's of television. The meaning of 'public service' could be left general and vague; under its broad umbrella, more or less all congenial programming avenues could be pursued; relatively few hard choices had to be faced. But the days of such open-ended latitude are now over. When programmes of many kinds are scheduled on commercial channels, public providers will be pressed hard to define more precisely than before the *raison d'être* of their own contributions.

Second, no models suited to the present condition of European public broadcasting have yet emerged from the analytical literature or operative systems elsewhere. The *US model of public television*, for example, of filling whatever gaps are left untended by private broadcasters, appears a recipe for marginalization and cultivation of an élitist image. Lacking a system-influencing capability, it can do little more than offer occasional oases to thirsty travellers in the commercial desert. Similar disadvantages attend the afore-mentioned *video publishing model* of public service provision. This was endorsed in the United Kingdom by the Peacock Committee on Financing the BBC (1986), when it recommended a gradual phasing out of the BBC, to be replaced by a Public Service Broadcasting Council, which would award grants to producers wishing to make worthwhile programmes that could not attract commercial finance. Such an approach, however, would surrender the opportunities that channels controlled by public corporations afford for public service *scheduling* – that is, presenting a diversity of experiences across a night's offerings and encouraging viewers to sample a programme on a subject they might enjoy, 'simply because it follows one they were already watching' (Green, 1991: 18). It also overlooks the need to assemble, in some programming areas at least (public affairs and light entertainment come to mind), a critical mass of talent under one organizational roof if (as Hearst argues in Chapter 5 above) high standards of programme quality are to be attained.

Third, the new role of public television must be compatible with the increased autonomy of viewers in multichannel conditions. After all, mass-mediated communications have no greater power than that of embossed and gilt-edged *invitations*: to come to the party (to attend); to bring a bottle (put something of oneself into it); to assume a role of some kind there (whether that of a fan, an information-seeking monitor, a horizon-widening experience seeker, a spectator, an escapee, or a mere passerby, dropping in); and to take on board some explicitly or implicitly built-in message.

Since in the new media environment, people will be receiving invitations to many more parties than they will have time to attend, the pursuit by public broadcasters of whatever mission they set for themselves will become more difficult and problematic. The very notion of a public purpose means they cannot set out simply to conform to the predetermined reception interests of the mass audience. Yet the degree of realization of any such purpose will turn on how many people have been induced to watch the programmes that reflect it.

How should the task be faced? Reflection on appropriate roles for public broadcasting may be approached from three standpoints: its relations to private competitors; its programming priorities; and its institutional status in society.

The Position of Public Broadcasters in a Commercial Setting

Hereafter, public broadcasters must be in both a competitive and a complementary relationship to private broadcasters. Their policies should be designed to strike a balance between these relations that subordinates neither to the other, while harnessing each to the other.

Competition arises with respect to products that companies distribute and consumers receive. In television, competitive success is predominantly measured with respect to programmes. Inevitably, one gauge of their success must be the amount and share of viewing. A public broadcaster who almost always caters only for minorities will have lost a significant part of the competitive battle. But broadcasting as a public service may not compete with private broadcasters only for high viewership. It should strive to ensure that the competition is understood, both internally and externally, in multi-dimensional terms. Politicians especially need this understanding if they are not to make crude estimates of relative success or failure. For individual programmes and for the structure of offerings as a whole, then, dimensions other than audience size should continually be stressed: quality, innovation, professionalism, standards, social relevance, serving a variety of interests, etc. That is why public broadcasters have an interest in, and should encourage the establishment of, vigorous forums of public accountability (see Chapter 14), in which both private and public broadcasters have to answer for their performance in light of multiple criteria.

The *complementary* function of public broadcasting arises, on the one hand, from the implacably narrowing imperatives of the market, and, on the other, from the significance for viewers, programme makers and society at large of preserving the values that private broadcasters tend to neglect. From an economic standpoint, complementarity is expressed in the fact that public broadcasting receives significant funding from public sources and is not directly dependent on economically calculated success. It may therefore more often do things that will not necessarily result in high viewer ratings. It may take risks with the innovative and less tried. It may distribute resources in such a way that lower-audience programmes can sparkle in production-value terms as brightly as higher-audience ones.

In other words, public broadcasters should *compete complementarily* with private broadcasters by offering a truly different mix of programming. This would combine thoughtful and involvement-worthy mass appeal programmes with programmes targeted at the more defined tastes of smaller but more committed audiences; a range of programme types in which none is consistently restricted to low budgets or relegated to minority viewing hours; and a greater incursion of surprises amidst the tried and true than private channels are likely to deliver. Above all, public broadcasting should distinguish itself by offering a variety of ways of depicting social reality – that is to reflect it, to comprehend it, to deplore and attack it, to enjoy it, or to redesign the concept of it. By making such variety available, discoveries are possible and curiosity has a field of activity. Only in such a manner can current viewpoints and preferences be refreshed and developed from a potentially wealthy supply instead of standing stagnant.

Public broadcasters must not only get the competition/complementarity relationship right, however. They must also find ways of so conveying their distinctive identities that understanding and support for their functions are generated in such terms. This underscores the trailer function of programme publicity. In it public broadcasters should emphasize the qualitative benefits of their offerings. They should seek to produce hallmark broadcasts and to publicize them as highlights, special events and outstanding features. These are productions that signal the special merits of a public service system – which may sometimes be programmes for an esoteric minority (opera or ballet or Greek drama, say) and sometimes for a majority (a Briton might think in this connection of certain *nonpareil* BBC comedies). It is also important that information and other challenging kinds of programmes should not be projected and stigmatized as uninteresting, heavy or boring. Trailers for them should instead strive to attract the attention of audience segments that might initially not expect to be interested in them.

Programming Priorities

The new role for public broadcasting must stem from a considered sense of priorities. Partly this is due to the strains imposed on limited resources by ever-rising television production costs. It is also inherent in the need to decide how best to differentiate public television from its private competitors.

Three models appear available at this level. One would prioritize *by programme type*, presuming that if commercial television concentrates on entertainment and topical news, public television should offer documentaries, plays, education, the arts and science. This, however, is a formula for decidedly boxing public television into a corner, offering almost nothing for those entertainment gratifications that are central (though not necessarily exclusive) in many viewers' expectations of television. US public television is an object lesson: having been forced into such a mould for historical and financial reasons, it is only now struggling to break out of it. More fundamentally, this model ignores the fact that in principle *all* kinds of programmes can differ from how private broadcasting tends to shape them.

Another model would prioritize *by audience target*, presuming that if commercial – and especially advertising-supported – television concentrates on mass appeal programmes, public television should serve the neglected minorities. Such a prescription is not only open to the same objections as those raised against differentiation by programme type; it also arbitrarily excludes the majority from the benefits of a public service approach. The equation between 'public' and 'universal' should not be lightly dismissed. When public broadcasting does justice to the needs it strives to meet, not selectively but as widely as possible, it enables an openness in the process through which views, insights and preferences initially shared by a few can also be found to be interesting and worthwhile by a majority. It is through such a dynamic component that public broadcasting can serve as a meaningful 'cultural forum' (Newcomb and Hirsch, 1983) and a factor in cultural development.

Only a third model would enable public broadcasting at one and the same time to be different, meet public needs and stay attuned to all viewers. It must be guided by a sense of *qualitative priorities*, differing from market-driven television not so much by the areas of programming presented as by the characteristics – of functions, gratifications, standards and quality – striven for in them, as well as by its cultivation of a reputation for accessibility to public concerns and responsiveness to public needs. Though no single policy outcome follows from this prescription, which must be applied differently in the varying cultures and conditions of diverse broadcasting systems, a number of emphases could flow from it.

Information provision

The audience's familiarity with certain events can readily be established through the news services of a private broadcasting system. But commercial broadcasting will tend all the more to televise an event, the more it is capable of attracting attention. This means that sensational and extraordinary events tend to be accorded a special rank. There is also a certain arbitrariness with respect to the socio-geographic region from which the news comes, favouring parochialism. Moreover, when the whole world is used as a resource for the display of extraordinary images, reality becomes distorted, forced toward those characterizations that vividness, simplicity and intensity tend to generate (Cohen et al., 1990).

The public system should distinguish itself through greater roundedness and depth of treatment in five directions. First, the information it provides should take into account those areas of reality, which, though not necessarily high in sensation value, are nevertheless relevant to how viewers live and especially to what is shaping the social conditions that determine how they may live.

Second, its reporting should ensure that the several dimensions of an event are recognizable. Mere revelation of an event does not satisfy needs for orientation or even simple understanding. If viewers do not wish to be reduced to slates momentarily imprinted with high-profile events that are quickly wiped away to make room for the next round of incidents; if they wish to obtain some control over what has been seen by forming their own impressions of its significance; then they need access to background, fuller information, surrounding contexts and relevant judgements of experts and others. Overall, the presentation of events should be guided by a sense of the questions to be raised about them to which answers, however problematic, are needed.

Third, viewer understanding and control also require awareness that a considerable number of events are staged, that is, intentionally arranged to foster certain impressions. It is not sufficient, however, to stress simply that this is often the case, which may do little more than breed disenchantment. Instead viewers must be in a position to read the staged scene as such – that is, to recognize the calculation and strategy behind it – and to go beyond it, helped by the affirmatively scrutinizing role of reporters, determined to draw publicists into meaningful comment on the issues of controversy concerned.

Fourth, public broadcasters should transcend the interests that the competing parties have in depicting themselves in certain ways and see to it that their contributions and standpoints join in debate, enabling the questions at issue to be substantively sifted. Such a dialogue should not always be confined to the best-equipped and ever-familiar protagonists. Also to be promoted is dialogue with non-professional interpretations and perspectives, since this can avoid a uniformly top-down formation of public agendas and facilitate the insertion of concerns that official commentators are tempted to ignore.

Fifth, opportunities to step out of the circle of immediacy and event-determined news should also be afforded, occasionally striving for a more analytical consideration of underlying trends and social processes. Here the emphasis would be more on connections and structures than on event-bound happenings.

Entertainment provision
Bases for a similar differentiation apply to television entertainment. Among commercial programmers, much competition is waged over attention-holding, production values (attractive stars, glossy sets, glamorous locations, pace, etc.) and sustaining tension. Stories are built around figures that can be speedily and universally understood and appreciated. Actors' local and social ties tend to be treated as theatrical props. Personalities are simplified into near-unidimensional stereotypes, only momentarily enriched to generate paradox or an unexpected story twist. The imagination is piqued as external stimulus, but there is little incentive for deeper reflection. The melodramatic tension that arises from scene to scene *is* the plot, instead of its being an outcome of some deeper development. Emotions are excited without imaginative faculties being put to work.

In the face of such tendencies, public television should not primarily set out to imitate the predominant commercial style. Given the high costs of entertainment programming, such an approach would amount to a squandering of public resources on *purely* competitive (and in no way complementary) ends. Entertainment in public channels should aim to stimulate and quicken imagination and thought, not shut it off. Its characters, even when standing for something emblematic, should have those less resolved qualities of complexity, potential and uncertainty that stamp real-life individuals. Its conflicts should invite reflection on interests, temperaments, taboos and preferences that originate in the real world and pose dilemmas that viewers can absorb as belonging to life as they know it or could imagine it. Images should tell a story about real persons, not just allegories. Neither should institutions that often provide the backcloth of television fiction (police, law, medicine, education, politics) always be painted in the same drastically simplifying strokes (see Turow, 1989, for a detailed analysis of misleading depictions of medicine in US network television). Since many people will probably tend to watch more entertainment as channels increase, the occasional provision in public television's fictional output of such a 'reality-righting' corrective to the distortions and banalities of commercial programming is particularly important.

Cultural self-determination
In Europe, commercial channels are likely to schedule a significant amount of US programming, available at relatively cheap prices with an already proven appeal. In the mixed television economy, it falls to public television to look to its society's more indigenous cultural needs. This is not to fly the flag of cultural sovereignty or to value the static preservation of some cultural *status quo*. The role envisaged is rather to enhance a society's ability to find for itself appropriate terms of adaptation and change in response to the incoming flow of international communication. In addition to coverage of national developments in sports, science, industry, the arts, etc., some priority follows for the cultivation of domestic talent – writers, dramatists, musicians, film-makers – in the programme commissioning efforts of public broadcasters. In multicultural societies (for example, Belgium, Switzerland and Spain) efforts are also called for to support linguistic diversity and to maintain the functionality of language as a bearer of cultural identity.

Innovation and the ability to surprise
Commercial television dances to strongly conformist and imitative tunes. Financial backers need assurances that every effort has been made in the programme-commissioning process to protect their investments and score ratings successes. Premiums are put on stars, formats, formulae, and themes that have worked in the past. The odds are stacked against creative risk-taking, which must struggle to pierce a prior climate of scepticism. Although multichannel competition also generates pressures on commercial programmers to find ways of distinguishing themselves from the clutter of all the rival offerings, such needs are more likely to be met by infusing the standardized approaches with presentation gimmicks than by departing from them.

In contrast, public television could assume the vocation of promoting freshness, a quality that can be applied to both the invigoration of old formulae and the generation of new programme ideas (Nossiter, 1986). Overall, the emphasis would be on programmes that are refreshingly different, make people sit up and take notice, awaken them to new experiences or encourage them to try out new notions. Such a philosophy would give public broadcasting the pioneering role of leading the way in new programme development, not abdicating it to the private sector.

Programme quality
In ratings-driven commercial broadcasting systems, powerful influences subvert and dilute *distinctive* meanings of 'quality' programming. It is subtly conflated with popularity, equated with what has proved itself in the ratings market by achieving hit status or attracting an above average level of viewing.

For their part, public broadcasters should hold out against this tendency and adhere to other, independent criteria of quality – fostering their identification; setting out to ascertain through research what producers and viewers regard as marks of quality; discussing the achievements and deficiencies of their schedules in quality terms; and aiming for a pallet of programming that incorporates as many standards of quality as possible. Such standards might include, not only the aforementioned criterion of freshness, but also: imaginativeness; an ability to illuminate controversy; authenticity (aiming to do justice to a subject, a problem, or a situation in terms of what it is really like, instead of distorting it for the sake of drama, attention holding or viewers' comfort); social relevance; expressive richness (operating artistically with more elements, at many levels, or at greater depth); and integrity (being shaped by a vision that has not been grossly violated, diluted or compromised to satisfy the quite different ideas of others).

The ability to attain such standards will turn partly on how programme makers are recruited and treated. In some European countries the public service broadcasting corporations had a particularly good record for fostering major talents and supporting their creativity with resources and encouragement. The more this tradition can be continued, the better the chance that high-quality programmes, appreciated by audiences as among their 'favourites', will often emerge.

An international presence
Much of the impetus behind the recent globalization of television has been commercial – and American. Nowhere has this been more strikingly evident than in the 24-hour news field, which is dominated by Ted Turner's CNN at present (as Hadenius from Sweden and Wolton from France have noted above). Though such an operation

has a global reach, its heart is in Atlanta, Georgia. Its programming tends to be stamped with a particular editorial standpoint and a certain way of exploring issues, events, and the actors involved in them. This threatens a diminution of plurality in the increasingly vital international opinion-forming arena (Hallin and Mancini, forthcoming). It therefore seems important for an alternative to be launched from Europe with as little delay as possible; that it be run under public direction; and that the news resources of the major public broadcasting corporations, including their extensive foreign correspondent networks, be pooled in its service. This might even be designed to pursue a non-uniform editorial policy – aiming to acquaint viewers with the many different perspectives taken in the world on major international events and conflicts.

The Social Character of Public Broadcasting

Unlike private television, which is predominantly accountable to the market, public television is rooted in the social system, from which it draws its existence. In charter and governance, it is thus a public institution and its primary funding sources are public.

There is also a close pragmatic tie of impact between all forms of television and the social system. Because of the amount of time that viewers spend with their sets, the level of resources devoted to programming, and its pivotal position in the calculations of would-be opinion formers, television has become an omnipresent institutional influence, touching, penetrating, even tending to bend all facets of organized social life to its rhythms and requirements. How television is organized and programmed is thus relevant to a host of societal goods: the realization of democracy through channels of discourse and choice, leadership and accountability; the vitality of culture; the quality of leisure; the interpretation of many social institutions to themselves and to each other (business, the military, education, labour, religion, science, medicine, etc.); and informal processes of acculturation, socialization and education (Blumler, 1989). But whereas commercial television can take such societal factors into account only rarely and incidentally (witness as object lesson its impoverishing role in US election campaigns), public television can build them more centrally into their programming policies.

Cultural functions

As a cultural institution, broadcasting projects an image of society and its activities. Public broadcasting should therefore define itself as an influential factor in cultural reproduction and renewal – and act accordingly. It thus has a responsibility to provide programming in culturally significant areas, to institute forums of cultural debate, to examine critically its own cultural contributions (and those of other media) and to maintain close ties with society's creative and artistic sectors. It should manifest this not only in activities directly related to transmission but also in other policies: support for independent producers, even when their work does not bring high ratings; support for programme archives; and development of other distribution channels, such as videocassettes and rental libraries.

Political functions

As a political institution, broadcasting provides an image of political life, its leading players, preoccupations and activities. In this sphere public broadcasting has the vocation of standing for the integrity and viewer utility of civic communication against the many (and still mounting) pressures that threaten to subvert it, including: sloganized messages and soundbites; advanced political advertising techniques; ever more sophisticated news management strategies; the down-grading of cognitive appeals; and the erosion of confidence in the information-processing capacities and interests of ordinary electors.

With the emergence of the dual broadcasting system, chances might also be sought to push back some of the political constraints under which monopoly public broadcasters have laboured in the past. With the advent of private channels and competition, public television should be able to put on programmes with more venturesome profiles without fear of the assumption that the fortunes of individual parties, groups or leaders could be seriously damaged by a single broadcast. More priority could be given to looking at and giving access to the marginal elements and lesser voices of society – not always falling back on major parties and mainstream standpoints. This could tap vital sources of social change and extend the province of broadcasting system norms of pluralism, choice and fairness more generously to groups that sometimes feel excluded from them. By the same token, in systems which sought to guarantee pluralism in the past by representing the main parties and affiliated social groups in public broadcasters' governing boards, opportunities for relaxation, more broadcaster discretion, journalistic autonomy – even structural reform – might be sought.

Social functions

As a social institution, public broadcasting is significant for a range of functions. One – with important implications for children's programming, which private television tends grossly to commercialize and trivialize – is that of socialization, or to serve as a trustee for the maturing development, quickening curiosity and educative needs of children and growing youngsters. A second is that of normative orientation, entailing broadcaster sensitivity to notions of standards, including a respect for the boundaries within which the chase for audiences should normally be contained (for example, not following commercial broadcasting into the more exploitative depths of 'tabloid television'). A third is that of multicultural understanding, representing the diverse groups of a pluralistic society to themselves and to each other. In addition, public broadcasting is significant for processes of both social change and social integration. As to the former, it should enable social critics to voice their views, not as 'free rides' or as exceptional token gestures to an enlarged marketplace of ideas, but as points of view to be seriously tested against other opinions and sources of evidence. Through occasional 'outreach' activities, the programming of public television may also be linked with social action in the community at large. As to the integrative function, it is no longer necessary for all persons, or as many as possible, to view the same programmes and, through subsequent conversations about them, help society to unite around the same symbolic offerings. Instead, public broadcasting should aim to contribute to social integration through its openness to diversity in how society is regarded and by the way in which different perspectives are creatively related to each other in its programming.

Is the Recipe Viable?

These notions of a public television order, outlined in normative terms, spring from the European tradition of socially committed liberty and hence do not shy away from emphases on fulfilment of media responsibilities beyond market demands. It is not enough, however, simply to lay down normative premises, since this does not ensure that they will be followed. In the face of many channels and rivals, fragmenting audiences, economy pressures and the ever-ready availability of cheap but well-produced Hollywood pro-grammes, public service principles could wither on the vine, increasingly becoming more a point of rhetorical reference and justification than an influence on practical action.

In the new situation, however, neither should the supports for a continuing public service vitality be under-estimated. These include the vigour and creativity of the European programming industry and the concern of many individual producers to make public service programmes. Their still relatively sturdy financial underpin-nings offer European broadcasters a material basis for continuing to serve the goals of quality, range, authentic civic communication and cultural challenge. Public broadcasting bodies, being single corporations and enjoying sole access to a substantial source of income (the licence fee), should find it easier to frame coherent policies for coping with multichannel existence than will their numerous commercial rivals, all competing on life-or-death terms for slices of a finite advertising pie. There is also the fact that the European audience has in effect been 'trained' to accept public service programming as something it is prepared to patronize along with the less demanding fare that it wants to enjoy as well. European broadcasters have attracted astonishingly large audiences at times.

Undoubtedly decisive for the future, however, will be whether European viewers' *expectations* of programming will change. Will they become so accustomed to an abundance of enticing 'snacks' that they will no longer recognize the value of 'haute cuisine' and lose their appetite for substantial and varied meals of carefully prepared courses? Although the future is unpredictable in this respect, it is essential for public broadcasters to appreciate, when facing it, that they will be involved in a competitive struggle over the formation and affirmation of such expectations. Through the provision of diverse, imaginatively enriching and challenging programmes, they must strive to keep alive the desire of viewers to look for alternatives to the more superficial satisfactions of commercial fare.

Much is at stake here – even internationally. If European public broadcasters manage to establish a distinctive profile *and* to ensure its success with their publics, this could serve as a model for television systems in other parts of the world. After all, the values and social functions that depend on how television is organized are not peculiar to Western Europe. Lessons could flow from success in upholding them for other democracies, as they increasingly realize that commercial television alone cannot satisfy a society's communication needs.

References

Blumler, Jay G. (1989) *The Role of Public Policy in the New Television Marketplace.* Washington, DC: The Benton Foundation.

Blumler, Jay G. and Nossiter, T.J. (1991) 'Broadcasting Finance in Transition: An International Comparison', in Jay G. Blumler and T.J. Nossiter (eds), *Broadcasting Finance in Transition: A Comparative Handbook.* New York and Oxford: Oxford University Press. pp. 405–26.

Cohen, Akiba, A., Adoni, Hanna and Bantz, Charles R. (1990) *Social Conflict and Television News.* Newbury Park, London and New Delhi: Sage.

Green, Damien (1991) *A Better BBC: Public Service Broadcasting in the '90s.* London: Centre for Policy Studies.

Hallin, Daniel C. and Mancini, Paolo (forthcoming) 'The Summit as Media Event: The Reagan–Gorbachev Meetings on U.S., Italian and Soviet Television', in Jay. G. Blumler, Jack M. McLeod and Karl Erik Rosengren (eds), *Comparatively Speaking . . .: Communication and Culture Across Space and Time.* Newbury Park, London and New Delhi: Sage.

Minow, Newton N. (1991) *How Vast the Wasteland Now?* New York: Gannett Foundation Media Center.

Newcomb, Horace and Hirsch, Paul (1983) 'Television as a Cultural Forum: Implications for Research', *Quarterly Review of Film Studies*, 8 (1): 45–55.

Nossiter, T.J. (1986) 'British Television: A Mixed Economy', in *Research on the Range and Quality of Broadcasting Services.* London: HMSO. pp. 1–71.

Peacock Committee (1986) *Report of the Committee on Financing the BBC.* Cmnd 9824. London: HMSO.

Smith, Anthony (1990) *Broadcasting and Society in 1990s Britain.* London: W.H. Smith.

Turow, Joseph (1989) *Playing Doctor: Television, Storytelling, and Medical Power.* New York and Oxford: Oxford University Press.

14

Toward Renewed Public Accountability in Broadcasting

Jay G. Blumler and Wolfgang Hoffmann-Riem

The preservation of vulnerable values in broadcasting must not stop short at the two approaches of (1) legal regulation and (2) revamped remits for strong public television bodies. A third leg is also required: the considered creation and activation of forums of public accountability.

Why is this important? 'Accountability' belongs to the family of democratic concepts. It applies especially to domains in which the competence of authority does not depend only on technical proficiency, but where the actions of decision-takers should be open to review and comment by those affected, because values significant for all are involved. Given the formative consequences of broadcasting for popular leisure, the fabric of culture and the quality of public life, clearly its controllers should be accountable. As Aufderheide (forthcoming) argues, civic participation in media affairs is itself a 'public interest standard in communications policy'. It follows that those who run and provide television and radio should continually be exposed to feedback, expressive of the interests of viewers and society as a whole, and be encouraged to take account of it. This embraces four related aims: bringing matters to light, by securing explanations and justifications from those responsible for the activities and policies they have pursued over a period; probing adequacy, by exposing the authorities to criticism and pressures for change; giving a hearing to alternative needs and ideas from outside official decision-taking circles; and 'inducing a sense of responsibility in those who are called to account' (Robson, 1960: 211).

Accountability 'Before the Revolution'

During the public service era, 'the thread of broadcast accountability' was 'spun strong' (Seymour-Ure, 1991: 245). Of course peer group standards and appraisals were a central factor in broadcasting governance. But the evolution of radio and television – what they should be doing, how well they were doing it and what needed to be changed – was also monitored by what Blumler and McQuail (writing when public television was unchallenged) termed 'an elaborate system of public accountability' (1965: 186). This included the following (with variations across societies):

1 Regular reports from public broadcasting boards, discussed predominantly in political forums.
2 Parliamentary debates in which opinions on the progress of broadcasting could be expressed.
3 Lively internal processes of debate and exchange among public broadcasting executives and programme makers over the adequacy of their goals and practices – for example, in conferences, the trade press and on the job.
4 The not infrequent eruption of public argument over controversial programme practices, standards and innovations.
5 Periodic, intensive and comprehensive reviews of the records of public broadcasting corporations by independent publicly appointed committees, often provoking 'grand public deliberations' on the future of broadcasting (Seymour-Ure, 1991: 212).

This system had characteristic weaknesses and strengths. The circle of 'licensed' participants – those entitled, encouraged and able to take part – was relatively narrow. At its core were politicians and broadcasters, to some extent each checking and balancing the other, occasionally joined by other informed contributors, such as élite columnists, culture critics, interest group spokespersons and media researchers in higher education. Often shut out were the voices of ordinary viewers and listeners, to whose *opinions* (as distinct from their *attendance*, measured by ratings), the system was largely indifferent (Shaw, 1991). Within the circle, however, a robust 'process of open criticism and riposte' (Seymour-Ure, 1991: 61) did ensue which probably made a difference to broadcaster behaviour. Of course, this was facilitated by more or less consensual agreement on the purposes that public broadcasting was supposed to serve.

Some of the underpinnings of this system, however, have been shaken by broadcasting system change. Responsibility for a significant amount of programming is being taken out of public hands. Multichannel proliferation is stretching monitoring capacity to the limit. Organizational processes of media concentration, conglomerization and internationalization are making the targets of accountability more difficult to reach. Principled consensus is riven by the public/private split.

Need for a New Model

The system of broadcasting accountability therefore needs to be refurbished with an eye to current conditions. This need arises from three sets of considerations.

One reflects the relative shakiness of the other two legs on which the public interest in television must stand. Regulation can usually set limits to the realization by others of their purposes, not determine to a significant degree what those purposes will be. The navigation by public broadcasters of the recommended course of 'competitive complementarity' could prove extremely difficult, resulting in many instances of misdirection, stalled engines, loss of a compass – and 'wrong man overboard'! Public interest concerns could be further sidelined by (a) insular attitudes among broadcasters of all stripes, including their tendency 'to take refuge, like a crack regiment, in [their presumed] professional excellence' (Shaw, 1991: 14) and (b) the urgencies and engrossing gamesmanship of intensified multichannel contention. As Smith (1990: 5) has pointed out: 'In the new more competitive system every one of the organisations which will . . . produce programmes is being made to live in a permanent state of contrived emergency [making it] difficult for any of them to represent themselves as pure examples of any particular policy.' To counter such influences, all parties must be enveloped in processes that will press them to look beyond their immediate goals and interests.

A second consideration concerns the fate of the audience, often ignored in the old system, still vulnerable to neglect in the new. Viewers' interests could be overshadowed by those of many others: lawyers, politicians, advertisers and sponsors, media moguls, professional broadcasters, etc. They could also be trivialized by the head-counting and attention-holding imperatives of market competition. As Ang warns, as a ratings discourse about the audience gains ground, its members tend to be reduced to numbers, classification schemes and variables, erasing from the 'field of discernment', then, 'any specific consideration of the meanings, saliences and impacts of television for people' (1991: 62) or 'the lived reality behind the ratings' (Jensen, 1987: 25). Clearly, forums will be needed in which richer accounts of viewers' interests can be expressed and broadcaster participants can be forcefully reminded of their 'real-people characteristics'.

Third, the accountability load will be much heavier in the new television system. Regulatory authorities will have to be kept up to the mark by 'accountability activists' in all sorts of ways. They will have to be prodded to take action over the practices of private television to which they might prefer to turn a blind eye. They must continually be asked how they intend to monitor those practices, and even be helped, by independently gathered information and independently conducted research, to monitor them. Above all, how they interpret and apply private broadcasters' franchise obligations must be closely checked for sufficiency and against temptations to succumb to tokenism.

An instructive example of this last point is afforded by recent developments in the regulation of children's television in the United States. On 18 October 1990 Congress passed a Children's Television Act, which included three main provisions: limits on the amount of advertising in children's programming screened by broadcast licensees and cable operators; a requirement on the Federal Communications Commission (FCC) to consider whether licensees had served the educational and informational needs of children when reviewing their franchise renewal applications; and a ban on programme-length commercials.

Except for the limit on permitted advertising time (10.5 minutes per hour on weekends and 12 minutes per hour on weekdays), none of this was straightforward. The FCC had to decide *when* to start and stop counting advertising in children's programmes; *what kinds* of programmes would qualify as meeting children's educational needs (and how the latter should be *conceived*); and precisely *what practices* should be ruled out by the ban on programme-length commercials (as well as how to *recognize* them). On all these points numerous public interest organizations submitted proposals and testimony, including summaries of social-science research on (a) processes of cognitive and emotional development in children, supporting the need for age-targeted educational programming, and (b) children's awareness of and responses to advertising, supporting tough measures against programming crafted to promote commercially sold toys.

In this battle the public interest advocates 'won some and lost some' of their objectives. They did not accept all the defeats as final, however, taking the further step of drawing the attention of the relevant congressional committees to what they regarded as shortcomings of certain FCC rulings. These included its failure to insist on age-specific educational provision; its readiness to accept even quite brief public service announcements as specimens of such programming; and its adoption of a very narrow definition of banned programme-length commercials (only programmes with paid advertisements for the very products featured in them).

We have elaborated this episode in some detail, because it usefully illustrates the kinds of problems with which our new-style accountability mechanisms must be geared to cope. It also underscores the need for those activating them to be armed with vigilance, relevant information and persistence (Kunkel, 1991).

Possible Ways Forward

Clearly, effective approaches to public accountability in Europe's mixed television economies must be more complicated and multifaceted than the former model. This is in line with world-wide tendencies in economic and social regulation generally to reduce or restructure the state's role without leaving the fields concerned to market forces alone. In those areas where market failure has been observed or is likely, various forms of self-regulation may be sought. Viewed in this light, public accountability in broadcasting, involving channels of discussion and appraisal, rights to participate and obligations to respond, as well as protection against power abuses – all without imperative Government intervention – might be thought of as a form of 'regulated self-regulation'.

A renewed public accountability system should be conceived as a set of interconnecting elements, however, no single one of which can do the whole job, with channels of overspill from one to the other and possibly some way of periodically bringing issues and trends together into an overall perspective. It seems to us that six elements could have a place in such a system.

First, thought might be given to procedures for strengthening public accountability on behalf of social values *inside* broadcasting organizations, both public and private. Their aim would be to enhance the autonomy and role in organizational decisions of media professionals (for example, journalists) on the assumption that their norms will, on balance, accord more often with social and creative values than will the attitudes and incentives of media owners and managers (Hoffmann-Riem, 1972; 1979; Kübler, 1973). Such an approach could take one or more of several forms:

1   Creation of a representative body of professionals to discuss organizational policy with management.
2   Rights to be informed in advance about certain specified kinds of decisions and to offer inputs to them.
3   Rights to veto certain decisions (for example, appointments to top editorial positions).
4   Rights to refuse to carry out policies on professional grounds.
5   Creation of a conciliation body to help resolve conflicts between professionals and management.

6 Creation of a mixed professional/management body to review recent output in light of creative standards.

These ideas are not put forward as a syndicalist manifesto for broadcasting but to illustrate the variety of ways, one or more of which could be tried, in which professional commitments could be mobilized behind the public interest in television. For private television companies, instituting such safeguards of professional autonomy could even be made a licensing condition.

Second, social-scientific research into mass communication could be enlisted in the accountability cause more often. Its strength is the independence, methodological rigour and relative objectivity of its insights into communication phenomena, whether derived from media content analyses, quantitative and qualitative audience surveys, observation attachments to programming units, or enquiries into audience effects. From an accountability standpoint, research on the production process would be especially valuable, particularly at a time of broadcasting system change, when independent examinations are needed of the impact on media workers of new and changing constraints and the kinds of output these are encouraging (or tending to rule out). More interchange between researchers and public interest advocates should be cultivated. Ways of summarizing relevant bodies of evidence for presentation to regulatory bodies and other broadcasting organizations should be developed. Support for policy-relevant media research in funding and access to information should be encouraged. Public boards might even be expected to comment in their periodic reports on pieces of broadcasting research that have come to their attention, including their possible policy implications.

A third avenue arises from the multiplicity of groups, whose causes, interests and public identities depend significantly on how they are ventilated over television and radio. Such groups should aim to play a more substantial part in the public accountability process than just indignantly complaining about something blatantly offensive to themselves. They should involve themselves more often in the discussion of broadcasting policy issues – perhaps 'taking off' from their own concerns but moving on toward critical consideration of the processes responsible. Broadcasting organizations might also be urged to put on programmes in which groups would have a chance to compare television coverage of their affairs with their own versions of reality – and to indicate in their reports how they have gone about this.

In a democratic society, however, care should be taken to ensure that this avenue is not continually dominated by the most powerful and well-organized groups with well-oiled access to the broadcasters and political authorities. Some receptivity to the concerns of less established groups, in a spirit of what Langenbucher and Mahle (1973) have termed 'reverse proportional representation', is desirable. As Melody has also pointed out, taking account of 'the perspective of those groups in society that may be significantly affected by the policies adopted, but which do not have a sufficiently organized financial vested interest to mount a representation . . . is necessary to ensure that in the final balancing of interests that underlies most policy decisions, consideration of the interests of important segments of the public are not omitted' (1990: 32).

Fourth, television and radio critics in the press and other media are vital cogs in the accountability wheel. Some of their writings appear regularly in prestigious organs, and what they have to say is often followed by media workers at all levels. They consequently have a potential for influence in spotting trends, upholding standards and sounding notes of alarm. It follows that they should not limit themselves simply to writing little essays on the pros and cons of individual programmes but should devote themselves to organizational developments, media politics and upcoming policy choices as well. Despite the regular appearance of such analytical pieces in a few publications (for example, *The Financial Times* in Britain and the *Süddeutsche Zeitung* and *Frankfurter Rundschau* in Germany), much European media criticism is inferior in this respect to its counterpart in the United States, where a number of authoritative columnists, like John J. O'Connor (*New York Times*), Tom Shales (*Washington Post*) and Howard Rosenberg (*Los Angeles Times*) play such a part with impressive insights, eloquence and judiciousness.

Fifth, it is no longer acceptable for discussion of broadcasting affairs to be monopolized by élites. To counter the many pressures that breed and entrench impoverished notions of what viewers expect from television, it is crucial for what we shall term 'citizens' organizations' to develop strategies and policies for involvement in broadcasting accountability.

It would be inappropriate to offer a detailed blueprint here for the accountability roles of such bodies, which have evolved a panoply of diverse organizational forms and functions in different European societies. At least four types may be distinguished. First, there are associations that look after the interests of consumers of products and services. These include bodies that mainly undertake product testing and are largely financed by magazine subscriptions – such as the Consumer Association in Britain (with equivalents in, for example, Belgium and France) – as well as ones that are funded by the Government to articulate, represent and lobby for the consumer interest in a wide range of policy and industrial spheres (as with the National Consumer Council in Britain and the Verbraucherzentralen in Germany). Second, in a number of continental countries, there are family-centred groups that occasionally cast an eye on media influences on family life, including child welfare (in Chapter 6, Mazzoleni mentions their recent role in Italian broadcasting). Third, religious organizations may also take an interest in media issues (see Lopez-Escobar, Chapter 11, for their role in Spain and Lopes da Silva, 1990, for Portugal – where the Catholic Church is even contemplating applying for a private television franchise). Finally, there are broadcasting-specific bodies that aim to represent the audience as such, like Telespectateurs in France, the Voice of the Listener in Britain and the Argentur für unterdrückte Nachrichten in Germany.

Although the priorities of such differently constituted bodies are bound to differ, they should give considered thought, when involving themselves in broadcasting questions, to the precise notion of the viewer's interest they intend to defend. They should not interpret this in a narrow sense, as if it were no different in principle from the consumer interest in how numerous other goods and services are supplied (see p. 3, Chapter 1). An example of the danger of shortchanging that interest actually arose in the United States in late 1990, when significant pressure on Congress to re-regulate cable television stemmed from consumer complaints about escalating subscription charges and poor service *without* any reference to such issues as stunted diversity, skimped quality or the cable operators' contemptuous treatment of public access channels.

Armed with a mature and independently conceived sense of what the interests of audience members involve, however, 'citizens' organizations' should aim to inform themselves more fully on broadcasting issues and to publicize their ideas and concerns actively. They can sponsor meetings, develop policy positions and issue papers and reports. They can form coalitions and undertake joint activities with other like-minded bodies. They can challenge simplistic and inadequate characterizations of viewers' interests whenever these surface in broadcasters' utterances and policy justifications. They can encourage better research into audience responses to and evaluations of programme materials. They might seek representation in consultative bodies and less derisory roles for such bodies in the policy process (see Lopez-Escobar, Chapter 11, for comment on how these have been side-tracked in Spain).

Thought might also be given to the prospects for representing the citizen/viewer interest more formally inside broadcasting systems.

In the consumer movement debate often arises over the relative merits of internalizing the defence of consumer interests within the organization of a service, or acting on the providers of the service as a pressure group from the outside. For broadcasting a mixture of both approaches could be best. However, a recognized institutional position has two advantages. One is the greater status and more defined responsibilities and powers that would go with it – for example, to serve as channels for complaints; to oversee codes of practice; to receive and comment on policy proposals before they are introduced; or to monitor overall performance and report. The other advantage is financial: the public funding of such functions would be enormously helpful, since most citizen and consumer organizations are chronically short of resources.[1]

Sixth, ways of occasionally overarching and integrating these various far-flung accountability elements may need to be invented. It is true that the 'old' accountability system had such a capacity, which certainly should be preserved and exploited, including the role of parliamentary debates on broadcasting and periodic reviews of broadcasting performance by independent public committees. The ambit of the traditional system was narrowly circumscribed, however, and it is doubtful whether it can encompass the full span of interests, voices, problems and ideas that should now be taken into account.

One possibility would be to establish a centre that could serve as a National Television Forum. (Of course in countries where broadcasting is organized on sub-national lines, as in Belgium, Germany, Spain and Switzerland, Regional Television Forums would also be appropriate.) Such a body might commission research, receive structurally relevant criticisms, receive reports from the system's other leading agencies and, above all, assume some responsibility for the agenda and quality of broadcasting policy debate. It could take a variety of forms. It might evolve out of an existing body for receiving complaints (for example, the Independent Authority for Programme Complaints in Switzerland; the Broadcasting Standards Council or the Broadcasting Complaints Commission in Britain); it might be assumed by a citizen-based accountability organ; or it might be set up afresh. Not to be confused with a regulatory authority, however, such an institution, though supported by public funds, should be armed with only a few limited powers, chiefly those of obtaining information and reports and ensuring participation in proceedings. Its *raison d'être* would be to mount discussions of broadcasting organization, policy and practice across a broad spectrum of relevant interests, including those of the broadcasters themselves.

In Conclusion: Accountability in Public and Private Television

These are all only a few conceivable suggestions. Whether they, or indeed other, approaches should be taken up must depend on the specific political, social, economic and cultural conditions of the countries concerned, particularly their political cultures and civic group structures.

The effectiveness of whatever accountability mechanisms are introduced will also vary across the different sectors of the emergent dual broadcasting order. It will presumably be easier to establish influential accountability forums for non-commercial broadcasting. The special programming mandate, the reliance on public funds, particularly the total or partial exemption from advertising finance, should enable public television to react flexibly to outside proposals and criticisms without always coming into conflict with economic imperatives. The new role for public service television described in Chapter 13 is necessarily tied to intensive public accountability. And at a time when the long-term future of public television is being called into question, its survival and prosperity prospects could be strengthened by its cultivation of responsiveness to public concerns.

Nevertheless, the public accountability of commercial television and those charged to regulate it is also vital. Conflicts will arise, of course, when responses to public pressures might threaten companies' ratings performances or what advertisers and sponsors are prepared to finance. Private television (and its regulators) must nevertheless be expected to withstand such conflicts. It has not been exempted from public interest obligations in any European country, and there is no reason to release it from them. Despite the increase in frequencies and channels, television broadcasters continue to use a public resource to transmit their programmes. The risk of an organizational abuse of the resulting power is one reason why the public has a legitimate interest in ensuring accountability to the greatest possible extent. Another arises from the fact that media freedom is not an absolute value but is inextricably coupled to numerous social consequences. The exercise of such a socially important freedom must take place in conditions of responsibility and accountability (Hoffmann-Riem, 1983). The new paths of public accountability discussed here, which are not based on state commands and controls but rely instead on interactive mechanisms of social self-regulation, are most flexible, allowing much respect to be paid to broadcasters' economic interests as well. They amount to a prospectus for reconciling freedom of broadcasting with public responsibility under conditions of modern television.

Note

1. We are grateful to Jeremy Mitchell, a Consumer Policy Adviser in Britain, for much useful information and comment on the subject of consumer organization and accountability.

References

Ang, Ien (1991) *Desperately Seeking the Audience*. London: Routledge.

Aufderheide, Patricia (forthcoming) 'Cable Television and the Public Interest', *Journal of Communication*.

Blumler, Jay G. and McQuail, Denis (1965) 'British Broadcasting: Its Purposes, Structure and Control', *Gazette*, 11 (2/3): 166–91.

Hoffmann-Riem, Wolfgang (1972) *Redktationsstatute im Rundfunk*. Baden-Baden: Nomos-Verlagsgesellschaft.

Hoffmann-Riem, Wolfgang (1979) *Innere Pressefreiheit als politische Aufgabe: Über die Bedingungen und Möglichkeiten arbeitsteiliger Aufgabenwahrnehmung in der Presse*. Neuwied: Luchterhand Verlag.

Hoffmann-Riem, Wolfgang (1983) 'Massenmedien', in Ernst Benda, Werner Maihofer and Hans-Jochen Vogel (eds), *Handbuch des Verfassungsrechts*. Berlin and New York: Walter de Gruyter. pp. 389–469.

Jensen, Klaus Bruhn (1987) 'Qualitative Audience Research: Towards an Integrative Approach to Reception', *Critical Studies in Mass Communication*, 4 (1): 21–36.

Kübler, Friedrich (1973) *Kommunikation und Verantwortung* Konstanz: Universitätsverlag.

Kunkel, Dale (1991) 'Comments of the Donald McGannon Communication Research Center to the Federal Communications Commission in the Matter of Policies and Rules Concerning Children's Television Programming'. New York: Fordham University.

Langenbucher, Wolfgang R. and Mahle, Walter A. (1973)' "Umkehrproporz" und kommunikative Relevanz: zur Zusammensetzung und Funktion der Rundfunkräte', *Publizistik* 18 (4): 322–30.

Lopes da Silva, Manuel José (1990) 'Vulnerable Values in Multichannel Television Systems: The Case of Portugal', paper presented at a conference on Vulnerable Values in Multichannel Television Systems: What European Policy Makers seek to Protect, Liège, Belgium.

Melody, William H. (1990) 'Communication Policy in the Global Information Economy', in Marjorie Ferguson (ed.), *Public Communication: The New Imperatives*. London, Newbury Park and New Delhi: Sage. pp. 16–39.

Robson, W.A. (1960) *Nationalized Industry and Public Ownership*. London: George Allen and Unwin.

Seymour-Ure, Colin (1991) *The British Press and Broadcasting since 1945*. Oxford: Basil Blackwell.

Shaw, Colin (1991) 'Media Accountability Systems: The Case of British Broadcasting', *Intermedia* 19 (1): 12–15.

Smith, Anthony (1990) *Broadcasting and Society in 1990s Britain*. London: W.H. Smith.

Index

Notes on the Contributors

Jay G. Blumler is Emeritus Professor of the University of Leeds, where he directed its Centre for Television Research, and Professor of Journalism at the University of Maryland. He is a Fellow and past President of the International Communication Association, Founding Editor of the *European Journal of Communication* and International Editor of the *Journal of Communication*. Widely published in political communication, he has led several European comparative media research teams, including work on TV roles in direct elections to the European Parliament (*Communicating to Voters*, Sage, 1983) and enquiries for the Peacock Committee on Financing the BBC (*Broadcasting Finance in Transition*, OUP, 1991). Jay G. Blumler is also Research Adviser to the Broadcasting Standards Council.

Stig Hadenius is a Professor of Journalism at Stockholm University. He has edited a regional newspaper and served as Secretary to the Parliamentary Committee on the Press (1972–5) and as Press Counsellor to the Swedish Embassy in Washington, DC (1979–83). His research interests and numerous publications deal with modern political history, Swedish news agencies, the structure and future of the party press, media policy and the role of journalism in politics. He is currently working on a book about press analysis of Gulf War developments.

Stephen Hearst is an independent broadcasting consultant and writer-producer for television, whose BBC career spanned over three decades and included responsibility for Arts Features in the 1960s and the running of Radio 3 in the 1970s. When he retired from the BBC in 1986 he was a Special Adviser to the Director-General and represented the Corporation on the Board of the Broadcasting Research Unit. He was awarded a CBE in 1979 and was a Visiting Fellow of the Institute for Advanced Studies at Edinburgh University in 1987.

Wolfgang Hoffmann-Riem is Director of the Hans Bredow Institute for Radio and Television in Hamburg, Professor of Constitutional and Administrative Law at the University of Hamburg, and Chairman of the German Association for Journalism and Communication

Scholarship. He has served on commissions of enquiry into media policy for the German Federal Parliament and the state parliament of Baden-Württemberg. Published widely in public law, sociology of law and the law of environmental protection, his recent media-related books include *Rundfunkrecht neben Wettbewerbsrecht* (1991) and *Rundfunkneuordnung in Ostdeutschland* (Hans Bredow Institute, 1991). He is currently working on a handbook of German media law and conducting a project of comparative research into the licensing and supervision of broadcasting in selected European and non-European countries.

Esteban Lopez-Escobar is Director of the Public Communication Department in the University of Navarra, Editor of *Communicación y Sociedad*, trustee of the International Institute of Communications, and Fellow of both the European Institute for the Media and the Annenberg Washington Program in Communications Policy. He is author of numerous works on international communications and new media policies, including *Analisis del 'nuevo orden' internacional de la informacion* (1978) and *La televisión por cable en Europa y América* (1986).

Gianpietro Mazzoleni is Associate Professor of Sociology of Communication at Salerno University, Italian member of the Euromedia Research Group and Corresponding Editor of the *European Journal of Communication*. An internationally acknowledged authority on the process of broadcasting system change in Italy, he has also researched and published in the fields of political and election-campaign communication, new communication technology adoption and comparative mass media systems.

Denis McQuail is Professor of Mass Communication at the University of Amsterdam and formerly Professor of Sociology at the University of Southampton. He co-directs the Euromedia Research Group, has taught at the University of Pennsylvania and held a Senior Research Fellowship at the Gannett Center for Media Studies at Columbia University. His research interests and publications cover a wide range, with particular reference recently to the impact and policy implications of new communication technology in Europe. Author of *Mass Communication Theory* (Sage, 1987), his most recent publication is *Media Performance: Mass Communication and the Public Interest*. (Sage, 1992).

Ulrich Saxer is Professor of the Department of Communication Research at the University of Zurich. From 1977 to 1981 he served on the Federal Commission of Experts for Media Policy in Switzerland; in 1980 he was a Visiting Professor in Mainz; and from 1983 to

1988 he headed a Research Programme for Local Radio in Switzerland. His main fields of writing and research are media policy, mass communication theory, sociology of mass communication, journalism research and media socialization.

Dominique Wolton is Director of Research at the CNRS in Paris and of its Laboratoire de Communication et Politique, Editor of *Hermes* and Corresponding Editor of the European Journal of Communication. Published widely in political communication and mass communication theory, his recent books include *Eloge du Grand Public: Une théorie critique de la télévision* (Flammarion, 1990) and (on the media in the Gulf War) *War game: l'information et la guerre* (Flammarion, 1991).

The Broadcasting Standards Council

The Broadcasting Standards Council's remit concerns the portrayal in television and radio programmes and broadcast advertisements of violence, sexual conduct and matters of taste and decency.

The Council was first established on a pre-statutory basis by the Government in May 1988. It became a statutory body under the Broadcasting Act 1990, with effect from 1 January 1991.

The Council has five main tasks:

1. To draw up and from time to time review a Code of Practice in consultation with the broadcasting authorities and others. The Broadcasting Act places a duty on the broadcasters to reflect the BSC's Code in their own codes and programmes guidelines. The BSC's Code was published in November 1989 and circulated widely among broadcasters, interested organisations and members of the public.

2. To monitor programmes and to make reports on the areas within the Council's remit.

3. To commission research into such matters as the nature and effects on attitudes and behaviour of the portrayal of violence and of sex in programmes and advertisements and standards of taste and decency.

4. To consider and make findings on complaints.

5. To represent the UK on international bodies concerned with setting standards for television programmes.

Broadcasting Standards Council
5–8 The Sanctuary
London SW1P 3JS

Tel: 071–233 0544
Fax: 071–233 0397

Broadcasting Standards Council Publications

A Code of Practice
November 1989
This publication is available free of charge from the Council

Broadcasting Standards Council Annual Report 1988–89 and
Code of Practice
Broadcasting Standards Council Annual Report 1989–90 and
1990–91
Available from the Council, £4.00

BSC Monograph Series

A Measure of Uncertainty – The Effects of the Mass Media
by Dr Guy Cumberbatch and Dr Dennis Howitt
Co-publishers John Libbey and Co Ltd, 1989, £18.00

Survivors and the Media
by Ann Shearer
Co-publishers John Libbey and Co Ltd, 1991, £7.50

A Matter of Manners? The Limits of Broadcast Language
edited by Andrea Millwood Hargrave
Co-publishers John Libbey and Co Ltd, 1991, £9.50

BSC Annual Reviews

Public Opinion and Broadcasting Standards – 1
Violence in Television Fiction
by Dr David Docherty
Co-publishers John Libbey and Co Ltd, 1990, £7.50

Public Opinion and Broadcasting Standards – 2
Taste and Decency in Broadcasting
by Andrea Millwood Hargrave
Co-publishers John Libbey and Co Ltd, 1991, £7.50

BSC Research Working Papers 1990

I. *Children, Television and Morality*
Dr Anne Sheppard, University of Leeds;

II. *Television and Fantasy: An Exploratory Study*
The Communications Research Group, Aston University;

III. *Morality, Television and the Pre-adolescent*
Research International, Young Minds;

IV. *Television Advertising and Sex Role Stereotyping*
The Communications Research Group, Aston University.

Working Papers available from the BSC, £3.00 per copy

Leaflets

Making Complaints
Available free of charge from the BSC

Future Publications

Women Viewing Violence: How Women Interpret Violence on Television
Film and Media Research Institute and Institute for the Study of Violence, University of Stirling

Public Opinion and Broadcasting Standards – 3
Sex and Sexuality
by Andrea Millwood Hargrave